Dedication

To President Corazon C. Aquino, for giving me the honor and privilege of working for her and serving the Filipino people.
– ESC

To Eugenia D. Apostol, feisty publisher and mentor who first led me to these stories.
– NSRC

To our grandchildren Diego, Emilio, Juliana—that they may grow up proud of their Filipino roots.
– ESC and NSRC

THE AQUINO LEGACY: AN ENDURING NARRATIVE
by Elfren Sicangco Cruz and Neni Sta. Romana Cruz

Published and exclusively distributed by
Imprint Publishing
26/F Rufino Pacific Tower, 6784 Ayala Avenue
San Lorenzo, Makati City 1200
Philippines
E-mail: imprintmnl@gmail.com

Editing by Joshene Bersales
Book design by R. Jordan P. Santos

First edition, November 2015

ISBN 978-621-95368-0-6

Printed in the Philippines

About the cover photo:
The tree with a yellow ribbon is one of many banaba trees on the
grounds of the Aquino Center and Museum in Tarlac. They all bear
yellow ribbons on special occasions.

The Aquino Legacy

AN ENDURING NARRATIVE

Elfren Sicangco Cruz & Neni Sta. Romana Cruz

IMPRINT PUBLISHING

Contents

MALACAÑAN PALACE
MANILA

FOREWORD

The 1986 People Power Revolution is an important chapter in the history of the Philippines; it was a time when the Filipino people united—in thoughts, in words, and in deeds—to end a repressive regime and wage a peaceful and non-violent campaign for liberation and justice. This is, of course, only one of the many facets of our narrative that demonstrates our love of country. With this chronicle by Elfren Sicangco Cruz and Neni Sta. Romana Cruz, both guiding lights in Philippine journalism and literature, I believe that the message of the EDSA Revolution and the characters behind its success will be conveyed to readers in a meaningful and objective way.

The Aquino Legacy: An Enduring Narrative is, indeed, a retrospective of the roles that my parents, the late Senator Benigno S. Aquino Jr. and the late President Corazon C. Aquino, played in our collective quest for freedom and democracy. It serves as a reliable source of information for Filipinos belonging to the millennial generation who may not be aware of how dire conditions were at the time and how we have, since then, moved forward as a people. It is an instrument for deepening their understanding of the Philippines—our history and our transformation from a land fettered by oppression, fear, and cruelty to a free nation empowered by a dynamic, resilient, and dignified citizenry.

It is always humbling to be mentioned in the same breath as my parents, whose legacy of faith, integrity, and equality I have sought to integrate in government. I do not bear this responsibility alone: My sisters, Ballsy, Pinky, Viel, and Kris, alongside the rest of the Filipino people, share my commitment to do great things for our nation.

People Power is defined by citizen engagement, social responsibility, and discerning involvement. I am hopeful that this publication will inspire more of our countrymen to contribute to our society, advance the welfare of our fellowmen, sustain the gains of our reforms, and uphold our Republic's revived

THE PRESIDENT OF THE PHILIPPINES

MALACAÑAN PALACE
MANILA

distinction on the global stage. Let us be each other's moral compass as we stay the course along the Daang Matuwid.

BENIGNO S. AQUINO III

MANILA
26 November 2015

THE PRESIDENT OF THE PHILIPPINES

Foreword by Pinky A. Abellada

We are very fortunate to be the offspring of Ninoy and Cory, two people who led exemplary lives publicly and privately. They gave so much of themselves for the restoration of our freedoms and for the strengthening of our institutions.

Yes, we had a far-from-normal life during the martial law years and Dad's incarceration, but Mom cushioned most of the blows for us. And yes, we were sometimes second to country in the priorities of our parents but we understood why we had to share them with others. Today, we continue to receive so much goodwill from their legacy, locally and internationally. My siblings will agree with me when I say that their guidance, values, and principles greatly shaped the people we are today. In fact, it is not uncommon that when confronted with challenges, we would look to Mom and Dad as role models.

We are very grateful to people who perpetuate their memory, more so if we know that the person knew one or both of our parents. When Neni contacted us for interviews for this book (and she was quite thorough with her questions!), we did our best to oblige. Neni had some light questions too, and it was quite fun answering them. After answering the questions, I would read how the others answered and it felt like one of those "dating game shows" where you get points for similar answers! Then when Neni wanted our husbands and children interviewed as well, we encouraged them to be as cooperative as possible. After all, we will not be around forever to tell our story. And if we tell our story as accurately as possible, attempts to distort history will not prosper.

The Aquino Legacy: An Enduring Narrative is the first book the family is involved with that looks at the lives of Ninoy, Cory plus PNoy. The fact that the book is meant for millennials ensures that today's youth will have a book on the Aquinos they can relate to, learn from, and hopefully, share with their children and grandchildren.

Pinky A. Abellada

PINKY AQUINO-ABELLADA

Acknowledgements

Karina A. Bolasco
Karen Lacsamana-Carrera
Omay Chikiamco
Aina SR Cruz
Roel SR Cruz
Lydia B. Echauz
Alfredo P. Hernandez, Jr.
Leticia M. Locsin (+)
Jo-Ann Q. Maglipon
Camille Martinez
Marisse Reyes McMurray
Victorio C. Valledor and Lockton Philippines Insurance and Reinsurance Brokers, Inc.
Miguel Tan
May Tobias-Papa
Jelson N. Young

Bookwatch
Business World
FOOD Magazine
Mr. & Ms. Magazine
Pacific Migration Journal, Vol. 8, Nos. 1-2, 1999
Philippine Daily Inquirer
Philippine Star
Sunday Inquirer Magazine
YES! Magazine

Preface

The idea for this book originally came from Elfren, who strongly felt that the contributions of Ninoy and Cory Aquino to the Filipino people's struggle for democracy are too significant to risk being forgotten. We feel that this is especially critical these days as history is in serious danger of being rewritten and altered by individuals who seek a kinder and more heroic portrayal of themselves in the memory of a nation. This has greater relevance today as the dark period of martial law is being dismissed and glossed over as an epoch that must now be forgotten. We feel this urgency even as some quarters urge us to "move on," as if the remembrance of things past and sordid and painful posed an obstacle to our progress and maturity as a nation. Many of us bear the scars of martial law—some more deeply than others. Many are burdened with traumatic stories that need to be told over and over again—for healing comes with every retelling.

These essays are written especially for the Millennial Generation or Generation Y, those who reached young adulthood around the year 2000. This is the generation that may only know Ninoy and Cory as the parents of Kris and PNoy or the faces on our currency bills. The group that may see the EDSA People Power Revolution as a peaceful and festive everybody's party on the traffic-choked highway.

This millennial generation, as future leaders and opinion makers of the land, must never forget the deplorable and unlamented years of martial law. This generation must never allow these to happen again if it truly values the meaning of democracy.

The lives of Ninoy and Cory Aquino may appear more like magical realism than stark reality, for truly, how does one weave such a drama even with the most imaginative conjuring? There is the charismatic opposition freedom fighter assured to be president of the land, suffering years of isolation and detention, then returns home from exile, only to be swiftly assassinated at his homecoming on the tarmac of the airport that now carries his name. There is the nonpolitician widowed wife forced to carry on her slain husband's anti-dictatorship struggle, and emerges as the president after the ouster of the dictator. And of course, there is their only son, as reluctant a presidential candidate as his mother, who becomes the country's fifteenth president ten months after his mother's death.

How can one family be fated to endure all that? But such are the incomprehensible ways of fate and destiny.

The Aquino Legacy: An Enduring Narrative has a deliberately chosen subtitle that attempts to capture the degree of untold pain and suffering that the family has lived with over the years, never quite gone even with the public commendation that was to come decades after. Their saga is more than timeless, their story as a family meant to be documented and remembered in history books.

Why another Aquino book? What is it that the public still does not know about Ninoy and Cory? Might this be just another retelling of the all too familiar yellow ribbon protests acknowledged by Berlin and the fall of its wall, the Velvet Revolution of the Czech Republic, and more recently, Hong Kong and its yellow umbrellas, as a nonviolent revolution to reap lessons from?

We as a people are often justifiably accused of being bereft of historical memory. Tragic mistakes of the past are unnecessarily repeated. It is not that today's youth and young professionals have forgotten what the People Power Revolution was all about—they never knew enough about it in the first place.

We do not mean to deify Ninoy and Cory Aquino as they themselves were the first ones to admit how mortal, how vulnerable, how flawed they were. We were not privileged to have met Ninoy, but Elfren had worked closely with President Cory in Malacañang for five years. Neni was the first Filipino journalist to sit down with Cory for an interview upon her return from Boston in 1983 (thanks to Eggie Apostol of *Mr. & Ms. Magazine* who sent her on that "big" assignment), and continued on to have close to two dozen one-on-one extended interviews and many private conversations, besides.

We make no claims that this is an exhaustive book. There remains much to study, explore, and analyze about the lives and times of Ninoy and Cory, and especially of PNoy, after he steps down in 2016.

Let this book allow today's millennials to approach the fascinating tale of the Cojuangco-Aquino family with greater interest and curiosity, and less trepidation about cold, hard-nosed historical facts. Straightforward historical accounts and commentaries have been juxtaposed with human interest essays, many of which have not seen publication before. We felt that the inclusion of the interviews with individuals closest to Ninoy and Cory would offer a fresh and a different perspective on them as revered national figures—and of PNoy as the highest official of the land.

To make this book in sync with millennial thinking and truly useful to students and their teachers, we have included Pres. Corazon C. Aquino's first State of the Nation Address in 1987 and her last State of the Nation Address in 1991. Included also are Sen. Benigno S. Aquino, Jr.'s undelivered arrival speech meant for August 21, 1983, Cory's and Ninoy's capsule biographies, and a bibliography of books written on them.

These essays would not have been possible without the total cooperation—though typically guarded, reluctant, and cautious for some members—of the family who, if they had their way, would have wanted less attention on themselves. (Neni had to convince and coax by teasing, "If President Cory trusted me through all those interviews I had with her, would you not?") Yet they were quick to respond, especially after Ballsy's exercise of her gentle but respected matriarchal clout, even granting an unexpected presidential interview strictly scheduled for an hour yet allowed to spill into another. And guess who of the Aquino children was the most elusive and the hardest to track down—the one with the Malacañang address or the sui generis sibling? But to all of them, the willing and the unwilling, we are truly privileged and deeply grateful. The access you allowed us was unexpected beyond words.

Special thanks to the talented millennials who helped put this book together for us: editor Joshene Bersales and book designer R. Jordan P. Santos who gave shape and form to our manuscript toward a volume that befits the subjects—and the audience it addresses.

We offer this book to the youth, to the millennials, for them to understand, value, and preserve the hard-fought historical gains in the restoration of democracy in 1986. It is a continuing myth that it was a miraculous, instant four-day revolution that overthrew the dreaded dictatorship. For the long, arduous struggle that climaxed in the much-publicized EDSA People Power Revolution actually began years back, in 1978, with the organization of LABAN (Lakas ng Bayan or People Power), Sen. Ninoy Aquino's political party, and the noise barrage for the Interim Batasang Pambansa elections. It may come as a rude awakening to the millennials that the freedom they enjoy today was not available to us during the dark years of martial law. There is no disputing that the struggle for democracy is unfinished and continues on today—a struggle that every citizen must partake in, to achieve a free and more equitable society for every Filipino.

ELFREN SICANGCO CRUZ
NENI STA. ROMANA CRUZ
26 November 2015

JUSTICE FOR NINOY! JUSTICE
FOR ALL VICTIMS OF POLITICAL
REPRESSION & MILITARY TERRORISM!!

"IT IS BETTER TO LIGHT A CANDLE THAN TO CURSE THE DARKNESS"

NAMFREL '84

194 DAYS SINCE
THE UNSOLVED MURDER

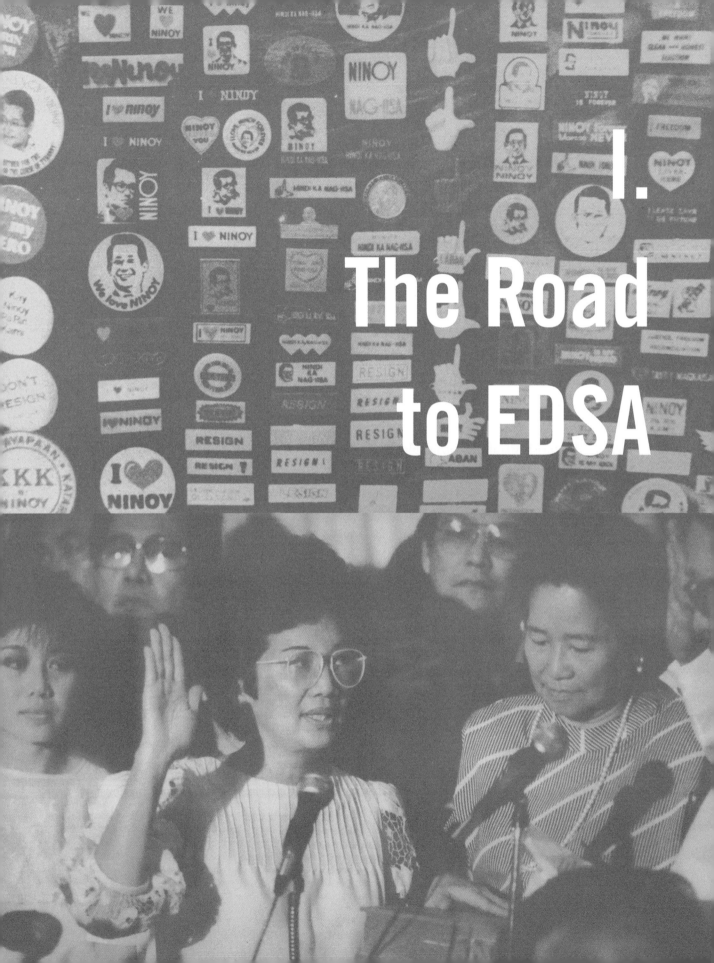

I.
The Road
to EDSA

The Road to EDSA

The classic definition of people power is "political pressure exercised through the demonstration of popular opinion," which ultimately forces the government into complete surrender. People power has traditionally been used to force governments, through nonviolent means, to accept political and social changes.

In the United States, the civil rights movement was based on civil disobedience and mass actions. The Philippine People Power Movement was a surprise to the rest of the world because it was rare for a dictatorship to be toppled through nonviolent means.

While the culmination of People Power was the massing of the people for four days in EDSA, this movement's beginnings can actually be traced many years back. The journey toward EDSA went through many different debates and disagreements on tactics and goals.

There were two debates in particular where the leadership of Ninoy and Cory Aquino played pivotal roles in charting the course that the Filipino people ultimately followed.

The first debate was on whether the Marcos martial rule could be toppled through nonviolent means. The communists had always advocated armed revolution as the only means. But their goal was not the restoration of democracy. It was to seize power and turn the Philippines into a communist state. At the beginning of Marcos's rule, the non-communist opposition groups and the middle forces resisted any call for an alliance with the left. But as the years of martial rule went on, there grew a belief that perhaps Marcos could be overthrown only through force.

The other major debate was on whether the opposition groups should participate or boycott the elections that Marcos allowed to be held during his rule. Again, the Left never agreed to participate in any election during the entire tenure of Marcos, and they were unrelenting. However, within the pro-democracy forces that sought to restore democracy through nonviolent means, there were respected voices arguing on both sides of the issue of boycott versus participation. It was the voice of Ninoy, and later Cory, that finally swayed the majority of the Filipino people to participate in those elections, despite the seemingly impossible odds. Those who participated in those elections had to suffer outright use of force, massive frauds, and the blatant use of government funds and resources.

For most Filipinos, the road to EDSA began in 1978 with the elections for the Interim Batasang Pambansa, and the Metro Manila Noise Barrage on April 6, 1978, which was the eve of the elections. The journey reached its highest point on February 25, 1986 when Cory Aquino was finally sworn in as the president of the Republic of the Philippines.

Historians will, hopefully, write the complete story that will allow Filipinos to appreciate the saga that started in 1978 and ended in 1986. I want to share some of the highlights of that period of our history. To use the words of Charles Dickens: "It was the best of times, it was the worst of times."

It was the story of personal sufferings and widespread social injustice. Many people who simply believed in freedom were jailed, or killed, or simply disappeared. At the same time, it showed the strength and dedication of a people whose commitment to freedom and justice could not be quelled by oppression and tyranny.

1978 Interim Batasang Pambansa Elections

Marcos was supposed to convene a 208-member legislative body in 1973 as mandated by his own constitution written after the declaration of martial law. He did not do so until six years later when he announced that there would be an election on April 7, 1978.

The main opposition party at that time, the Liberal Party, announced that it would participate under certain conditions. These demands were the lifting of martial law, the release of political prisoners, freedom of speech and assembly, and the guarantee that participants in the electoral process would not be arrested. Marcos rejected all of these demands. Furthermore, he announced that elections would be by bloc voting. The leaders of the Liberal Party decided to boycott the elections.

Ninoy Aquino was then still in jail. According to Cory Aquino, Ninoy thought about his position and decided to participate because the campaign was the only forum made available to him to speak to the Filipino people.

The main electoral battleground was Metro Manila where twenty-one seats were at stake. The Marcos political party was the Kilusang Bagong Lipunan (KBL) led by Imelda Marcos. The opposition group was a new one called Lakas ng Bayan and its acronym and battle cry was LABAN. It was a battle cry that still resonates today as a manifestation of the Filipino fighting spirit even in the face of tremendous odds.

Cory Aquino gave a press conference in Times Street to announce the twenty-one candidates of LABAN led by Ninoy Aquino. Its first rally was in the courtyard of St. Andrew's Church in Parañaque. Aside from the candidates and their companions, only around two dozen spectators came to listen. Obviously, the population was still full of fears about possible punishments from the martial law regime against those sympathetic to the opposition.

LABAN Stalwart

Jaime Ferrer once told me that he volunteered to host the first rally in Parañaque because he and his family not only lived there, but their roots were also in that community. He felt that his neighbors would not let him down. But even he underestimated the power of fear. However, they decided to continue with the rally because they noticed that although people remained in their homes, they still listened by their windows and doorways.

Then on March 10, 1978, Ninoy was allowed to have his first and only television appearance. It would be taped in the morning and aired at 7:30 p.m. on Channel 4. Somehow, the news about his appearance spread quickly by word of mouth. But that evening, the streets of Metro Manila were almost empty as people stayed home to listen. It was a master performance.

After that evening, the number of people attending LABAN events began to balloon to tens of thousands. Several rallies had to be scheduled simultaneously. Marcos had obviously underestimated Ninoy Aquino. And the first signs of people power were already being seen in the streets of Metro Manila.

Noise Barrage

There are different stories about the original sources of the noise barrage on the eve of the elections. There was supposed to be a ban on all election activity. I had joined a group that was planning to conduct an Operation Quick Count (OQC). We were still naively thinking that the elections in Metro Manila would have a semblance of legality.

A few days before the elections, I attended a small meeting at the Mofire office of Butz Aquino in San Juan. It was there that I heard about the call for a noise barrage. The pamphlet I got said that the barrage should last for thirty minutes. The noise should be loud enough for Marcos to hear in Malacañang and for Ninoy to hear in Fort Bonifacio.

On the night of April 6, I attended a meeting to plan for the OQC the following day. Nobody was talking about the noise barrage. But I noticed that after around 8:00 p.m., small groups of people were beginning to leave quietly. My friend Ninoy Gutierrez turned to me quietly and whispered that it was time to leave and I could join him in his car. I instinctively knew he was joining the noise demonstration. As we went out, a few others joined us in the car.

We first went around Timog and the Scout streets. Then we went to Cubao and then Greenhills. Everywhere we went, there was an explosion of noise. We decided to go to Makati, Mayor Yabut's territory. On Pasay Road, there were very few cars but thousands of people were on the streets banging pots and cans. It was supposed to last thirty minutes but it lasted until early morning. We saw policemen were simply standing around. It was another form of peaceful rebellion that we had discovered—unplanned, spontaneous, but a striking expression of people power.

We thought the election was won. But the next day, we were unprepared for Marcos's oppressive response. I was assigned to monitor elections in southern Manila and Makati. We soon discovered that in most schools, gates were closed after the counting started. Soldiers guarded the entrances. In many precincts, returns were accomplished even before the counting had begun. It was only in St. Scholastica's College where the nuns were able to let the public view the counting. We gave up trying to get results. We vowed that next time, we would be prepared. But the next opportunity would only come after six more years of waiting.

The Year 1983

On August 21, 1983, Ninoy Aquino was assassinated upon his arrival in the Philippines. He had decided to return from exile in the United States.

While in exile, he had said that never in the history of the Filipino people have they suffered from greater political and economic wants. In his statement to a subcommittee on Asian and Pacific Affairs of the U.S. House of Representatives, he articulated his political views:

> I have concluded that revolution and violence exact the highest price in terms of human values and human lives in the struggle for freedom. In the end there are really no victors, only victims.
>
> I have decided to pursue my freedom struggle through the path of non-violence, fully cognizant that this may be the longer and the more arduous road.
>
> We are already the worst economic performer in Southeast Asia. Revolution would take us back thirty or even forty years and we may well end up the basket case in the region.

Tens of thousands lined up to pay homage during Ninoy's wake. On August 31, 1983, the funeral procession that started at Sto. Domingo Church in Quezon City finally reached the Manila Memorial Park in Parañaque, after eleven hours. More than a million people lined the streets to watch the funeral procession. Once again, people had come out in the streets as a moving form of homage to a martyr and a protest to this brazen act of violence.

The stage was now set for the next phase of people power. Protest groups started mushrooming and public demonstrations were being held all over the country. Almost every Friday, Ayala Avenue became the site of a rally with yellow confetti raining down from office buildings. At first, soldiers and policemen tried to prohibit these rallies but eventually they had to give up.

The Filipino people were becoming more committed and more courageous. **LABAN** and **NINOY!** were still the battle cry. But these had been joined by a new one: **CORY!**

1984 Batasang Pambansa Elections

The year 1984 marked the end of the term of the assemblymen. The debate on participation versus boycott took center stage again. The left was clearly intent on boycotting the elections. But the memory of the abuses during the 1978 elections was a reminder that Marcos would literally do anything to win the elections.

There were many respected voices that advocated an election boycott. This group included admired human rights lawyers. Two opposition parties had emerged—PDP-LABAN and UNIDO. But within the PDP-LABAN there was also a debate on whether to participate or boycott the election.

Then Cory Aquino declared on Radio Veritas that she was in favor of participation. Her call was to give nonviolence and participation in the election process one more chance. The two political parties decided to participate. Cory Aquino went around the country urging participation and endorsing opposition candidates.

On election day, people were now more prepared. In Parañaque and other areas, watchers went through rigorous training. People were ready to accompany ballot boxes from the precinct to the city hall and guard the ballot boxes with their lives.

Of the more than 200 delegates, 55 opposition delegates were elected in spite of the use of "guns, goons and gold" by the Marcos forces.

1986 Presidential Snap Election

The next presidential election was scheduled in 1987. However, as early as 1985 there were already rumors of the possibility of a snap election. Jaime Cardinal Sin was now taking a more active role in the movement to force Marcos to resign. It was time to end his "critical collaboration" with the Marcos rule.

The Reagan government was still fully supportive of Marcos in spite of the widespread human rights abuses and the massive fraud and terrorism that marked every election. But the crowds in the protest rallies were growing and were spreading outside Metro Manila. There was also a consensus that Cory Aquino was the only person who could unify the people and defeat Marcos.

Cory Aquino announced that she would consider running for president only if she was presented with a million signatures asking her to run, and if Marcos would call for a snap election. A "Million Signatures" campaign was then initiated by Chino Roces and the newly organized Cory Aquino for President Movement.

The conjugal dictatorship had brought the Philippines to the brink of an economic collapse. Then, in October 1985, Reagan sent U.S. Senator Laxalt as his personal envoy to the Philippines. During his visit, Sen. Paul Laxalt mentioned that a snap election could prove that the Filipino people supported Marcos. In a television interview, Marcos took the bait and announced he was holding a snap election.

But even after a million signatures were presented to her, Cory did not announce her candidacy immediately. It was only at the end of November that she finally made her decision. She was clearly reluctant to run, but later she explained: "The will of the people was the cross I have to bear."

Cory Aquino and Doy Laurel were the presidential and vice presidential candidates of a unified pro-democracy movement. Marcos and Tolentino ran under the banner of the Kilusang Bagong Lipunan. The opposition campaign had no media coverage and the candidates had to speak at dozens of rallies everyday. But the rallies and motorcades brought millions to the streets, church courtyards, basketball courts, street corners, and any place brave enough to host opposition rallies.

The Marcos forces resorted to their usual tactics of widespread vote buying, intimidation, ballot box snatching, tampered election returns, and disenfranchisement of voters in opposition bailiwicks. In many areas, volunteer watchers from the opposition groups and the National Citizen's Movement for Free Elections (NAMFREL) were beaten up.

After the election, it was clear that Cory Aquino had won but the election count was being altered. The Commission on Elections (COMELEC) count showed Marcos with a narrow lead, but the NAMFREL showed Cory leading by more than a million votes.

On February 9, 1986, two days after the election, the state-run television showed thirty computer technicians led by Linda Kapunan, suddenly standing up and walking out of the COMELEC tabulation center at the Philippine International Convention Center (PICC), with computer diskettes in hand. They later announced that they were protesting the manipulation of election results to favor the Marcos candidacy.

Two days later, on February 11, 1986, former Antique governor and a Cory campaign leader, Evelio Javier, was shot and killed after being chased through the streets of the provincial capital. The Catholic Bishops Conference of the Philippines condemned the government and said, ". . . if such a government does not of itself freely correct the evil it has inflicted on the people, then it is our serious moral obligation as a people to make it do so."

These events had set the stage for the final phase of the people power movement.

Tagumpay ng Bayan

The Batasang Pambansa finally declared Marcos as the official winner. The question in everybody's mind was, "What do we do now?"

Cory Aquino decided it was time to call the people to another rally. Veteran politicians protested, saying it might make matters worse and that fear of persecution would result in a low turnout. But Cory insisted that she felt the people were waiting for a call for action.

A group of opposition leaders from the political, cause-oriented, and business sectors met in the Cojuangco Building in Makati to discuss the venue. Cory wanted the rally to be held in Luneta. There was near-unanimous disapproval. As someone pointed out, it would take a million people to fill up Luneta.

Plaza Miranda and Liwasang Bonifacio could be filled with 20,000 to 50,000 diehard supporters. The business community proposed Ayala Avenue and promised to bring down their employees from their offices. But Cory said it had to be in Luneta so that we could find out whether the people were still prepared to continue the fight or were ready to surrender.

On February 16, 1986, the *Tagumpay ng Bayan* rally was held at the Luneta. The crowd was estimated to have reached two million. In her address, Cory called for a boycott of firms and publications identified with Marcos and his cronies. She also announced a civil disobedience campaign that would include a refusal to pay taxes.

The Filipino people were now preparing for more rallies and acts of civil disobedience, including a possible general strike. On Saturday, February 22, 1986, meetings were being held in small groups throughout the nation to prepare everyone for the coming week. Cory Aquino left Metro Manila to go to Cebu and other provincial cities to carry her message of continuing the struggle for freedom.

Four Days of EDSA

The story of those four days in EDSA has been told and retold in many books.

Cory Aquino was in Cebu City on the first day. After a night in the Carmelite convent, she flew back to Manila on the second day. She stayed in the house of her sister, Josephine Cojuangco Reyes in Wack Wack. She felt the place was more secure and it was right next to EDSA.

Everyone was urging her to stay secluded for fear that Marcos or his minions would make an attempt to assassinate her. But on the third day, a Monday, Cory Aquino disregarded all advice and ran out to the car and had herself driven to the POEA building located at the corner of EDSA and Ortigas Avenue.

Standing on the front steps of the POEA building, she told the crowd to remain vigilant because Marcos was still in the country. She also noted that this people power movement was unprecedented because this time, it was the civilian population who were protecting the military.

There was a growing consensus that Cory Aquino needed to be sworn in as president before any military junta could be set up. The people massing all over the Philippines also needed to see that there would be a peaceful transition once Marcos departed from Malacañang.

At around 11 a.m. on February 25, 1986, in Club Filipino, Corazon Aquino was sworn in as president of the Republic of the Philippines. After her short inaugural speech, she and her children went to Manila Memorial Park to visit the tomb of Ninoy Aquino.

On that April day in 1978, when the LABAN candidates, with Ninoy Aquino as their leader, held the first people power rally with less than fifty people in St. Andrew's Church courtyard, no one ever imagined that the journey would end with more than two and half million people massing at EDSA.

Some say that Cory once said: "When I become president, there will be dancing in the streets." There are others who say that what she actually said was: "When I become president, there will be democracy in the streets."

I say that when Cory Aquino became president, there was both. **(ESC)**

Making Democracy Work

I t is true that the immediate cause that forced Marcos to flee the country was the four-day People Power Revolution. But this historic event was the climax of a long series of other revolutionary struggles which I call the Road to EDSA.

On the night of January 22, 1986, when Cardinal Sin asked the people to go to EDSA, I was one of those who immediately went there. While there were just a few thousands of us in EDSA, the response was quick, as most of those who came first were part of organized groups.

There was no social media at that time. However, these organized groups had their own networks and means of quickly reaching each other. But because there was no media support and communication networks were limited, it was not surprising that the groups were small in numbers. However, there were so many of these groups and they were so widespread that together, they could rally thousands on very short notice.

Religious orders, priests, nuns, and brothers were ideal because they lived together and they had the numbers. Furthermore, their networks went beyond their members and included students in Catholic schools, parishioners, and members of Catholic lay organizations. They were used to organizing and were very disciplined. It is no wonder they were at the forefront of the EDSA Revolution.

For example, my own journey to EDSA started in 1978 during the Batasang Pambansa elections. I was then an active member of the Manila Jaycees and we had volunteered to join the Operation Quick Count of the Philippine Jaycees. That was when I first met Butz Aquino who was a Capitol Jaycee. The night before the election, we were at the Quezon City headquarters attending a meeting. A small typewritten note was being circulated that said Ninoy Aquino, who was then in jail, was asking the people to organize a thirty-minute noise barrage as a sign of protest.

Around nine in the evening, people started quietly leaving the room. My friend, Ninoy Gutierrez, told me to come with him and find a group we could join. We did not invite anyone else because we were not sure whom to trust. These were the days of martial law. When we went out, it seemed as if the entire metropolis was taking part in the protest. Cars were going around blowing their horns and we joined one caravan. We were confident then that the opposition would win in the next election.

But it was a rude awakening. In one school which was a polling place, the opposition watchers were told to leave. In another school, army soldiers closed the gates during the counting. Only in one school I went to—St. Scholastica's College—did the counting proceed publicly. The nuns there stood their ground and refused to be intimidated.

That was when I realized that it would take more than one noise barrage or rally to topple the dictatorship. But I learned, from the nuns' example, that an organized group with the courage to stand its ground could be more effective than any speech. This was, to my mind, the forerunner of NAMFREL, maintaining its position in subsequent elections under the dictatorship.

For the revolution to succeed, there has to be a cause for which the overwhelming majority of the people would be willing to go to jail or even sacrifice their lives for, if necessary. The restoration of democracy and overthrowing of the Marcos dictatorship were such causes.

There also had to be an emotional event and a charismatic leader that would bring together the different revolutionary forces and inspire groups to organize themselves. The assassination of Ninoy Aquino was such an event, and groups were unified under the leadership of his widow, Corazon Aquino.

There also has to be organizations on the ground to serve as a nucleus in any confrontation with the ruling powers, like in a rally. It was, therefore, critical that existing institutions like the Catholic Church and Protestant denominations joined the cause. These institutions have a following that could reach all social classes, including the poor.

The Makati confetti rallies were successful because of the support of the business groups. Business and civic groups were also the primary organizers of NAMFREL. The electoral campaign during the snap election took off because political opposition parties like PDP-LABAN and UNIDO were organized. Cause-oriented groups and nongovernment organizations (NGOs) became active mobilizers of rally participants.

The participation of youth groups was essential because they have built-in organizations like student councils and other campus organizations. And in organizing the masses, I discovered that there were organizations in the urban poor areas that could also be tapped.

The EDSA People Power Movement was not just civil disobedience. It was a revolution—a movement for radical change. It achieved its primary goal, which was the restoration of the democratic system to this country.

Now we hear people questioning whether democracy really works. I even heard a nun say on television that she preferred the country to be run by professionals rather than by elected officials. But who will choose the professionals who will run this country?

For those who tell me that they prefer a dictatorship, I always ask them to give me the name of the person that they propose to be the dictator.

Democracy will work. It just requires collective will, leaders who believe in democratic ideals, and the active support of the very same groups that toppled the Marcos dictatorship and made the EDSA People Power Revolution a reality.

Time has a tendency to wash over horrible moments in history. This is why we must never forget. We must constantly reinforce the legacy of EDSA, and keep reminding ourselves that when push comes to shove, we are a people who will fight for freedom and democracy at all costs. **(ESC)**

Never Again

Will another Marcos return to Malacañang as president? This is not the first time that there have been attempts and talks of a Marcos restoration. On August 20, 1999, former president Corazon Aquino addressed a rally on Ayala Avenue, Makati protesting a charter change attempt by then president Ejercito Estrada. There was a public perception that the call for charter change was really to pave the way for a Marcos restoration.

Here are excerpts of Cory Aquino's speech addressed to the public and more specifically to President Estrada:

> When Marcos men threatened me during my campaign rally for the snap election in Basilan—"Cory, *isang bala ka lang.*"—I stood my ground and answered, "Marcos, *isang balota ka lang.*"
>
> Mr. President, do not worry about us being afraid. We have been threatened by experts.
>
> We have faced bullets outside the silver screen and faced down tanks with only rosaries in our hands.
>
> But there are things of which we are afraid. We are afraid of the evils that may tear up the country again.

Mr. President, you say, "Be not afraid of breaking loose from the past."

Mr. President, we are afraid of the past breaking loose in the present with a Marcos restoration.

Mr. President, it is not just the future, but the present that calls for courage, clarity of vision, and concord. It calls for vigilance against the return of a past this nation paid so high a price—in blood, sweat, toil and tears—to escape.

President Corazon Aquino concluded her speech with the following words:

We are a peaceful people, but a freedom loving and moral nation as well. Right and wrong are beyond political calculation.

Our children must see that stealing does not cease to be wrong because the loot is successfully hidden. Our children must see that the mastermind is not innocent because his hired guns are afraid to linger him. Our children must see that might does not make right but that, given time and determination, right is irresistible.

We will not surrender the guarantees and good government for which we paid dearly.

We will not allow those who plundered our country to return to power no matter who they think their best friend is. The electoral mandate extends no farther than the candidate himself.

We will not so easily allow the dismantling of what took the democratic resistance many years to recover under martial law, and succeeding years after EDSA to rebuild:

Our democracy from the grip of tyranny;

Our country from the pockets of thieves;

Our economic wealth that was stolen and mortgaged the people who are back in power today.

President Estrada should not take this rally personally. This is not a fight against him. He has been president only one year. He was only mayor, not martial law administrator during the Marcos regime.

This is a fight against a fourteen-year dictatorship and a dark legacy that refuses to die.

We are told to forgive and forget. Surely, the President understands why it is extremely difficult for us to just forgive and forget such deep wrongs done to our country, since he finds it hard to forgive and forget wrongs done to him.

Let me say it now: There will never, *never* be a Marcos restoration, not by hook or by crook. This country will always be free and will always be the country of the People Power Revolution.

Fourteen years and eleven months after this speech was delivered, the heir apparent Bongbong Marcos has been implicated in the Priority Development Assistance Fund (PDAF) schemes, including allegedly giving Php100 million to Napoles NGOs. This is a potential plunder case which can put him in the same detention center as Senators Bong Revilla and Jinggoy Estrada.

An arrest warrant for plunder has also been issued for the primary martial law administrator during the Marcos years. Juan Ponce Enrile was Minister of Defense during the entire martial law period except for its final four days.

But on her own personal journey to her private Land of Oz, Imelda Romualdez Marcos continues to have the absurd fantasy that the Philippines and the Filipino people deserve to have another Marcos as president.

We say to that: never again! **(ESC)**

Preserving the Legacy of People Power

I was a Tuesday morning three decades ago, the exact date was February 25, 1986. Along with more than a million other Filipinos, we had been staying in EDSA since Saturday. That morning, I was told that Corazon Aquino was going to take her oath as president of the Republic of the Philippines. Finally, the fourteen-year Marcos rule built on lies, oppression, and massive corruption would come to an end.

Along with several friends and people we connected with, I had been sleeping in my car parked on a side street of EDSA. Food was available because people kept bringing and distributing all kinds of food. Among those that I banded with were party mates from PDP-LABAN, colleagues from the Jaime Ferrer for Assemblyman Movement in Parañaque City, former friends from my La Salle college days, and associates in the business world. I was fortunate that I had been active in the Cory Aquino for President Movement and, therefore, had met a lot of opposition leaders. We formed a natural network during those critical four days in EDSA.

I decided to walk to Club Filipino to witness what I knew would be a historical occasion. When I got there, the room where the oath taking was going to be held was already crowded. The entire premises of Club Filipino was also jampacked. I decided to wait at a street near the Greenhills Shopping Center, right in front of Club Filipino, for some companions who were fortunate to have found space inside the room.

After the ceremony, Nene Pimentel, Jaime Ferrer, Dante Tinga, Zaf Respicio, Lito Lorenzana, and I decided to go somewhere and discuss what had just taken place. We also reflected on what would happen next.

The inaugural speech of President Aquino on February 25, 1986 was brief but, as always, communicated her message in a memorable way. Here is her speech:

> My brothers and sisters, I am grateful to the authority you have given me today. And I promise to offer all that I can do to serve you.
>
> It is fitting and proper that, as our people lost their rights and liberties at midnight fourteen years ago, the people should formally recover those lost rights and liberties in the full light of day.
>
> Ninoy believed that only the united strength of the Filipino people would suffice to overturn a tyranny so evil and so well organized. The brutal murder of Ninoy created that unity in strength that has come to be known as *Lakas ng Bayan*—People Power.
>
> People Power shattered the dictatorship, protected those in the military that chose freedom, and today has established a government dedicated to this protection and meaningful fulfilment of our rights and liberties.
>
> We became exiles, we Filipinos who are at home only in freedom, when Marcos destroyed the republic fourteen years ago.
>
> Now, by God's grace and the power of the people, we are free again.
>
> We want to make a special appeal to those who have not yet joined us. Do not engage in any further action against the people and instead, be among those who will lend a hand to rebuild the country.

There is now a new generation of Filipinos—the millennial generation—who has very little knowledge of the Marcos dictatorship. And then there are the principal beneficiaries of the Marcos rule—family, cronies, and sycophants—who are trying to rewrite history.

It is critical to remind our people that the Marcos martial law rule was built on lies, oppression, and unparalleled corruption.

The most brazen lie was when Marcos said he was imposing martial law for the good of the Filipino people. The truth was that when Marcos became president in 1965, the Philippines was the second richest country in Asia, next only to Japan. When he was finally ousted, the country had become the "sick man of Asia." Marcos imposed martial law because he knew that in a democratic election he was going to lose. But he and his family wanted to keep their power and wealth intact for succeeding Marcos generations.

Marcos maintained his power through the use of arbitrary arrest, detention, salvaging, and torture. He had tens of thousands, including opposition leaders like Diokno and Tañada, and publishers like Chino Roces, arrested. Then Ninoy Aquino was also detained, exiled, and assassinated.

One of the principal implementers of martial law, aside from Gen. Fabian Ver, was Defense Minister Juan Ponce Enrile. In 1982, Enrile was quoted as saying: "We presume the priests and nuns charged with subversive activities are guilty until the courts decide whether they are guilty or not."

Justice was a travesty under the Marcos rule. The Supreme Court Justice Enrique Fernando had publicly and servilely held an umbrella over Imelda Romualdez Marcos's head.

Recently, Presidential Commission on Good Government (PCHH) chair Andy Bautista has given a partial snapshot of the wealth the Marcoses looted during their rule. The ill-gotten wealth hidden in secret bank accounts are estimated anywhere from $5 to 10 billion. These amounts do not include what the Marcoses spent during their twenty-five years in power. Imelda's spending splurges in the major shopping centers of the world were legendary. Her shoe collection has become a standard joke by many comedians.

Every EDSA Anniversary celebration, I always repeat Corazon Aquino's speech in 1999, which concludes with:

> Let me say it now: there will never be a Marcos restoration, not by hook or by crook. This country will always be free and it will always be the country of the People Power Revolution.

This truth is something that the millennial generation needs to learn and understand. It is something that must not be rewritten, but taught in classrooms and other venues. It is one of the most important legacies that the old generation can leave to the new one. **(ESC)**

II.
Remembering
Ninoy

Ninoy's Martyrdom

Every August 21, Filipinos commemorate the martyrdom of Ninoy Aquino, which triggered the People Power Revolution that led to the downfall of the Marcos dictatorship and the restoration of democracy in the Philippines.

There are many types of heroic deeds and heroes. Some are military commanders like George Washington, philosophers like Voltaire, and scientists like Einstein.

Then there are heroes who suffer persecution and death for espousing a cause they believe in. Such heroes continue to fight for and remain committed to a cause, even as they are fully aware of the risks and can foresee possible retaliation by their opponents. Such heroes we call martyrs, and their death because of their adherence to a cause, martyrdom.

Although there have been martyrs throughout history, their numbers are very few because their ultimate fate—death—is considered by many as too great a price to pay. Martyrs do not seek death, but they are willing to die rather than renounce their beliefs. But it is also true that martyrdom serves as the ultimate motivation for others to continue fighting for their cause.

St. Joan of Arc was convicted of heresy and burned at the stake on May 30, 1431, after a conspiracy by foes of Charles VII and the English. Twenty-five years after her death at the age of nineteen, her heresy conviction was overturned. In 1920, she was canonized as a saint. It was her sacrifice that restored the French monarchy and finally drove the English out of

France. Her brief life and her brutal death—her martyrdom—fascinated eminent writers like Voltaire, Mark Twain, Anatole France, and George Bernard Shaw.

In 1535, Thomas More was tried for treason for refusing to sign an oath recognizing King Henry VIII's divorce from Catherine of Aragon in order to marry Anne Boleyn. Had More agreed to take the oath, his life would have been spared. But he refused and he was beheaded. In 1935, More was canonized a saint.

Mahatma Gandhi preached and practiced the doctrine of nonviolent resistance to all forms of oppression. He used his formidable leadership skills to help attain independence for India. He also struggled to prevent his country from being divided into two nations, one Muslim and the other Hindu.

In 1948, as he stepped out to greet some people, Godse, a Hindu extremist, shot him three times. His death, unfortunately, did not prevent the partition of India. But today he is still recognized as the inspiration and embodiment of nonviolent resistance even if he suffered a violent death.

Martin Luther King, Jr. organized and inspired numerous acts of civil disobedience, sit-ins, and marches for civil rights. He received the Nobel Prize in 1964, the youngest recipient at that time. In 1968, he was shot and killed by a white racist who was later identified as James Earl Ray. When he was still alive, he had said that whoever gave the eulogy for him should make no mention of the hundreds of awards he had received. Instead, he wanted that person to say that he had been a "drum major for peace and a drum major for righteousness."

Dr. Jose Rizal wrote two books, *Noli Me Tangere* and *El Filibusterismo*. While in prison, he wrote the poem "*Mi Ultimo Adios*." His writings became part of the inspiration for the Philippine revolution. But it was his public execution that became the symbol of Spanish oppression and Filipinos' struggle for freedom.

Ninoy Aquino's death has all the characteristics of martyrdom. Like St. Thomas More, Ninoy could have saved himself by staying in exile and swearing allegiance to a tyrannical ruler. But he refused and decided to come home, fully aware of the possible consequences.

Like Joan of Arc and Mahatma Gandhi, Ninoy suffered a violent death. Upon his arrival in the Philippines, he was shot to death as soon as he stepped on the last step of the service stairway.

Like Martin Luther King, Jr., the death of Ninoy provided more inspiration for more civil disobedience and marches that eventually became known as the People Power Movement.

Finally, like Dr. Jose Rizal, Ninoy's execution became the symbol of the Marcos tyranny and further fueled the courage and commitment to freedom of the Filipino people. Two scenes—Rizal being shot by Spanish soldiers in Luneta and Ninoy's body lying still on the airport tarmac—are among the most distinguished images in Philippine history. These two scenes have also epitomized the ideals of Filipino heroism and love of freedom. **(ESC)**

Ninoy: Man of Courage

How can a single individual fight tyranny and inspire people to restore democracy to their nation? How can a single man restore pride to a nation and leave the legacy that the Filipino is worth dying for? There are very few stories in the Philippine saga as inspiring as that of Ninoy Aquino.

Today, one question often asked is what makes for successful government in a democracy. There are many voices with different views that have tried to present coherent answers to this issue.

There are visionaries, who believe the Philippines must first create a genuinely new social order before there can be a truly successful democracy. This requires removing the monopoly of power from the elite by granting the middle and lower classes equal access to economic and political power.

However, this process of transformation can be attained only after generations of education and reform. The shortcut has always been the axiom that every immediate change in the social order is inaugurated by a phase of revolutionary violence. According to the revolutionary writer, Regis Debray, "Force is the ultimate arbiter of social change not simply because no possessing class gives up real power without a struggle, but also because no popular movement which fails to challenge the ruling power's monopoly of violence will be capable of the social energy necessary to invent a totally new order of society."

There is no question that force has always been decisive in changing or in maintaining the social order. The problem, therefore, is not so much acknowledging the decisive role of force as determining the form that it should take. Will the revolution come in the form of a popular uprising or a military coup d'état?

But are there less violent alternatives? Br. Armin Luistro, FSC, secretary of the Department of Education, believes the answer lies in "restoring faith in democracy." The path to this requires the supreme sacrifice by our leaders to give up not just power but also the quest for more of it. This is a message echoed by spiritual leaders in this country and by those who still seek change through the constitutional process.

The irony in this whole debate is that our political leaders, like former president Gloria Macapagal-Arroyo, Speaker Jose de Venecia, and oppositionists like Ejercito Estrada and Susan Roces, all argue that their primary reason for grabbing power. is the welfare of the poor. They also claim that they are not to blame for the current state of poverty and social injustice. In fact, their proposed solution, as in the case of a parliamentary form of government, is to increase their power by centralizing it in one body—the Congress.

The problem seems to lie in what is meant by "good government." Benito Mussolini, former prime minister of Italy, was said to have a good government because he made the trains run on time. However, in the end, his own people turned on him and caused his death.

The present regime seems to measure good governance in terms of budget deficits, Moody ratings, and the ability to stay in power. The congressional group believes the national budget should be converted into a national pork barrel fund because they contend they know best what their constituents want. In fact, to them, the Philippines is merely a collection of congressional districts.

Then, we have the different interest groups with their own views. The business sector, of course, believes that whatever is good for business is good for the country. Therefore, minimum wages, workers' benefits, and the right of workers to organize are considered evil propositions that will lead to national economic disaster.

In management, we are taught that an organization is judged on the basis of results and not efforts. Also, the final judges are the customers or constituents who are the real reasons for the existence of an organization.

In a democracy, a successful government is judged on the basis of its results, by the majority of the population without sacrificing the interests of the minority.

If the majority of the population believes poverty alleviation, job creation, and social justice matter more than anything else, then the present government, executive and legislative, must be judged as a failure. For those who believe that education, the environment, and peace and order are the most important indicators of good government, then this government is also an unsuccessful government.

In the end, it will be the people who will make the final decision. The only question is whose voice will serve as their inspiration. Will it be the voice of a genuine hero or another charlatan who will lead us to another period of suffering?

Ninoy Aquino has joined the ranks of Filipino immortals like Rizal, Mabini, Quezon, and Magsaysay. It can only be hoped that people will continue to be inspired by his heroism which saved a nation from a dictatorship. Wherever this great man is now, he will know that his sacrifice will remain as a beacon of hope for a suffering people. His colossal courage will certainly continue to inspire those who still want to make a difference in the lives of Filipinos. **(ESC)**

The Ideal Opposition Senator

Every August 21, Filipinos pause to remember the many faces of the greatness of former senator Benigno "Ninoy" Aquino, Jr. Having served in the Cabinet of his widow, President Corazon Aquino, I have seen him through the eyes of his family. Because of this, I choose to remember him as one of the great personalities who once made the Philippine Senate a bulwark of democracy and a gathering of visionary national leaders.

There was a period in our history when the opposition in the Senate was comprised of men of stature. Even during the presidency of the very popular Ramon Magsaysay, the Senate opposition was led by two intellectual giants, Senators Claro M. Recto and Lorenzo Tañada. Their speeches spoke of differences in the political philosophies and national visions from that of the administration at the time. I do not think anybody will attribute their role in history to the committees they chaired or the projects they funded through their pork barrel.

After Recto's retirement, Tañada was joined by his fellow La Sallian, Senator Jose W. Diokno. Together with other opposition senators, they showed that it was possible to have brilliant politicians who also possessed personal integrity and would fight for social justice and equal opportunity for all.

During the Marcos presidency, prior to the martial law years, the opposition included leaders like Gerry Roxas and Soc Rodrigo.

In the 1967 election, with Marcos utilizing all his power and using Machiavellian methods, the young—barely thirty-five years old—Ninoy Aquino was the only opposition candidate elected to the Senate. He later said that his first two years in the Senate were very tough because he was trying very hard to prove that he was worthy of his seat. Nick Joaquin quotes Ninoy talking about those years:

> My God, I was forced to study to learn every trick in the book. I memorized the rules of the Senate; I burned the midnight oil going over the old Senate Journals, reading up on old debates. I was determined to be a good parliamentarian. I was averaging eighteen hours a day reading, reading. I had a staff lining up things for me to read and I'd come home with a bulging briefcase and sit down and read again . . . and I was trained by a great fiscalizer, Ambrosio Padilla, who was in his seat when the bell rang at five and stayed there until eleven in the evening, who asked no quarter and gave no quarter and went over every bill like a fine-toothed comb . . . . Most of all I learned from Tañada. Before making an attack I'd prepare an outline of it and submit it to Tañada and he'd grade it . . . (he) was an exacting mentor but he gave me the discipline to be a good prosecutor.

In these few words, the neophyte senator was already exhibiting certain facets of his future greatness. He understood that greatness did not come from being glamorous, although he was considered to be a celebrity. Nor did it come from simply grabbing power even though he was the scion of a powerful political clan. He was willing to undergo the rigors of intellectual learning and the discipline required to educate himself. At the same time, he had the wisdom to choose the right mentors and the humility to listen to them.

Indeed, Ninoy Aquino was an ideal opposition senator that other politicians should strive to emulate and be remembered for. **(ESC)**

Ninoy: Not a Mere Exile

His exile to the United States was a learning experience for Ninoy Aquino, who was considered as the most prominent critic of the Marcos administration. Aquino experienced much freedom in exile, but it did not occur to him to stay permanently in the United States. In fact, he was plagued by the thought that he might be a mere exile if he stayed away from the country for too long. When he returned to the Philippines, it is said that his commitment to the nonviolent path of change was one of the lessons of his exile. Aquino was not just a mere exile for the Filipinos. Rather, he was instrumental in the People Power Revolution that restored democracy in the country.

Before the Exile

This Wonder Boy's careers in journalism and politics were phenomenal and legendary enough to have earned him a niche in history. But it was Ninoy's unofficial role as leader of the opposition and foil to an overstaying dictator, from the Camp Crame and Fort Bonifacio detention camps to a near-idyllic Boston exile to a tragic martyrdom at the tarmac, that has earned him a unique place in contemporary history.

Even as the eight-year-old Ninoy complained about an "uneventful" existence, there was nothing orthodox about his life. Born to a political and landed family from Tarlac on November 27, 1932 to Senator Benigno S. Aquino, Sr. and Aurora A. Aquino, Ninoy grew up thinking it was not uncommon to have a prominent father and a distinguished paternal grandfather, Gen. Servillano Aquino, a revolutionary who fought both the Spaniards and the Americans.

But then too, Ninoy was no ordinary child, he of the legendary precocity and loquaciousness. When his grandfather-general would visit their home in New Manila, the observant grandson was awed that the general was known to be such a sharpshooter. But he also wondered out loud how that was possible, when he had eyes which were slightly crossed. Ninoy asked him bluntly, to his mother's consternation, "How did you become a general with those eyes?" (Joaquin, 1983: 189).

As a child, Ninoy was always out in the streets, and knew the latest gossip in the neighborhood since he socialized with everyone. Whenever the family would go home to their Concepcion, Tarlac hometown, within an hour he would have gathered the latest update on everyone. This earned him the nickname T-V-T (Tribune, Vanguardia, Taliba—the era's major newspaper chain) because he always had his own neighborhood scoops and was news-conscious. He will be a reporter someday, his father foresaw.

Comfortable with company, whether it be his peers or grown-ups, whatever their station in life, the young Ninoy was never self-conscious about entertaining his father's callers, always an endless stream for those in public office. He would be nestled in the middle of the company, carrying on a conversation with the adult guests, truly living up to his description as precocious and loquacious. It was typical of him to engage the drivers of these prominent guests in animated conversation. And whenever there was any street gathering or assembly, one could be sure Ninoy would be in the midst of it.

But there were unpleasant lessons to be learned, too, the beginning of his orientation in the ways and wiles of politics, during those years of his youth. For suddenly, the boy who had grown up as a prince was now regarded as a pariah (Joaquin, 1983: 191). He smarted from the public perception of his father as Japanese collaborator and this brought him in affinity with the Laurel children, including Salvador or Doy, whose own father was similarly accused. (Doy would later become vice president in the Aquino administration.)

It was another painful blow when his father attempted a political comeback and failed. In 1947, his father died in his arms while watching a boxing bout and the fifteen-year-old Ninoy vainly tried to take him in a taxi to a hospital (Dalisay and Azurin, 1993: 25). Even before this loss, Ninoy, he who never had a childhood because the circumstances of his life dictated that he grow up much too prematurely, had already seen his father as a fallen hero. The setbacks his father felt were also felt as intensely by the young son. And how it repelled him that as his father lay in state, there was a series of necrological services paying the dead man the highest tribute. Ninoy recalled, "I thought it was all baloney, all a sham . . . it was my first time to learn bitterness . . . . That would make me a real loner" (Joaquin, 1983: 194).

Ninoy fell into deep melancholy, but soon found himself thrown again into the world of politics when he campaigned for family friend Jose Laurel, who ran and lost the presidency to Elpidio Quirino in 1949. Thus began Ninoy's phenomenal career in the worlds of journalism and politics. At seventeen, lured by the excitement of media, he applied for a job with the then leading daily, *The Manila Times*. He knew that he was hired as a copy boy by the publisher, Chino Roces, only because their fathers had been friends. He had little more than spunk and his youth to offer, because he could not write a grammatically correct sentence. He learned the ropes quickly because he carefully studied the edited copies that he carried back and forth in the office, seeing firsthand the conventions of writing in newspapering. He went on to cover the Korean War and to receive the Philippine Legion of Honor for Meritorious Service as war correspondent at the age of eighteen. A few years later, at the age of twenty-three, he won another Legion of Honor medal after negotiating the surrender of Southeast Asia's top communist leader, Huk supremo Luis Taruc.

At age 23, he was the country's youngest municipal mayor, the youngest vice governor at 27, and also the youngest governor at age 29. At 35, in 1967, he became the youngest senator of the Republic, the only senatorial opposition candidate to have emerged unscathed by the Marcos machinery. Little wonder then that Ferdinand Marcos was keeping a close eye on the upstart Ninoy Aquino, who he knew would be a potential threat to his overriding ambition and lust for power. Ninoy's political victories at the polls did not come easy, for his opponents always questioned his age eligibility. With every election, the issue became a tired but rehashed one—did the age requirement stipulate it for the age of the candidate on the day of election or the age on the day of proclamation in office? That meant a world of difference for Ninoy, whose birthday fell on November 27, two weeks after election day.

Even when Ninoy was mayor, then president Marcos regarded him as an archenemy, calling him a communist and a "Huk-coddler," favorite epithets especially reserved by Marcos for the wonder boy. Ninoy credits his election to the Senate to Marcos and his accusations, for it led him to be remembered in the public consciousness. He was determined to make a name for himself in the Senate, especially proud that his own father had been a member of the same legislative body. He delivered one fiery speech after another, warning about the making of a Marcos-styled garrison state as early as 1968. The tongue that even his mother could not hold in check as a child was even more unrestrained now, to the delight of media and the citizenry. All the time, Ninoy Aquino was sending signals to President Marcos that "by force of performance and personality," he would succeed him as president of the land (Dalisay and Azurin, 1993: 41).

Among Aquino's memorable speeches—all delivered eloquently and at a speed difficult to match, as if he always had more to say than there was time for—was his September 13, 1972 exposition of Oplan Sagittarius, a government plan to declare martial law, to a nation beset by much social and civil unrest.

Eight days later, on September 21, Marcos did declare martial law. It was no coincidence that the very first "enemy of the state" to be arrested without charges and brought to a military detention camp was Ninoy. Thus began for Ninoy a most trying eight-year period when he was deprived of all his rights as a citizen—but during which he began a spiritual journey and transformation and led an often lonely struggle from his detention cell. He poignantly described the emptiness of his existence: "For seven years, I did not see the moon and stars" (De Quiros, 1997: 440). Marcos thought that the gregarious and outspoken senator would finally be silenced by isolating him from his family and constituents, but Ninoy proved even more eloquent stripped of the trappings of power.

He waged a forty-day hunger strike in 1975 in protest of the military tribunal—kangaroo court, he called it—that was trying him and also in solidarity with all the other victims of oppression and injustice of the regime. In 1977, he was sentenced to death by firing squad for subversion, illegal possession of firearms, and murder. With the opposition against the Marcos dictatorship growing, the dictator knew that he had to find a graceful way to get the charismatic opposition leader out of the scene. In December 1979, while on a brief Christmas furlough at his home, Ninoy was offered freedom by Marcos if he left the country. Ninoy discussed this with friends who advised him to go to the United States (Komisar, 1987: 45). But there came no official order on the exile proposal.

After a heart attack in March 1980, which he suffered while undergoing his routinary jog in detention, Ninoy was rushed to the Philippine Heart Center. When his doctors recommended heart surgery, he requested presidential permission to travel abroad in May. He was granted permission, subject to the approval of the Supreme Court. It was during Mrs. Imelda Marcos's visit to him at Philippine Heart Center when the idea of leaving for the U.S. for surgery was discussed and facilitated. Permission to travel did not come without certain conditions. Ninoy was allowed to leave for the U.S., where he would undergo a triple heart bypass at the Baylor University Medical Center in Dallas, Texas, only with some members of the family. Son Noynoy, who was completing his college studies at the Ateneo de Manila, stayed behind and it was a welcome circumstance that daughter Pinky was based in Hong Kong. Both children quietly joined the rest of the family eventually. It was also stipulated that he would return to the Philippines immediately, presumably to detention camp, after his recovery and that he was not to engage in political activities while abroad.

Exile as Freedom

Only eighty-seven days after release, Ninoy reneged on his oath of silence. "A pact with the devil is no pact at all. My goal is to restore freedom to my people," was how he justified his continued crusading (White, 1989: 114). He delivered an impassioned speech to the Asia Society in New York City and in the first three months abroad, had networked with other Filipino opposition leaders in exile. They were one in their demand for Marcos to step down and dismantle the martial law regime as a prerequisite to national unity (White, 1989: 114).

Ninoy's three-year exile in Boston began. When he recovered from his triple bypass operation, he was invited to a fellowship at Harvard University's Center for International Affairs. This was followed by another fellowship at the Massachusetts Institute of Technology's Center for International Affairs. To his family, these last three years of his life were also the happiest years of their family life.

Despite the fact that this was a tranquil and blissful period, in sharp contrast to the seven years and seven months of detention, Ninoy never entertained any thoughts of taking up permanent exile in the U.S. "We knew it was just a transition period, we knew it would not be forever," said eldest daughter Ballsy Aquino-Cruz (Interview, 14 November 1998). She said it was not a luxurious lifestyle, but a frugal one with only the bare necessities, for although the affluent Cojuangcos, Cory's family, would send her financial assistance, the only regular income earner abroad was Pinky, then working for IBM. It was not like her mother to ask her family for any help, Ballsy shared. Her mother would buy the most economical meat cuts in the market, never complaining about the $100 weekly food budget she had to live with, always managing to creatively make ends meet. The family did not bother to prepare storm windows nor improve the heating system for the gracious 1920s Newton home that was the Boston home they rented, because they knew they could be returning to the Philippines anytime. It had much ambience, but was not very comfortable during the harsh Boston winters. "*Alsa balutan*" (literally, packed and ready to leave) was how Ballsy describes the survival mode the family had to be in. It was hardly the lifestyle of the "steak commandos" that exiles in the First World were often called, with a touch of derision.

Former President Cory Aquino, in writing on her life with Ninoy, reiterated this awareness of the transitoriness of life in Boston:

> Throughout our three years in the U.S., we were always aware that our life there was temporary. Ninoy never ceased talking about the Philippines. Ninoy had many reasons for wanting to return, among the most compelling were the deteriorating political situation in the country, combined with the rumored poor state of the President's health" (C. Aquino, 1986a: 37).

It must have been this consciousness that made Ninoy and Cory make the most of their time together as a family, something that took getting used to because Ninoy had been an absentee father for some time. He found time to be a father to Kris, who was only two when her father's incarceration began. Ballsy recalled how patient he had become and somehow tried to make up for all the years he lost as a family man. Prior to his incarceration, the children could only remember their mother as the more active parent because their father was preoccupied with his political career.

Friends who saw the exiled Ninoy for the first time in Boston were struck by his dignified mien, a far cry from the brash politician that he once was. They were even more surprised at his mellowing, for there emerged a more suave and cosmopolitan man, almost diplomat-like. How could he have shed off all traces of the years of detention, they wondered.

But even if they were thousands of miles away from the Philippines and Marcos, the family knew they had to be as vigilant and security-conscious as they were in Manila and were even certain they were under surveillance and their telephones bugged. This was proven when Ninoy tore his Achilles' heel tendon while alighting from a car and thus had to wear a cast. Immediately after came a friendly call from a defense official back home, asking how things were and by the way, was Ninoy faring well after the accident?

Still and all, Boston and Harvard were a feast for Ninoy's mind and heart. As Cory reminisced:

> Boston was paradise. He was free and you have to have had Ninoy's experience in prison to appreciate what freedom means. In Boston too, Ninoy developed his mind further. Harvard was a dream come true, Ninoy would

often say, and without his detention in Fort Bonifacio, Harvard would never
have happened. That was Ninoy. He always saw the bright side of everything.
(C. Aquino, 1986a: 37)

Because he thrived in interacting with people, Ninoy's Boston home was always a busy hive.
There were the members of the Filipino community who made the Aquinos feel so welcome.
Ballsy recalled that when they first arrived there, long-time resident Mary Rose Jacinto
Ezpeleta, herself a family member of an affluent steel magnate forced into exile during the
Marcos years, introduced them to other Filipinos. There was a constant stream of guests, largely
Ninoy's friends from the Philippines, to be picked up at the airport so that Ballsy and Pinky felt
they might as well be running a taxi service. Ballsy, Pinky, and Viel finally decided to move to
the attic so that their second-floor bedrooms would be permanent guest rooms. That was far
less complicated and disconcerting than having to make room for houseguests every so often.
But there was still the beddings laundry to worry about with every coming and going. It was
Kris, then nine, who squealed to her mother that she overheard her father persuading guests
who were already billeted at a hotel to please move to their house instead, lest Cory "be so hurt."
And to add insult to injury, Ninoy would tease Cory by making sure she was within hearing
distance when he would "apologize" to the guests at dinner, "*Pasensiya na kayo, si Cory lang ang
nagluto*" (Our apologies, it was only Cory who cooked). All these she would take in good humor,
because she also knew that when she was not listening, he would pay her cooking such lavish
compliments (Sta. Romana Cruz, 1996: 30-31).

Ballsy continues to be amused by recollections of her father's hospitality often gone way out
of bounds, his eagerness to meet old friends, friends of his children, even mere acquaintances
from home. He was the tireless tour guide who wore his guests out with his characteristic talent
at being raconteur. Even when his foot was in a cast and he had to depend on a crutch to walk,
Ninoy had to drive to the airport to pick up fellow freedom fighter and statesman Lorenzo
Tañada, Sr. In typical Ninoy Aquino fashion, Ninoy did not stop talking politics and in the next
breath was pointing out this and that interesting sight during the drive to Newton, until Tañada
begged him to please concentrate on the road because his newly-arrived guest was getting so
nervous.

A crusader of democracy that he was, Ballsy says that at home, he was a complete autocrat,
making decisions independent of all family members, including his wife. He did not feel the
need to carry on democratic discussions. The members of the family were simply expected to

abide by his decision and trust that it was done in the best interest. She recounts that her mother said, almost with pride, that she was uncomplaining about following him and was just happy and content having Ninoy for a husband. Cory was in awe of Ninoy and his intelligence during their courtship years—and that high regard persisted during their marriage. It was not in a complaining tone when she described her husband as a male chauvinist. In an interview with Gail Sheehy for *Parade Magazine* of the Washington Post, Cory said, "He never wanted it said that I was influencing him in anything." This, Cory did not mind at all because she enjoyed her private role. "I figured, 'Look, you can do your thing in public life. I'm going to make sure that these children of ours will turn out to be good and responsible citizens'" (Belmonte, 1986: 37a).

She confessed to having been intimidated being part of the party circuit in Boston, when she and Ninoy associated with intellectuals who talked not of books they had read, but of those they had written. Ninoy thrived, but Cory lived blissfully content in her legendary husband's shadow. Because she chose to stay in the background, the image of Cory preparing coffee, quiches, peking duck, and chicken liver pate was perpetuated. But who can resist the influence of a Ninoy? One cannot really be such a neophyte politician when one is married to a master like Ninoy, admitted Cory. "I suppose it is all osmosis, since I also come from a political family" (Sta. Romana Cruz, 1998: 292).

It was a matter of choice that Cory shunned being on center stage. But there were opportunities for her to show her independent spirit, the quiet courage and dignity that saw her through the painful years when her husband was in detention. Scott Thompson, an American professor who knew the Aquinos well then, remembers a dinner he hosted for the couple. He suggested after dinner that the ladies leave the men to their cigars. The idea did not sit well with Cory, who wanted to stay just where she was—and unabashedly made her sentiments known without any fuss: ". . . she knew, as the guest of honor's wife and a woman of wealth and breeding, that she could get away with it" (Policarpio, 1986: 80).

Throughout the three years of his exile, Ninoy never lost sight of his dream to see the restoration of democracy in the country. As an exile in the U.S., he joined another senator and well-known oppositionist, Raul Manglapus. Together, they wrote to Vice-President George Bush in reaction to the American official's lamented remarks to the dictator Marcos, "We love your adherence to democratic principles—and to the democratic processes." Aquino and Manglapus reminded Bush upon his arrival in Manila for a scheduled visit: "Kindly keep in mind that your every word of praise for the Marcos dictatorship and your every appearance and published picture with the dictator will deepen the cynicism of the Filipino people and drive more of their countrymen to the arms of the radical left" (Manglapus,1986: 230). Although they were both outspoken Marcos critics working toward the same goal, Ninoy declined Manglapus's offer of the presidency of the Movement for a Free Philippines, which Manglapus founded and headed (Manglapus, 1986: xxiii).

It was not all sweetness and light in Harvard, for while there, the Marcos regime filed, in addition to his already existing death sentence, two more subversion charges against him and publicly announced that he would be served arrest warrants the minute he stepped on Philippine soil (B. Aquino, 1983: 58). But the distance and the clime of the academe gave Ninoy "the leisure and atmosphere to reflect on the meaning of his prison years for his country. And it was from our home in Newton, so close to Harvard, that he made his final trip to bring home the fruit of his reflections" (C. Aquino, 1986c).

A difficult issue Ninoy had to reckon with during his exile was deciding between the violent and nonviolent options for the dismantling of the Marcos dictatorship. Should Marcos's ruthlessness be matched by violence? It seemed the only way to remove the dictator from office. He devoted hours of academic research studying the use of violence toward national liberation.

By coming home the way he did, it was obvious what his preferred option was.

Ninoy's plan to come home, frightening to his family who knew it meant walking right back to detention, was met with much speculation in Manila, the same way his sudden departure to the U.S. was. Many even suspected that he did not really have any health problem, but had settled for a deal with the Marcoses. This time, his return home was under suspicion, for why would he give up the comforts of a Boston lifestyle?

When he made known his plans to return home to friends, among them, fellow detainee and media personality Jose Mari Velez and *Free Press* publisher Teodoro Locsin, Sr., he made it clear that nothing could change his mind. Not the foreshadowing of what awaited him in Manila, spoken by Imelda Marcos herself, at a meeting with Ninoy in New York. Not Velez's concern for his life or freedom. His mind was set, "I'm willing to give up my freedom and go back to Bonifacio for just ten minutes of Mr. Marcos's time. I have to convince him that unless he (Marcos) immediately starts us back on the road to Democracy through fair and honest elections, the Philippines faces the grim and bloody prospects of a military takeover and a revolution" (Maramba,1984:92-93).

Not Locsin Sr.'s reminder of another solitary confinement or house arrest or even of the grim scenario, "Suppose you are shot?" stopped him. Instead, his proud answer was, "If they had not recalled Rizal and shot him, he would have ended his life as a mere exile. He would be nothing in our history . . . . If they make the mistake of killing me or shooting me, they will make me a hero and they will lose and I will win" (Dalisay and Azurin, 1993: 47).

In a letter datelined San Francisco on February 21, 1983 to Senator Estrada Kalaw, Ninoy said, "I am seriously considering returning to our country soon. I think my usefulness in America has come to an end. And I think, I'll be able to help the opposition from there more effectively than from the safety of America" (B. Aquino, 1983: 48).

The Return of Ninoy: From Subversive to Hero

Far from being a hasty decision the journey home was one that had long been premeditated. Keeping in touch with fellow exiles in the U.S. and comrades back home, Ninoy was always eager for any developments in the political situation. Among his usual questions were: What did the young students think of him, beyond a figure from the past who was now a member of the opposition? Did people think he was a steak commando? Did they think he could advance the cause of freedom better in the United States or was it now time to go home? How dangerous was it to do so? (Maramba, 1984: 122).

Ninoy's prepared and undelivered arrival statement speaks of the consequences and folly of his homecoming: "I have prepared for the worst . . . and return to an uncertain future" (B. Aquino, 1983: 68). He had presumed solitary confinement or death by firing squad. The image of the returning hero's grim and startled expression as he was being led out of the China Airlines plane from Taipei by uniformed military escorts had been captured on videotape and replayed many times over, then on television, and today in people's memories. It tells us that while reality was far worse than he himself predicted, Ninoy was truly ready to die for the Filipino who to him was worth dying for.

In the article "Ninoy & the group of 28," Tony Gatmaitan reveals the negotiations between Ninoy and a group of twenty-eight financiers who were willing to support Ninoy's program of anti-Marcos mass mobilization. He wrote: "The group of 28 still believes that Ninoy Aquino was shot because in three years he had become a total warrior. He came home better prepared for a confrontation rather than for negotiations. He came home for negotiations, yes, but if that failed he was fully prepared for confrontation" (1986: 9).

The festive homecoming planned for the exile returning with a passport bearing the name of Marcial Bonifacio (for martial law and Fort Bonifacio, where he was detained), was suddenly transformed into a tragic event with the white figure of the martyred hero sprawled on the tarmac, murdered by the very same soldiers meant to safeguard his life.

That Sunday in 1983, the 21st of August, marked the beginning of the end for the Marcos regime, for the death of the returning exile elicited unprecedented waves of protest and mass action, calling for an end to the dictatorship. The gunshots that killed Ninoy may as well have been heard all over the world, for the assassination elicited much support internationally. Rather than being stilled and silenced, Ninoy and the voice of the opposition gained new life. Ninoy died as he lived, it has been often said, for he spoke fast, ate fast, thought fast, always racing against time. And he may as well have styled his death, for it was as he wanted, "swift and fast" (Maramba, 1984: 87).

After that Sunday afternoon, the Filipinos were never the same again.

The murder of Ninoy was more than what the long-suffering Filipinos were willing to take. They paid tribute to Ninoy as he lay in his casket bloodied and wounded, in the same blood-streaked white safari suit he came home in. Two million fearless Filipinos led him to his final resting place in Parañaque in a funeral procession that took all of eleven hours.

The death of Ninoy became the symbol of the struggle for justice and reconciliation. And the yellow ribbons and buntings festooned on trees became the color of the revolution that culminated in the EDSA People Power three years after his death.

In contrast to his pledge of nonviolence and reconciliation, Ninoy Aquino's homecoming took a bizarre turn. His good intentions were foiled by his assassin's bullets. Yet his death was not altogether meaningless, for it accomplished what Ninoy sought. As his widow recalled in an August 21 commemoration, "What happened to us after Ninoy's death was completely unexpected. There were no reassurances that if he went home, our people will rally around him . . . I knew that a great change was taking place . . . ." (C. Aquino, 1998).

Cory was almost stunned to see upon the family's arrival in Manila a group of media persons waiting to interview her—and tens of thousands of people patiently on queue to pay Ninoy their last respects. This was incredulous, because in his lifetime, speaking to a crowd of 500 people was already significant.

The people had awakened from apathy and although logically the reigning president's might and power ought to have prevailed, it proved vulnerable in the face of weekly protest rallies initially staged in Makati, yellow confetti marches, and continuing people's protests, with thumbs and forefingers forming the letter "L," after Ninoy's Laban party.

Cory, shy and reticent in a previous existence when she was "merely" Ninoy's spouse, now found herself under the harsh limelight of publicity and celebritydom. Just by being Ninoy's wife, she became the symbol of the struggle for truth, justice, and reconciliation and emerged the charismatic leader who brought the factious forces of the opposition together.

Three years after Ninoy's martyrdom, a revolution took place not in a battlefield but on a highway, not with firearms, but with the interlocked arms of comrades fighting for freedom through prayers and sheer unity of spirit. It was a peaceful three-day revolution that led Marcos out of Malacañang into his own shameful exile in Hawaii, "a revolution with a laughing face," it was called (Magno, 1998: 274). It was an event that the whole world watched because it was the very first time in history that civilians were called upon to defend the military.

Also referred to as the EDSA Revolution, EDSA stands for Epifanio delos Santos Avenue, a major highway in Metro Manila. This was where masses of people gathered to show support for the military leadership who broke away from Marcos. Filipinos proved themselves worthy of the sacrifice as they came out in full force to show that "*Ninoy, hindi ka nag-iisa*" (Ninoy, you are not alone).

And in a chronology of events that even the most skillful fiction writers could not have imagined nor crafted the scope and grandeur of, the courageous woman in yellow who once upon a time was known only as a compliant housewife serving coffee to her husband's constant stream of guests, had been elected president of the Philippines. As the housewife turned opposition leader turned president said in a speech months after her having assumed office, "I don't think that I need to say how much I wished for myself and for my children that it had been Ninoy standing there being sworn in. Yet I understood why it could not be" (C. Aquino, 1986b).

The euphoria that was the EDSA revolution has waxed and waned over the years. Many have expressed disillusionment about the lost opportunities for true democracy and greatness, while some are sharply critical of the Aquino administration for what is perceived as having made no serious attempt at regaining the greatness so long in coming to this country. Was it not accomplishment enough to have reestablished the democratic institutions totally lost during the dictatorship? Was it not sufficient to have restored democracy and effected a peaceful transition from President Aquino to President Ramos? Was it not a measure of strength to have survived seven coup attempts?

EDSA may still remain the unfinished revolution, but its gains cannot be diminished. Democracy for most parts of the world is never so easily attained. It needs to be the handiwork of the entire citizenry. **(NSRC)**

References

Aquino, Benigno S., Jr. 1983. *Letters—Prison and Exile.* Metro Manila: Aquino Family and La Ignaciana Apostolic Center.

Aquino, Corazon C. 1998. "A Call for Transformation, Courage & Selflessness." Speech at EDSA Shrine, 21 August.

———. 1986a. "My Life with Ninoy," *1985-86 Fookien Times Yearbook*, 36-37.

———. 1986b. "Non-Violence: The Key to Peace." Speech at Harvard University, 22 September, Boston, Massachusetts.

———. 1986c. "A Sentimental Journey." Speech at a dinner hosted by Boston Mayor Ramon Flynn, 20 September, Boston, Massachusetts.

Belmonte, Betty Go. 1986. Editor's Note, *1985-86 Fookien Times Philippine Yearbook*, 37a.

Burton, Sandra. 1989. *Impossible Dream: The Marcoses, the Aquinos, and the Unfinished Revolution.* New York: Warner Books.

Crisostomo, Isabelo T. 1986. *Cory: Profile of a President.* Quezon City: J. Kriz Publishing Enterprises.

Dalisay, Jose Y., Jr. and Arnold M. Azurin. 1993. "Benigno S. Aquino, Jr.: The Making of a Martyr." In *Six Modern Filipino Heroes.* Edited by Asuncion David Maramba. Metro Manila: Anvil Publishing, Inc.

De Quiros, Conrad. 1997. *Dead Aim: How Marcos Ambushed Philippine Democracy.* Pasig City: Foundation for Worldwide People Power, Inc.

Gatmaitan, Tony. 1986. "Ninoy and the Group of 28," *Sunday Inquirer Magazine*, 24 August 1986.

Joaquin, Nick. 1983. *The Aquinos of Tarlac: An Essay on History as Three Generations.* Metro Manila: Cacho Hermanos, Inc.

Komisar, Lucy. 1987. *Cory Aquino: The Story of a Revolution.* New York: George Brazillier, Inc.

Magno, Alexander R. 1998. "The Aquino Assassination." In *A Nation Reborn, Vol. 9: Kasaysayan: The Story of the Filipino People.* Edited by Jose Y. Dalisay, Jr. Manila: Asia Publishing Company, Ltd.

Manglapus, Raul S. 1986. *A Pen for Democracy.* Manila: Movement for a Free Philippines.

Maramba, Asuncion David, ed. 1984. *Ninoy Aquino: The Man, the Legend.* Mandaluyong: Cacho Hermanos.

Mercado, Monina Allarey. 1993. *People Power, An Eyewitness History: The Philippine Revolution of 1986.* Manila: Writers and Readers Publishing, Inc. and Tenth Avenue Editions, Inc.

———. 1986. *Ninoy: Ideals and Ideologies 1932-1983.* Edited by Socorro Enage Sapnit. Metro Manila: Benigno S. Aquino Jr. Foundation, Inc.

Policarpio, Alfonso P., Jr. 1986. *Ninoy: The Willing Martyr.* Manila: Isaiah Books.

Sta. Romana-Cruz, Neni. 1998. "Cory Aquino, Citizen." In *A Nation Reborn, Volume 9. Kasaysayan: The Story of the Filipino People.* Edited by Jose Y. Dalisay, Jr. Manila: Asia Publishing Company, Ltd.

———. 1996. "Recipes of the Smart and Famous: Ninoy's Favorites," *Food,* I (11):28-32.

White, Mel. 1989. *Aquino.* USA: Word Publishing.

Life With Ninoy

Cory Cojuangco Aquino jested that the only things that wanted in her otherwise blissful twenty-nine-year marriage to Ninoy were a few unconventional and boring moments.

She, with unusual restraint, had alternately mystified and embarrassed those who openly wept in indignation over the Black Sunday incident at the airport. Could she be for real, many wondered as they bore the anger and the bitterness that this extraordinary widow was expected to manifest, but didn't.

But then, in Cory's life, nothing has ever conformed to the normal and the predictable.

Once upon a time, when she was seventeen and a freshman at Mount Saint Vincent in New York, a Catholic school run by the Sisters of Charity, she dreamt old-fashioned dreams of a conventional marriage to someone much older and wiser than she. This was why she rebuffed Ninoy's especially warm airmailed tidings with a stereotyped, "Let's just be friends!"

Cory had been educated abroad since age thirteen, together with her two brothers and three sisters. Despite the long years in the States, the children came home each year for their vacations. It was at one of the usual rounds of bienvenidas when seventeen-year-old Cory first became aware of this young charmer Ninoy, also seventeen.

Even so, Ninoy did not quite meet the stipulated age requirement in Cory's romantic dreams. But that did not discourage him. In true Ninoy Aquino fashion, he merely let time pass quietly. Two summers or so later, Cory had softened, realizing that despite the age deficiency, Ninoy was far more intelligent than any of the older men she had hoped to marry.

Returning home for good after graduating with a bachelor's degree in French and Math (the unorthodox combination because she wanted to be different), Cory tried to satisfy her perennial fascination with law by attending law classes for a full year and a half. This she had to forego with her eventual marriage to Ninoy.

Tarlac folks deemed the union of two of its most influential families a most fortunate and ideal one. At any rate, it was inevitable that Ninoy and Cory should meet, since Cory's father, Don Pepe, was the godfather of Ninoy's sister, Lupita.

Cory and Ninoy had long agreed that they first met at a birthday party of Ninoy's father. But there was little significance to the event for, Cory laughed, "We were both nine and what do nine-year-olds think about?"

As everyone who knew Ninoy was aware, he was a political, public person and thrived on crowds, while Cory was the exact opposite. Never was this sharp incompatibility put to a greater test than during their first years of marriage—a true baptism of fire, she called it.

A year after marriage, soon after their first child was born, Ninoy was elected mayor of Concepcion, Tarlac. While Cory could not campaign because of her baby, she nevertheless had to live according to people's expectations of a mayor's wife.

That meant accompanying the sick to Manila for hospital care with the Aquino car doubling as ambulance, and attending all the wakes in town. What she found the most difficult was visiting the dead and sometimes waiting for coffins to be nailed to completion and having nightmares afterward over such long waiting scenes when the dead seemed as impatient as the living. While devoutly complying with these responsibilities, Cory found herself buttressing her spirit with the thought, "No one forced me into this way of life. I made the choice."

What also took an inordinate amount of getting used to, especially for a New York-reared girl, was Concepcion's electric power supply, which was available only twelve hours a day. Most difficult for Cory was allowing herself to be public property. "It was such a small town that everyone minded each other's business. Everyone knew what we had for lunch," recalled the very private Cory.

The next and only other time Cory had to campaign more vigorously was when Ninoy ran for the Senate. This seemed imperative, in spite of the couple's vow early in their marriage that each would continue to do what each could do best: Ninoy, his public service, and Cory, caring for home and children.

Despite what may have seemed a major irreconcilable difference, Cory never felt this was a serious threat to their marriage. It merely seemed the most natural thing that both she and Ninoy had enough old-fashioned sterling love to sustain the complexities of an unconventional marriage. To Cory, marriage meant forever. It was a path she had taken and there was no turning back.

Besides, Cory candidly claimed, "With his charm, you could not stay angry with him for long. He would turn everything into a joke." For instance, Ninoy had never stopped teasing her for her initial coyness when she first discouraged the infatuated young man. Cory said of that rebuff, "It was probably the only time in his life that anyone ever turned him down."

On those occasions when Ninoy was into fiery anti-establishment tirades, Cory would go through the often futile motions of attempting to temper him. But speaking as someone who knew Ninoy too well, she said her attitude was one of resignation. "Who can ever dissuade him from doing something once he had made his mind up?" Through all these, Ninoy would remind her, "At least, you can never say there is ever a dull moment in this marriage." Cory has often told him that she would do anything precisely to get such moments.

It is strange and sad that they had to get away to enjoy such simple joys! Cory remembered fondly the periodic Hong Kong trips (the last one was in 1981) they took as a family, more a necessity than a luxury, for it was during those times when Ninoy suddenly found the time to be with his children all day. On unusual evenings when Ninoy would be relatively free in Manila, Cory and he would go to the movies, any kind of movie, for which they had such a passion. In Boston, the family would complain of the cold or feign sheer exhaustion because Ninoy always enjoyed going out.

The last three years the Aquinos lived in the warmth of family togetherness in Newton, Boston, were idyllic years in many ways, compared with the splintered family set-up during detention at Fort Bonifacio. But it was not all that comfortable and easy at the start. Cory and Ninoy, after somehow having gotten used to living apart, needed to get used to the idea of living together once more. "While the children had only me for so long, there was their father now whom they had to relate to and regard as the authority figure. Especially for Kris who had never known what it was to have a home with a father, this was a special experience."

"I had to be good at cooking and cleaning to survive in Boston," revealed Cory, whose lifestyle never required her to do tasks that a retinue of hired hands could so easily do. One of her biggest thrills in the States was eating out just anywhere. For that meant freeing her of one less meal to prepare, and the children, of dishes to wash. Even in a place not in the usual path of tourists, the Aquinos' typical New England home never ran out of visiting friends who would stay for a day or so. There was such a continuous stream that Cory sometimes wished out loud for disposable beddings.

For extraordinary and hardy as her spirit may be, Cory never aspired to be a stereotyped all-suffering, all-enduring wife. She felt perfectly free to speak out her thoughts to Ninoy, especially when the going was rough.

An inevitability that arose as a consequence of Ninoy's detention for many years was his loss of employment. While it may be difficult to conceive that a Cojuangco heiress should ever need to reckon with the economics of survival, Cory said this was part of the reality they had to accept. She may have taken comfort in the prospect of security, in having a dear and fortunately large family, both Ninoy's and hers, to fall back on, should help be truly necessary. Don Pepe had once admonished his children to continue to assist one another especially during times when one of them may, because of certain circumstances, be unable to work. But Ninoy was proud and would not hear of any form of material assistance. "We have always lived comfortably, never luxuriously, and it has always been through Ninoy's efforts."

It is this very same openness that has allowed Cory to interpret freely Ninoy's repeated request in his lifetime that he be interred in Tarlac. To reach a happy compromise because she herself preferred the convenience of visiting the dead in the city, they had agreed matter-of-factly that whoever would be left behind would have the final choice. And Cory felt she had made the right choice, for although Tarlac is a cherished place, one could not visit as regularly as one would want to.

While in Boston, she would wonder out loud to Ninoy what intellectual discussions would again accompany the dinners to which they were invited. It was after all such an intellectual mecca that the usual cocktail party talk would not be "What books have you read?" but "What books have you written?"

Ninoy, observed to have undergone a full flowering of his intellectual gifts during his three-year exile, considered such speculations trivial. This widely-read man would tell her what he had always been convinced of, that whatever form of competition there is in the world all boils down really to the number of books one has read. And Ninoy knew he was far ahead in that race.

On Cory's part, she felt that her being a good listener went well with what such Boston intellectuals needed.

Is she apolitical? Many people have wondered. Cory said, "I may not be a politician. But it would have been such a pity for someone who has been exposed to Ninoy not to be one. I feel l owe the country something."

Soon after their father's death, while recollecting their last days of relative tranquillity in Boston, the children were regretting that they were not more willing subjects to the newsmen and photographers who flocked to their home, assiduously covering their father's pre-departure weeks. Then, like Kris and Pinky, they would have had many more recent photos with their dad. Viel, considered to be the shyest of them all, is remembered to have said, "Another photographer again!" and quickly retreated to her bedroom. Though they avoid publicity, they have been taught that their status in life gives them the responsibility to share their blessings with others.

Soon, life did begin to normalize in Times Street. Cory was eager to start life anew, to see her four older kids settled in their jobs, to see Kris adjusted to her life as a seventh grader at the International School. Two days after the funeral, Cory was enrolling Kris at IS, once more lending credence to her brave words, "I have done all my crying in Boston. Besides, when you cry, then things don't get done."

The tears may not be evident, but the pain was. Typical of Cory, hers was an inconsolable grief that must be kept private. "I do not wish to cry in front of my children. They have enough pressures to cope with. Other people too seem uncomfortable when they see you in tears."

People who were heartbroken at the sight of the once fiery and flamboyant Ninoy in his bloodied bush jacket feared that his appearance may inflict more unnecessary sorrow on his family. Cory saw nothing of what many thought unpretty. "He looked much better than I expected. I guess when you love someone, you only see the beautiful."

Her heart may have been scarred, even battered—but still she struggled to keep it whole and full. **(NSRC)**

"Dad in White, Lying Dead on the Tarmac"

I distinctly remember the sense of anticipation and uncertainty at the meeting of the Women Writers in Media Now (WOMEN) the day before Ninoy Aquino's expected arrival

WOMEN is a group of journalists organized in 1981 by Marra Pl. Lanot, Mila Astorga Garcia, and Jo-Ann Q. Maglipon. Initially, the members came together to hone their craft and critique each other's writings. But the growing climate of suppression in the country led them to join the struggle for freedom from the dictatorship. They did what they knew best and wrote the stories of fellow citizens stripped of human rights—and some of them paid the price for it. It is a badge of courage they proudly wear today—that they were summoned to military court hearings for their writings.

As had become a regular practice of the group, we met at Odette Alcantara's lovely and welcoming Heritage Art Center in Cubao, Quezon City. Odette was a feisty woman warrior and, in her later years, an environmentalist with whom we shared many causes. At that August 20 meeting, there was indecisiveness about meeting Ninoy at the airport. We did not wish to add to what was sure to be a large homecoming crowd, and we were absolutely confident that there would be subsequent protest rallies under his leadership that we would certainly join. We felt that at worst, he would be thrown back in detention.

More than three decades later, Ninoy's death still angers and resurrects anti-Marcos sentiments in many people. Did the regime really feel it could get away with murder, that the citizenry would simply be cowed into silence? August 21, 1983 drastically changed the course of Philippine history, led to the dictator's undoing, and the return of our democracy.

When one cannot but yield to the strong feelings of antipathy that this nightmare brings, one appreciates and marvels at the absence of negative feelings in Ninoy's children—President Noynoy Aquino, Ballsy Cruz, Pinky Abellada, and Viel Dee—at the recollection of that day.

In his first-ever visit to their Newton home in 2014, ironically on the anniversary date of martial law, PNoy recalled what it was like back then. In an atypical emotional speech in Boston College, he shared:

> In the early morning hours of August 21, 1983, I was watching CNN, waiting to see if they had any news about Dad's arrival. I will never forget the face of the reporter when he said that, upon the arrival of opposition leader Benigno Aquino, shots were heard, and he was seen lying in a pool of blood.
>
> This most unexpected news was such a shock that I lost all sensation, and lost track of space and time until the phone rang. I scrambled to get to the phone before any of my sisters or my mother, all of whom were upstairs, could answer it. It was a Filipino-American friend from the West Coast, and by her somber tone, I immediately knew something was wrong, but she wouldn't tell me anything. When I got upstairs, I found them all awake, and also tuned on to the news, knowing nothing definite, waiting for messages from friends and allies.

The news was broken to them by Takeo Iguchi, the Japanese consul at the time and a friend of the older Aquino, who heard the news through a Japanese politician, who was informed by a Japanese reporter on the plane with the late senator.

"This was one of our family's lowest points. As the only son, I felt an overwhelming urge to exact an eye for an eye."

Viel remembers what it was like for her in their home in Newton, Boston—a comfortable and secure environment that her father left for much uncertainty and danger back home.

"I was awakened in the middle of the night with the shocking news and even though it was a very warm summer night (and we had no air conditioning in the room), I suddenly was shivering cold."

Ballsy and Pinky share (along with many of us) the enduring image of "Dad in white, lying dead on the tarmac." No other words are needed to convey the tragedy of the assassination, preserved in that timeless image.

It is apparent that, armed with their mother's deep faith and prayerfulness, they do not dwell on the past and have learned to always look to the future with optimism.

It is a blessing for the family that it was also because of that day that their special long-time friendship with respected theologian Fr. Catalino Arevalo, SJ, began. He was then on leave from the Ateneo and was studying in Boston College across from their Newton home. When an American fellow Jesuit informed him about the assassination, he felt he had to offer his help to the slain ex-senator's family, whom he had never met. He says he must have met Cory in his youth because his best friend during his Ateneo school days was Monching Cojuangco, a cousin of Cory's, in whose Baguio home he would spend summers.

Back in Manila, Father Arevalo celebrated the first Mass for Ninoy in October 1983. Since then, he became Cory's spiritual adviser, and continues to be the invited priest with his thoughtful homilies at family commemorations. Pinky teases that that knock on the door of the Newton home must be a gesture Fr. Arevalo regrets, as he has not been able to walk out again. To this day, the respected Jesuit theologian deeply feels the loss of Cory Aquino, tearing up as he recalls the many conversations with her. All he can say in total admiration and respect is, "I truly miss her."

It must provide the members of Ninoy's family much consolation that through the three decades, they have never been alone in their commemoration—long before it became a national holiday. To every celebration of the Mass at the Manila Memorial Park, faithful Ninoy followers from all walks of life would come unbidden. Cory would always say that this faithful attendance was heartwarming and beyond all expectations, that the crowd had done its share and when her turn came, it would no longer be necessary to be ever present as well. That has been left unheeded, of course.

It is said that when Cory was buying a memorial plot for her husband, she turned down the plots in the more private and secluded areas where the mausoleums of the elite were, saying even then that Ninoy had to be where people could easily visit.

To Ninoy's children, there is such comfort in the public remembering of a man "who gave up his life so that his countrymen would regain their lost freedoms." Let his life, and death, ensure that we will "never forget the horrors of a dictatorship and martial law and prevent its repeat."

What are the lessons learned from their father? Pinky speaks of "his big heart and his love for country and love for people from all walks of life." Eldest daughter Ballsy keeps those lessons close to her heart—and many others she still prefers to keep mysteriously private. **(NSRC)**

The Political Role Model

Each time we talk of elections, we lament the lack of political heroes—politicians who can serve as role models for our children.

Political heroes are those who have used their leadership to bring critical issues to the attention of his or her people and convince them to get involved in helping make this world a better place for everyone and for future generations.

It is always difficult to choose a present leader as a hero because there will be groups that will always oppose any current leader. But Filipinos face a unique and critical moment in the history of their country. They will now choose the political leaders who will either bring us back to the old days of systemic corruption and crony capitalism, or those who will lead the country to its golden age. With all the corruption in politics, it is easy to keep pointing the finger at all the bad guys and forget that it is still possible to have good guys—even heroes—in politics.

Philippine history has a gallery of heroes. But it is very rare for a politician to be hailed as a national hero. Even presidents have seldom been considered heroic figures in our history. The two presidents generally acknowledged as heroes are Ramon Magsaysay and Corazon Aquino. Both were never considered as being in the mold of typical politicians. Magsaysay was more known as a guerrilla leader and as secretary of defense when he was able to suppress the growing Communist rebellion. During his 1953 presidential campaign, his campaign jingle's most famous line was: "Our democracy will die *kung wala si Magsaysay.*"

Cory never ran for any government position before she ran for the presidency against Marcos in 1986. Her campaign was more of a crusade than an electoral campaign. Marcos used guns, goons, and gold to defeat her. But Marcos had to resort to blatant cheating to try and stay in power. Aquino's victory was the result of a People Power Movement, not a victory based on a political machinery or campaign funds.

Ninoy Aquino was such a rare person. He was a thoroughbred politician who became a national hero by exercising political leadership. Even his martyrdom was a political act if we again define politicians as those who use their leadership in order to attain a national vision for the people.

He was elected as mayor of his hometown and then ran and won as a congressman. Finally, in 1967, he survived a Nacionalista landslide and became the lone Liberal to win in the senatorial elections. His popularity made him the most logical candidate to replace Marcos as the president of the Philippines.

Ninoy did not have a private army nor did he start an insurrectionist movement to topple the government. He did not believe in an armed revolution. He had faith in the democratic process and the rule of law. Even in jail, he remained the most popular political personality in the nation. Marcos always considered him as the most dangerous opponent of the martial law regime.

Even as a senator, Ninoy was already establishing that rare distinction of a politician also becoming a statesman. His most famous speeches could be full of criticism but always contained elements of a political ideology. On August 25, 1971, on the floor of the Senate, Ninoy gave a speech defending himself from charges of being a communist. But his speech also included these lines:

> If the inexpressible cruelties of official oppression and repression cannot cow us, the tyranny upon us will fail. In the end I say, tyranny will bend to moral justice. Official injustice is still the Filipinos' burden. It is their government's shame. The demand of the hour is upon us, my countrymen, and it is simple: We must weld; separately, I must warn, we shall perish.
>
> Greatness, Mr. President, is not willed, it is earned. It is not a crown put on one's head, it is given by a people as a tribute to a leader. If Mr. Marcos has ruled selflessly and wisely, when the historians write the chapter of Philippine life under his rule, they will pause and say of him: "There lived a

great man, a great president who made a priesthood out of the presidency."
This, I know is a great challenge and an overwhelming responsibility.
Unhappily Mr. Marcos, who started off with a pledge to lead this nation to
a great-again society, has failed to come up to the measure.

There is one characteristic that separates the political hero from the run-of-the-mill
politician. The hero politician stands for a set of beliefs or values that is clearly manifested
in his political life, thus lending him credibility. This belief, however, must be clearly
communicated to the people.

The run-of-the-mill politician is one who sells himself or herself to the public based on
promises or being against something or somebody. It is easy, for example, to be against the
BBL but what is it that opponents of the BBL stand for and what is their alternative proposal?

On August 21, 1983, Ninoy returned to the Philippines after being exiled by the
Marcos regime. Upon arrival, he was immediately arrested while descending from the plane
surrounded by military escorts. Unknown to most Filipinos, he had a speech ready for his
homecoming. The speech was never delivered.

In his prepared speech, he outlined some of his political beliefs. He said:

> National reconciliation and unity can be achieved but only with justice,
> including justice for our Muslim and Ifugao brothers . . . . Subversion stems
> from economic, social and political causes and will not be solved by purely
> military solutions. It can be curbed not with ever increasing repression but
> with a more equitable distribution of wealth, more democracy, and more
> freedom and for the economy to get going once again, the workingman
> must be given his just and rightful share of his labor and to the owners and
> managers must be restored the hope where there is so much uncertainty if
> not despair.

These are ideals that are still relevant to this day. In fact, these messages are also found in
the writings of Pope Francis.

Ninoy ended his prepared speech with these words: "I return from exile and to an
uncertain future with only determination and faith to offer—faith in our people and faith in
God." He was prepared to give up his life for the values that he espoused.

Benigno "Ninoy" Aquino was a Filipino politician who had an ideology, an ability to communicate his personal values and political beliefs, and had the courage to sacrifice his life for his people. He is a political hero and role model for our young people today who need to believe that heroism can still thrive in the world of government and politics. **(ESC)**

Looking for Another Ninoy

Throughout history, the Filipino people have been searching for a great leader who possesses both charisma and the qualities of a hero. Things are no different today.

Many historians have been reluctant to see history in terms of "great men." Thinkers believe that circumstances play an important role. But there are also historians and thinkers who believe that there are certain qualities that enable leaders to mold the social forces around them.

I have often wondered what would have happened if Ninoy had survived that assassination attempt. Would he have become the great leader the Philippines continues to look up to?

The German sociologist Max Weber said that in a personality-based leadership (versus institutional-based), the leader can exercise leadership in one of three ways.

The first would be legal authority based on accepted laws and procedures. This is the authority that former president Gloria Macapagal-Arroyo had exercised.

The second is traditional authority based on the established belief "in the sanctity of immemorial traditions" such as patriarchal or spiritual authority. This is clearly the basis for the authority of the Catholic bishops and other religious leaders.

However, these two types of power are most effective when either one is combined with charismatic authority. According to Weber, charisma is a "quality of an individual personality by virtue of which he is set apart from ordinary men and women and treated as endowed with the supernatural or superhuman."

Central to the qualities of a charismatic leader is the power to persuade through communications skills.

Certainly Ninoy Aquino was charismatic. I can still remember, back in 1978, before the sham Batasang Pambansa elections, in one short thirty-minute television interview, Ninoy inspired a whole populace to come out in the streets and conduct a noise barrage throughout the night in the whole of Metro Manila. This was during the height of the dictatorial power of the Marcos regime.

But our country is also looking for a hero. We are looking for a person "distinguished for valor, fortitude, or bold enterprise; someone regarded as having displayed great courage or exceptionally noble or manly qualities, or who has done a deed or deed showing him to possess such qualities."

During martial law, when almost every opposition leader had been released or exiled, Ninoy remained defiant even while suffering the worst imprisonment in Fort Magsaysay. Even the threat of execution failed to force him to collaborate with the Marcos regime or even just to promise to keep silent.

But his truly great and heroic deed was when, after a comfortable exiled life in Boston, he decided to come back to the Philippines despite the knowledge that he was risking his life.

Today, the greatest obstacle to the life of human dignity for the Filipino masses is the feudal structure that is dominant in our society.

The term "feudal" refers to the relationship between a lord and his vassals or servants. Feudalism is the prevailing structure in every aspect of our nation's life—in politics, business, military, media, and even religion. The only difference is that there are lords who treat their vassals better than other lords.

For most Filipinos, the only recourse seems to be to seek to be of value to a feudal lord. For those who refuse to become vassals, there are only three alternatives.

The first is to rebel and go to the mountains. The second is to immigrate. The third is to continue struggling for a seemingly lost cause of changing the feudal structure of the country.

The great Filipino leader must have a guiding vision, as well as the passion and courage to change the social structure of this country in spite of the opposition he will face from the entrenched elites and other interest groups currently in the ruling clique of this country.

The great Filipino leader must also have the integrity to enforce the laws of this land, the same integrity displayed by Supreme Court Justice Adolf Azcuna when he publicly said that the proposed memorandum of agreement on ancestral domain between the government and the separatist Moro Islamic Liberation Front (MILF) is "on its face, patently illegal under our laws."

We are looking for a leader who will truly believe that there should be no lords or vassals in this country and that all Filipinos are truly equal and must be treated equally in terms of economic and educational opportunities, and have equal access to social justice.

When Ninoy Aquino said that the Filipino is worth dying for, surely he saw each Filipino as equal to one another. Three decades after his death, the Filipino people are still looking for another Ninoy. **(ESC)**

Reference:

Weber, Max. *Economy and Society.* USA: University of California Press, 1978

We Need Heroes like Ninoy

On August 21, 1983, Ninoy Aquino was assassinated upon his return to the Philippines. During those thirty months between that date and February 25, 1986 when Corazon Aquino took her oath as president of the Republic of the Philippines, the nation marched and demonstrated against the forces of the Marcos dictatorship. This is the period historians now recall as the People Power struggle for freedom and democracy.

The creativity of the People Power Movement was a very marked distinction of this struggle as compared to armed revolutions. This creativity was demonstrated not just in apparel and the color yellow but in slogans and songs. Among songs that literally became anthems of the struggle against the Marcos dictatorship were "Tie a Yellow Ribbon," the tale of a prisoner coming home; "Impossible Dream," said to be the Aquinos' favorite song; and "Bayan Ko," a patriotic song banned by the American colonizers, the Japanese invaders, and the Marcos forces.

There was one song that seemed to be dedicated to Ninoy. Popularized by Bonnie Tyler, the lyrics were so meaningful for that period. The chorus for "I Need A Hero" goes:

I need a hero, I'm holding out for a hero
Till the morning light

He's gotta be sure
 And it's gotta be soon
And he's gotta be larger than life.

The country in 1983 was desperate for a hero. To understand why the martyrdom and heroism of Ninoy Aquino created such a tidal wave of emotional response, it is important to appreciate the condition of the Filipino nation before August 21, 1983.

The only way to describe the "before" period would be to use Dickensian imagery. For the Philippines, it was the worst of times. It was the age of Imeldific extravagances and foolishness. It was the season of Darkness when Marcos abolished human rights and made freedom a crime against the state. It was the winter of Despair when cronyism became the norm and no one seemed to have the courage to speak against the evil that had befallen the country. It seemed that for the Filipino people, there was nothing before us.

After August 21, 1983, there was a dramatic change as the yellow armbands and confetti became visible all over the country. It was now a season of Light as speakers began to publicly denounce human rights violations and the persecutions of those who advocated for democracy. It was now the spring of Hope as the end of the Marcos regime became a possibility. It seemed that, suddenly, we had everything before us.

In her speech on August 21, 1998, during the fifteenth death anniversary of Ninoy, Cory said:

> I have asked many people—most of whom never knew Ninoy—why they came to the wake. Some said they were ashamed of themselves for being so fearful of the dictator, and were sorry they had not found the courage to stand up and be counted earlier. They felt if they had shown more courage, maybe Ninoy need not have died. Others have said they were outraged and had had enough. Still many came, simply to pray and grieve quietly with me and my family. Rich and poor, the powerful and the powerless, they kept coming in endless lines to pay tribute to Ninoy, convincing me that *hindi ako nag-iisa.*
>
> At that point, I believe that Ninoy's death triggered a long-awaited transformation in many Filipinos. We finally found the collective courage to rise against a dictatorship after years of shameful and fearful stupor.

No longer were we going to be lulled by the clever machinations of a regime bent on staying in power forever and plundering the nation. The protests started. Telephone directories and yellow fabrics were suddenly in short supply. It was a non-violent protest movement run through photocopiers, Betamax tapes, confetti rallies, and noise barrages in Makati, and the alternative press. Some thought the protests would not last. But as Filipinos have done many times in the past, we proved the skeptics wrong.

Courage, like cowardice, was infectious and the Filipino people rose in defiance. This same courage carried us all through 1986. When rampant cheating and violence marred the snap election of February 7, 1896, we as a people again demonstrated our collective courage.

There were many defining moments in Ninoy's journey toward martyrdom and heroism. One event no one should forget was in 1973, when Ninoy defied the Military Commission that was appointed by Marcos to try him. Here is part of his opening statement:

I have therefore decided not to participate in these proceedings: First, because this ritual is an unconscionable mockery and second, because every part of my being—my heart and mind and soul—yes, every part of my being—is against any form of dictatorship. I agree we must have public order and national discipline if this country is to move forward. But peace and order without freedom is nothing more than slavery. Discipline without justice is merely another name for oppression.

I believe we can have lasting peace and prosperity only if we build a social order based on freedom and justice. My non-participation is therefore an act of protest against the structures of injustice that brought us here. It is also an act of faith in the ultimate victory of right over wrong, of good over evil. In all humility, I say it is a rare privilege to share with the Motherland her bondage, her anguish, her every pain and suffering.

When the country needed a hero, Ninoy Aquino came. Some have described the biggest contribution of heroes as "saving the soul of a nation."

Today, the Priority Development Assistance Fund (PDAF) scam that brought tears to Cardinal Tagle; the sex-for-flight scandal where oppressed Filipinas bravely confronted, publicly, their persecutor; the continuing crusade against smugglers and tax evaders; and the seemingly snail pace of much-needed judicial reforms, should remind us that the struggle to save Filipinos is far from over.

We must, again, unite as a nation and show our common outrage against corrupt officials, tax evaders, smugglers, criminals, and justices who abuse their powers. We must become our own heroes, just as Ninoy had been, three decades ago. **(ESC)**

P TWO-FIFTY

Mr.&.Ms.

MAR. 2, 1984 • **25**th of a series

194 DAYS SINCE
THE UNSOLVED MURDER

for Justice and National Reconciliation

Y AQUINO:
to prepare for
vigorous participation'

BossLady.

Sec. Elfren Cruz

Pls. give the Unday
Elementary School a
two-classroom
school house.

CA

III.
The Cory
Years

Cory Aquino

I leave it to historians and future books to talk about how the course of Philippine history was dramatically changed by the presidency of Corazon Aquino.

There will be other major historical events in the future. But the drama and glory of the Cory Aquino period will never be replicated.

In one short term, she led a nation from oppressive dictatorship to democracy. She led the economy's transition from crony capitalism to free enterprise and allowed entrepreneurship to expand. She restored the freedom which we now take for granted and she made human rights once more a right and not just a privilege.

She introduced personal faith and morality as a basis of governance to a political society which considered materialism and pragmatism as the basic rules in politics. She willingly gave up power twice. The first time was when she decided to restore Congress and case legislation through executive orders. The second time was when she decided not to run for president in spite of appeals for her to do so. Perhaps, future politicians will learn that clinging to power will eventually earn the ire of people and the condemnation of future generations.

There were, of course, powerful forces who refused to accept their loss of power and would continue to fight to regain their former status. This struggle led to many moments of courage which she continuously displayed without fanfare and publicity stunts.

A hundred years from now, people will likely continue to remember her for being the first People Power President in the world; for remaining as the moral conscience of her people even after her presidency; and for her many other great deeds. **(ESC)**

How I Met Cory Aquino

My first one-on-one encounter with Cory was in early 1984, when I visited her in the Cojuangco Building to invite her to be the speaker at the general assembly of the Parañaque-Las Piñas chapter of PDP-Laban. I had already met her on several occasions by then, most recently when I accompanied opposition leaders like Jaime Ferrer and Nene Pimentel.

There were three things that I remembered about that event. First, it was our chairman, Jaime Ferrer, who instructed me to invite her and then said to me that she would be the next president of the Philippines. Second, my wife reminded me that she had already met Cory. She was the first Filipino journalist to interview Cory upon her return to the Philippines after the assassination of Ninoy in 1983. It was an urgent assignment for the *Mr. & Ms.* magazine, published and edited by Eggie Apostol, to counter the controlled press during the Marcos years.

Last, I remembered how nervous I was and how gracious Cory was when I visited her. I remembered thinking that she was as charismatic as her husband but in a different and more quiet way.

The assembly was held at the Tropical Palace Hotel in BF Homes. I was tasked to introduce her, and I ended my introduction by announcing: "The next president of the Republic of the Philippines, Corazon Aquino." After her talk, she called me aside and quietly scolded me for the introduction, and told me never to do that again.

The years 1984 to 1985 were the prelude to the People Power Revolution of 1986. Those were the years when rallies were weekly affairs. There were frequent encounters with the police and even armed forces units. I was then PDP-Laban's deputy secretary-general for Metro Manila. In that capacity, I was reporting to Representative Peping Cojuangco, the party secretary-general for the same region.

I was then juggling my time between working for the party, organizing rallies, working for a living, and maintaining a family life with my wife and our three children—Tanya, Roel, and Aina. I was also spending a lot of time in the Cojuangco Building because that was the site of the party secretariat and the nerve center for many of the opposition's rallies and protest movements. I, therefore, had many opportunities to see and even exchange greetings with Cory.

However, whenever people ask me how I was able to establish a working relationship with her, I would tell them it was really a chance assignment.

After Marcos declared a snap presidential election, I decided to resign from my job and work full time for the campaign. Let me add that my wife gave her full consent to this decision.

At first, my involvement was on organizing and looking for potential poll watchers in the subdivisions of Parañaque. Then one day, Peping Cojuangco called a meeting of young PDP-Laban leaders to help organize and energize the Million Signatures for the Cory campaign. I was there to represent Parañaque-Las Piñas. Among those also present were Jojo Binay who represented Makati; Joey Lina, Manila; Jun Simon, Quezon City; Mario Raymundo, Pasig; among others. In the Parañaque subdivisions, I was able to recruit volunteers to set up registration tables outside churches and distribute leaflets at the subdivision gates.

At the beginning of the official campaign period, a campaign secretariat was organized by Paul Aquino. Its main headquarters was in the Valgosons Building along Pasong Tamo in Makati.

One day, Paul Aquino called a small group to a meeting. He basically said that Cory would soon be campaigning in Metro Manila. At that time, we had zero access to mass media except through a few courageous publishers like Eggie Apostol and Betty Go Belmonte. The only way for our candidate's message to reach the people was for her to speak in as many rallies as possible.

Metro Manila was very critical because it was hoped that this area would be able to compensate for the massive cheating and intimidation by the Marcos forces in the provincial areas. There was a need for a volunteer to organize the scheduling of all of Cory's campaign appearances to maximize exposure to as many people as possible. However, for security reasons, she had to be home before midnight.

Therefore, there was also a need to plan the route carefully so a series of rallies could be held in adjacent areas and our candidate could speak immediately upon arrival at the rally site and then leave immediately after speaking. This required close coordination with the rally organizers at each site.

During that meeting, I ended up being appointed to head the task force. My memory of the exact events is not clear because I cannot remember whether I volunteered or I was asked to volunteer by Paul Aquino. But I do remember that the first person I asked to join me was Rey Tan, who had been actively involved in organizing protest rallies.

In planning the rally schedules and routes, I met with the rally organizers, most of whom became local or national political leaders after the restoration of democracy. They were, of course, the Ferrer brothers, Jaime and Janet, of Parañaque; Joey Lina and Mel Lopez of Manila; Neptali Gonzales and his daughter in Mandaluyong; Del Rosario in Navotas; Binay in Makati; Martinez in Caloocan; Oreta in Malabon; Tinga in Taguig; Mercado, Muñoz-Palma, Romulo, and Simon in Quezon City; and many others.

I also coordinated with the Cory Aquino Media Bureau and worked with people like Rene Saguisag, Teddy Boy Locsin, and Billy Esposo, who also worked closely with me when we managed the Jaime Ferrer for Assemblyman campaign in 1984.

Then one day, Paul Aquino called and said that since I was the one who had planned the routes and schedules and met with the rally site organizers, I should ride with Cory in the campaign van during her campaign sorties in Metro Manila. He instructed me to meet and coordinate with Eldon Cruz, the husband of Ballsy.

Those days and nights spent riding in that campaign van were dramatic and historical stories in themselves. But let me just end this memory walk with three brief recollections.

First, the schedule was followed and the rally organizers cooperated enthusiastically. Second, Cory was always home before midnight. Third, when she attended the rally in Parañaque, I was asked to introduce her to the crowd. I ended my introduction by saying: "Corazon Aquino, the next president of the Republic of the Philippines." This time, she no longer scolded me.

In 1987, there was a PDP-Laban national assembly at the Ninoy Aquino Stadium in Manila. I was then head of her Presidential Management Staff. I was asked to introduce her and I did so by simply announcing to the assembly: "Corazon Aquino, the President of the Republic of the Philippines." **(ESC)**

Working for President Cory

One of my proudest memories is that I was one of the few lucky ones who started working for President Cory on Day One of her presidency. That was the day after Marcos fled the country and Corazon Aquino became the new head of the Philippine government.

The night Marcos fled the Philippines, several of us were in a house in Wack Wack with Cory. When the news came that the dictator had fled and the martial law regime had ended, a thanksgiving Mass was held. Afterward, she announced some cabinet appointments, including Joker Arroyo as Executive Secretary.

Some time that evening, Joker called and told me to report to him the following day. We started working without any title or official appointment. Malacañang was still being "de-bombed" and was shut down for security reasons. For the first few months, the Office of the President was in the Cojuangco Building in Makati. During those early days, the technical staff serving the president was composed of two people—Joker and me.

But it was an easy transition because during the campaign days, I had already met the people—like Margie Juico, Maria Montelibano, Teddy Boy Locsin, Rene Saguisag—who would compose her personal and media staff.

The restoration of democracy had been a long struggle. Combating the forces that were trying to topple the democratic institutions being rebuilt proved equally daunting. There were coup attempts like the "God Save the Queen" plot, which led to the dismissal of Juan Ponce Enrile as Minister of Defense. There were others, like the one led by Gringo Honasan, during which the near-fatal shooting of the president's son, Noynoy, happened. During that coup attempt, many staff members and I had to live and sleep in Malacañang for a week.

There were also many high points. There were the rallies where people gathered to support her presidency in spite of threats from coup plotters. There were the accolades from the world, and the speech to the United States where senior American political leaders pinned Cory dolls on their coats when they attended the joint session to listen to her.

There was the convening of the Philippine constitutional assembly and the first democratic elections, after which she voluntarily gave her legislative powers to the new Congress. I was with her as she literally toured the country meeting with different groups—from cultural minorities to business leaders to ordinary citizens. I was with her visiting areas devastated by natural calamities, from the Baguio earthquake to floods.

I witnessed her resolving policy debates and political conflicts. But my favorite stories are those times she focused on directly helping the poor. She saw the poor as individuals with different needs and not just as economic indicators or poverty rates.

She instructed me to set up a structure whereby a certain percentage of revenues of the Philippine Amusement and Gaming Corporation (PAGCOR) would be channeled directly to projects for the poor. That was why we created the President's Social Fund.

Her instructions were that all the funds would be for projects that had a direct impact on the lives of the poor. We had to specify the final beneficiaries. The funding would also be coursed through NGOs and all the undertakings would be what we now call microprojects. These included classrooms, potable water systems, footbridges and livelihood projects.

Cory Aquino was a Lady—always courteous and polite. I never saw her humiliate or embarrass anyone or raise her voice in anger in public. One time, when two cabinet officials were having a vigorous policy debate in front of the whole cabinet, she simply told them they were giving her a headache and the debate immediately ended.

But for those who worked for her, we knew when a decision was final and that she was getting upset. With me it was when her tone, in saying my name, changed to a simple, curt "Elfren." Then there were also times when her lips would tighten and we knew she was becoming upset and it was time to move on.

That was just one of the many times when we knew the Lady was also the Boss. **(ESC)**

The Boss Lady

I n my job as Cory Aquino's PMS head, I was lucky to have personally witnessed her concern for the many other "minor" decisions that had such profound effects on the lives of ordinary Filipinos.

I recall one anecdote of how she felt that bureaucracy should never stand in the way of helping those who needed assistance.

The year was 1988 and the president had a radio program. One of the tasks of the PMS was to process all the requests for assistance and suggest answers. Here was one request we received:

> I am Mr. Estepanio Cabreros, head teacher of Pagangan Elementary School, living in Pagangan, Aleosan, Cotabato. Being the head teacher of this school, our number one problem is the water system that the children are hard-up bringing their water supply because our artesian supply is sometimes out of order.

After thorough research and consultation with other departments, here is the proposed answer we sent to President Aquino:

Thank you Mr. Cabreros of the Pangan Elementary School, Aleosan, Cotabato. Regarding the problem with your school's artesian well and multi-purpose workshop, I advise you to approach your mayor or the local developments council so that these projects will be endorsed to the regional development council for possible inclusion in the program of the Department of Public Works and Highway and Department of Education, Culture and Sports.

The following day, my proposed answer was sent back to me with a handwritten note at the bottom which said:

Elfren Cruz, Pls take care of the artesian well. CA

I remember showing that note to all my staff and we understood that our role was not to be part of the bureaucracy but to help those who were being burdened *by* the bureaucracy.

President Aquino, even then, worked very well with NGOs and was very interested in projects that included school buildings, potable water systems, livelihood projects, and other pro-poor projects. On October 19, 1989, for instance, she sent me this handwritten note:

Elfren Cruz.

CCPAP presented me with a comprehensive program for the three Samar provinces. In line with our commitment to serve the bottom 30%, please set aside the necessary amounts. Please coordinate with Bert Villanueva.

Thanks! CAquino.

But she was also very practical and had a sense of what was really needed. One time we sent a list of projects for her approval. I thought we already understood her priorities. It included a list of potable water system projects, including one project whose beneficiaries included 9,000 families in thirty-one barangays in Paoay, Ilocos Norte.

She approved all the projects except for one proposal for clothing materials for hospital patients' gowns in several government hospitals nationwide. Again, there was a handwritten note which said:

> Maybe, we should give free medicines first before hospital gowns and pajamas.

But there were also many light moments. Normally, I would receive instructions written on official Malacañang stationery. Sometimes I would receive handwritten notes on personal stationery with the name Corazon Aquino at the top or in simple yellow post-its. I was, therefore, very amused when a couple of times, I received instructions written on a post-it which carried the heading "Boss Lady." It was obviously given to her, but my wife continues to say that those are the most charming notes I ever received from her.

The years I served President Aquino will remain as the most rewarding and glorious period of my life. I shall always be grateful to her for giving me the opportunity to serve the Filipino people and to work in service to a true heroine. **(ESC)**

The Cory Charisma

For nearly three decades, Corazon Cojuangco Aquino exercised power—for a few years as the legally elected president, but for a much longer period, before and after her presidency—using solely her "charismatic" leadership.

"Charisma" has been defined as the quality of an individual by virtue of which he or she is set apart from ordinary men and women and treated as endowed with supernatural, superhuman, or at least specifically exceptional qualities.

The ancient Greeks often thought of charisma as a gift from the gods. But modern definition more frequently alludes to charisma as a personal leadership involving personal magnetism that permits leaders to arouse fervent popular devotion and enthusiasm.

Leaders come in varying types of personality. Most of them use identifiable personality tricks and props. Winston Churchill and Fidel V. Ramos both use the cigar as props. But Churchill had the V (for victory) sign while Ramos had the upright thumb sign. Roosevelt used the "fireside chats" while Martin Luther King used biblical phrases in his civil rights speeches.

Corazon Aquino had the yellow color and the *laban* signs as her populist trademarks. Her son, Noynoy Aquino, still uses yellow as his official color but the *laban* sign has been replaced by the yellow ribbon.

But central to the charismatic leader's repertoire is the power to persuade through communication skills. Charisma can influence others and arouse their enthusiasm.

During the movement to replace the Marcos dictatorship with democratic institutions, many opposition leaders had the opportunity to speak to the people as rallies and marches were becoming more numerous. But no one had the ability to arouse the kind of enthusiastic reception that Cory could. She did not speak in the loud, bombastic style of the traditional politician. Nor did she speak in the angry tone common among speakers espousing leftist ideology.

When she spoke, however, the listener could visualize a vivid picture of the sufferings and sacrifices of Ninoy and his family. And when she would end that what motivated her husband was his faith and belief that the Filipino was worth dying for, the listener could empathize with her.

The ancient view that someone is either born with charisma or not is very different from the modern one. Although some persons might have a predisposition to acquiring it, there is considerable evidence that charisma is not something one is born with. Charisma is not given to a person and it is not an inherited or inborn quality. It is something that develops over time.

I did not have the privilege of knowing President Aquino before she came back in 1983. I remember seeing her in some of the LABAN meetings during the 1978 Batasang Pambansa elections when her husband galvanized the opposition with one television interview.

But I was later told that those who knew her then could never imagine that she would eventually develop into a truly remarkable charismatic leader of the Filipino people.

It is possible, therefore, for leaders to develop charisma, although certainly only very rarely is this done successfully. But charisma, combined with hard work, the right attitude, and even a little bit of luck can have an impact of influencing and motivating, no matter how hopeless the situation might look.

During the dark days of the Marcos dictatorship, the possibility of a peaceful transition to democracy seemed like a hopeless cause. There were several moral and hardworking leaders of the opposition at that time. But there was one person who combined hard work, an inflexible moral standard, and charismatic leadership that fortunately emerged to lead her people in a nonviolent crusade that culminated in the rebirth of Philippine democracy. **(ESC)**

The Cory Aquino Leadership

L eadership is at its best when the vision is strategic, the voice persuasive, and the results tangible." This is the Corazon Aquino leadership that restored freedom and dignity to the Filipino.

With only a few exceptions, such as the leadership of Manuel L. Quezon and Corazon Aquino, Philippine history has become a case study of how selfish and shortsighted leaders in politics, business, and religion can destroy the economy and the moral fever of any society.

But where do we find the leaders who will lead us to a golden age that we have longed for and prayed for?

People have been talking and writing about leadership from the beginning of the history. Warnings about the evil consequences of wrong leadership are as old as the Bible. In Matthew 15:14, the Good Book warns, "If the blind lead the blind, both shall fall into the ditch."

One of the most profound lessons on leadership came from a management guru, Warren Bennis, who wrote that leadership cannot be taught. He said: "More leaders have been made by accident, circumstances, sheer grit or will than have been made by all the leadership courses put together. Developing character and vision is the way leaders invent themselves."

We are all aware that Cory never intended to become a national leader. But a combination of events put her in a position where she could be, not just a national symbol, but also the national leader if she possessed the right qualities. Fortunately, she did possess them.

Thousands of books and case studies have been written about leadership. Dozens of leadership characteristics have been proposed. Out of the many I have read, there seems to be five that consistently appeared on everyone's list.

A leader must be forward-looking or a visionary, possess the virtue of honesty or integrity, inspiring, competent, and have the courage and will to surmount any challenge.

But among these characteristics, it is particularly the ability to be forward-looking and to inspire a shared vision that elevated someone from being a credible individual to being a true leader.

Cory showed she had courage when she dared to speak publicly against the martial law forces of the Marcos dictatorship. Time and again, she proved that she and her family were icons of integrity. The millions who listened to her, from the crowds in Luneta to the halls of the U.S. Congress, were always moved by her speeches. She showed tremendous political skills and organizational capabilities as she welded the many disparate opposition forces into a single group during the snap election. She led the transformation of the nation's economic and political system from cronyism to democracy.

When Cory transformed her mission from that of avenging her husband's death to a crusade for the restoration of democracy and human rights, she became a leader of her people and the embodiment of their vision of a nation for their children.

But leadership is also not just about characteristics and personality traits. Leadership is an event, not only a trait. It is about what you do with who you are, more than just about who you are.

There is such a thing, as writer Michael Useem says, a leadership moment which happens at a time when a leader's credibility and reputation is on the line, when the fate or fortune of others depends on what the leader will do. This leadership moment happens when a decision is made to serve a greater good.

For Cory, there were many such leadership moments. One was when she decided to run for president under a martial law regime. Then she decided to convene a constitution and allow Congress to be elected when she could have ruled by decree for a longer period. There was also her decision not to leave Malacañang at the height of the Honasan-led coup attempt.

But her defining moment was when she decided not to run for reelection in 1992 in spite of overwhelming evidence that she could have won a second term.

One of the greatest gifts that Corazon Aquino has left us with is the legacy of a leadership that symbolized and expressed what was truly the best in the Filipino. We can only pray and hope that she has left behind in other people, especially her family, the conviction and the will to carry on. **(ESC)**

Reference:

Bennis, Warren. *On Becoming a Leader.* USA: Warren Bennis Inc., 1989

Cory's Last Day as President

There was something nostalgic and vaguely familiar about driving to Times Street in Quezon City at lunchtime on June 30, 1992. Yellow ribbons welcomed the homecoming of the neighborhood's most prominent resident. And if passersby wondered what the fuss was all about, the streamer on the gate from the women of Negros Occidental, effusively thanking Pres. Cory Aquino for a job well done, was a sure giveaway.

While media and the nation watched and wondered about President Ramos's first afternoon in Malacañang, old friends and loyal Cory supporters spent the afternoon with Citizen Cory at her family home.

What was originally meant to be a quiet and private lunch with her family turned out to be an impromptu mini-reunion of Cojuangco Building habitués during the snap election season.

It was heartwarming to see individuals trooping to Times Street to express to the former president in so many subtle ways how much she continues to be esteemed and valued. It was a display of affection more meaningful now that she, sans title, no longer has center stage. A delegation of twenty-five women from Negros Occidental had made prior arrangements with eldest daughter Ballsy that they wanted to be the first to greet President Cory when she returned to her home, just to thank her for helping improve their lives. That was all their visit was about, so that they had to be persuaded to join the Elar's catered lunch for a hundred. Another group from Los Baños brought her a blooming orchid named after her, on a driftwood. There was Ms. Elvira Chan of Metrobank, who only met Ms. Aquino after Ninoy's murder and has remained a faithful friend since.

The gathering was also a chance to open her newly renovated home to well-wishers. She was amused that many people, her hairdresser included, have been feeling sorry that all Cory was returning to was this unpretentious-looking bungalow. The simple facade remained, but a pleasant transformation has occurred in the interior to befit a former president and to remedy the leaking roof and rusty pipes. According to close family friend and Museo ng Malacañang Foundation head Reggie Coseteng, who oversaw the renovations guided only by the presidential specification of a clean, well-lighted look at the lowest cost possible, the repairs began as early as January 1992. Coseteng was credited with having supervised the work every single day. Family-owned Mariwasa supplied the white living and dining room tiles and the kitchen tiles, manufactured using *lahar*.

The receiving area that served Ninoy and his endless stream of walk-in visitors well has acquired an air of stateliness. Flowers from many well-wishers brightened up the place even more with its all-white look and minimal Orientalia accents. When Ballsy told her mother that there was now enough space for entertaining a hundred guests, Citizen Cory, certainly not yet missing the receptions she has had to host, hoped out loud that she would not have to play host as often.

But she was a gracious host that afternoon, her exuberance and sense of relief at having been unburdened so evident. She was eager to talk, bubbling over with details having little to do now with affairs of the state.

Was it a lonely ride home after the inaugural ceremony? What were her thoughts? Recapturing those moments made her temporarily pensive. But it was clear that she did not wish to indulge in any reminiscing. She had a feeling of liberation from endless criticism, was all Citizen Cory was willing to say, the only time a cloud crossed her face that afternoon. Besides, she related that in the car that had her, Kris and Col. Voltaire Gazmin, her attention was focused on Kris, who could not contain herself after her personal security bid her goodbye. She had to comfort Kris, who had suddenly become sentimental. She herself was so touched at the final goodbye in a series of staggered farewells. This, she admitted, made it easier for her. Second daughter Pinky teased that from the way Kris was weeping, you would think it was a take for one of her movies.

The afternoon was not meant for any sadness, only joy and anticipation at all that the future held in promise for Citizen Cory. The boxes of memorabilia had to be sorted out and arranged for public viewing. There was the speaking engagement in Hong Kong in mid-July for a Zonta conference, a commitment she made in 1991. There was another international conference in Seville in September where the world's women leaders, like Margaret Thatcher, Benazir Bhutto, and President Aquino, have been invited to speak on women and democracy, a topic that she confidently said she could speak on extemporaneously now. After that, an expo visit and a trip to other parts of Europe with Kris. While she had imposed a moratorium on speaking engagements, it was certain that this would be temporary and short-lived. There was the writing of her memoirs to complete, and there were offers to translate these into other languages for serialization. The Benigno S. Aquino Foundation awaited her personal involvement again. And there were the livelihood projects she wished to initiate, encouraged by the success of the collaboration with NGOs in her experience with the President's Social Fund.

But for now, she was allowed a break, so she could indulge in grandmothering and the simple joys of again being "anonymous," if that was at all possible. While her house was ready for her, her garden has not been started, the greening of which the plant lover in her was eager to effect.

She spilled over with tales about her two eldest grandsons, Jiggy Cruz and Miguel Abellada, who for the past months, had been constantly asking if she were still president. On his last Sunday in Arlegui, Jiggy bade the house goodbye, waxing sentimental, "I will miss you." Miguel was wondering why many of his lola's boxes were going to Tarlac. Did she really need all those luggage for a simple provincial trip? And having seen nothing but boxes recently, both felt absolute pity for their grandmother, concerned that past June 30, she would be out in the streets, homeless, and with nothing but those boxes to her name. But Monday night, on their lola's first night back at Times, as they were happily jumping on her bed, their lola cautiously asked which they preferred, the Times or Arlegui home. To her relief, neither was nursing an Arlegui hangover.

When Kris expressed concern that her condominium unit would be empty for the duration of their trip to Europe, her mother playfully suggested that if she wanted to, she could rent it out then—but could Kris be sure that her legendary wardrobe would not be borrowed as well?

The conversation went on to the former president's fear as she waited to be picked up by the incoming president for the joint ride to Luneta, that her own car might not follow, leaving her stranded there; President Ramos's not quite stolen inaugural kiss because he had bade permission two weeks ago; the warm conversation she had with former vice president Doy Laurel at the grandstand, regarding each other's plans; the quiet satisfaction that the day's peaceful transition happened at all.

For friends who have had to stay at arm's length during the Malacañang years, it may had been initially awkward to relate to her now, for how did one interact with someone who was still your head of state an hour ago? But because Citizen Cory signaled both tone and mood by being casual and breezy, it felt like postponed and disrupted relationships could resume once more.

The friends in attendance were given a collector's item of a ball pen in blue, white, and Cory yellow, compliments of Virgie Ramos of Gift Gate, especially produced to mark a new chapter in Citizen Cory's life. It need not have carried the "Cory Aquino" inscription because one cannot use it without a yellow bud opening up to reveal a tiny, bespectacled and unmistakably Cory doll at the top. Purely coincidental that while the Cory rag doll was born as she began her political career, another doll variation should mark its end.

Yes, on that day, many other beginnings beckoned for Cory Aquino. **(NSRC)**

The Beginning
of the Cory Legend

Corazon Aquino passed away on August 1, 2009 at 3:18 in the morning. The cause was advanced colon cancer and she had been hospitalized for more than a month. Her son, Benigno Aquino III, said that the cancer had spread and she was too weak to continue therapy. She was seventy-six.

The messages of grief and love came from people of all walks of life and from all over the world. Her security escort of twenty years, Melchor Mamaril, gave a very touching eulogy. "I feel a sense of wonder and at the same time, I realized that her treatment raised my dignity as a person. She gave me self-respect, self-worth, and self-confidence. And even when she lay dying in bed, she was always concerned about us. She would always ask if we had eaten already. One could always see her compassionate heart for all those in need."

President Barack Obama said he was deeply saddened by her death: "She played a crucial role in Philippine history, moving the country to democratic rule through a non-violent People Power Movement . . . . Her courage, determination and moral leadership are an inspiration to us and exemplify the best in the Filipino nation."

Hillary Clinton, then U.S. Secretary of State, sent a message: "Cory Aquino was beloved by her nation and admired by the world for her extraordinary courage after the assassination of her husband and later, during her service as president. She helped bring democracy back to the Philippines after many years of authoritarian rule with a faith in her country and its people that never wavered."

The year 2009 also commemorated the thirtieth year of the martyrdom of Ninoy Aquino, whose funeral procession from Sto. Domingo Church to Manila Memorial Park brought millions of people to the streets of Metro Manila. This was the beginning of People Power, the start of many demonstrations in the face of intimidation and harassment by the police and military forces of the Marcos dictatorship.

This was also the beginning of the ascent of Cory as the inspiration and the leader of the movement for the restoration of democracy and freedom to this country.

There have been many stories written about her since that time until after her death. But one story, seldom told but worth recalling, is the first interview with Cory by a local journalist after her husband 's assassination.

At that time, the media was totally controlled by Marcos and his cronies. The independent press could best be described as a "mosquito" press and was published "underground." Its publishers and writers were constantly being arrested or harassed.

Then a personality magazine, *Mr. & Ms.*, decided to publish a Special Edition series, beginning with the assassination of Ninoy and a full-length article on Cory. The local journalist whom the publisher Eggie Apostol chose for that historic first interview was Neni Sta. Romana Cruz. Here, in her own words, is the story of that first interview:

> I was in the company of *Mr. & Ms.* publisher Eggie Apostol, who had arranged an exclusive interview that she wanted me to do for the *Mr. & Ms.* Special Edition which was launched immediately after the Aquino assassination. She picked me up and we proceeded to the Aquino residence on Times Street. It was so soon after Ninoy was buried because the nine-day Masses at Sto. Domingo Church were still going on. All the major broadsheets were part of the Marcos propaganda machinery and were scared to give Ninoy Aquino and his family any publicity lest they displease those in power.
>
> But Eggie was eager to outscoop everyone and to promote truth and justice by letting the public know what lay beneath the staid and inaccurate news coverage of the national dailies and the broadcasting stations.
>
> The interview was in the living room. She was in black, looked tired and drawn, but was restrained and calm. I was struck by her humility and more

so by her recognition of my maiden name, pointing out that my mother's family, the Luceros, are related to the Cojuangcos, something I vaguely knew through my elders who knew her family and used to mention it. It seemed almost ridiculous that a prominent member of the clan should be the one pointing out the kinship with a lesser known member of the family tree.

She made me feel so at ease and I seemed to be mourning more than she was. I kept thinking, how can this frail woman endure it all? She was easy to interview because she wanted her story to be heard."

In one part of the article, Neni wrote: "People who were heartbroken at the sight of the once fiery and flamboyant Ninoy in his bloodied bush jacket feared that his appearance may inflict more unnecessary sorrow on his family. Cory saw nothing of what many thought was unpretty. She said, 'He looked much better than I expected. I guess when you love someone you only see the beautiful.'

On that August day in 1983, did Cory sense what her future would be? Here was what Neni wrote: "There are many things Cory looks forward to—from the mundane task of unpacking (she cannot even quite recall, is it a week or two weeks that they have been home?), of even having the luxury of time to cry, sort things out (a necessity, she has told Kris), to the momentous ones of compiling her husband's writings into a book, and working closely with a biographer for Ninoy's story.

But she was destined to be more than just an editor and writer. Unknown to her, the Cory legend had begun. She would be the subject of countless stories and articles. Her destiny would one day make her the icon of People Power and democracy in the Philippines and throughout the world. **(ESC)**

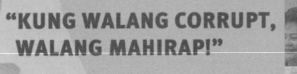

"KUNG WALANG CORRUPT, WALANG MAHIRAP!"

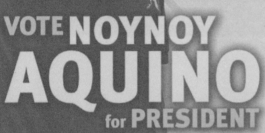

VOTE NOYNOY AQUINO for PRESIDENT

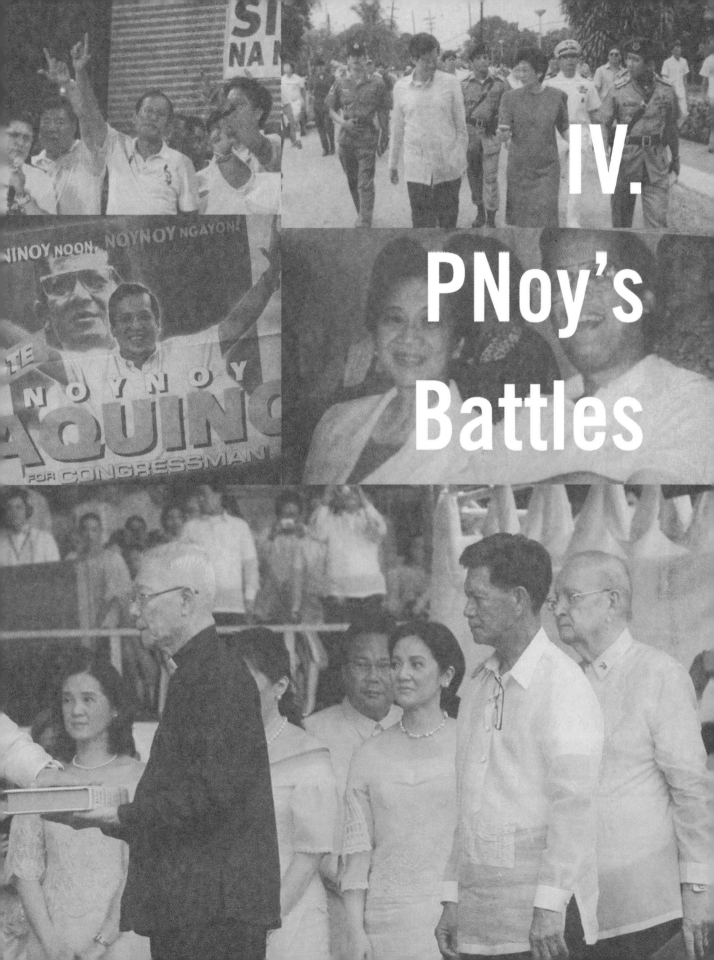

IV.
PNoy's Battles

Noynoy Aquino Speaks Out

Even under the most normal of circumstances, being the namesake of one's father carries with it an intrinsic burden and responsibility. But when that parent is not only a popular public figure but also a legend elevated to heroic proportions, the task of living up to a name becomes doubly difficult.

For Noynoy Aquino, the only son of Cory and Ninoy, such a scenario is a bit too simple and inaccurate because it is incomplete. He is Benigno III, there being two other Benignos before him—his father and his father's father—to contend with. As a citizen imbued with nationalism and a sense of mission for his country, there is his paternal grandfather's father, Servillano Aquino, a Katipunero, to look up to as model.

That Noynoy sees nothing formidable in the role he has long discovered to be evolving for someone with his lineage could only be a gauge of a thoroughly wholesome upbringing. Since early childhood, without anyone, least of all his father, pointing it out to him, Noynoy has experienced a serious obligation to pursue what his ancestors stood for. It may have been all a delusion, he says, but in a philosophical tone, he paraphrases biblical wisdom in turn quoted by Schumacher in his bestseller *Small is Beautiful*, "You ask why a lot is asked of you. You should ask why a lot has been given you." That, more than anything else, has crystallized for Noynoy the answers to the usual identity questions that plague youth:

"My experience [in life], the people I meet, the many blessings I have had, all point to a duty that all these must be repaid to both my parents and society." These words may sound too grave and solemn, but they ring with such earnestness and sincerity when Noynoy confesses that he has never consciously planned to follow anyone's footsteps.

He has long conceded that he can never attempt to match what his dad was, especially in the political sphere. Besides, for a more practical reason, "no matter how good you become, you will always fall far below the measure."

Especially when the criteria are far above the ordinary. His Lolo Servillano was arrested by the Americans for his revolutionary activities in the Katipunan. His Lolo Benigno was a hard-hitting Speaker of the House and was arrested after the war. All that his own father suffered of course is now part of contemporary Philippine history.

Given his family's record of arrests, does Noynoy fear a similar fate for himself? The question is not directly answered but his leanings become apparent. "It is all a simple choice. You can either keep quiet, fall for the illusion of security and comfort, and be a traitor to the principles and convictions sacrificed before you. Or you can speak up and be counted. Then there is at least the chance of winning, of surviving the struggle."

The amazing thing about Noynoy is that he has not always been his father's son, this courageous young man with such hopes and dreams for the future, knowing the accompanying demands and sacrifices his new-found task entails.

He was twelve and in seventh grade at the Ateneo when his father was arrested. Noynoy uses surprisingly mild words for this upheaval in his family life. "There was a real change in the environment," a statement that also embraces what was a rude political awakening for him.

The impressionable young boy looked around him and became deeply disturbed by what he saw. Events which have left enduring unpleasant images were those involving his father's associates who shifted alliances for what looked like mere personal convenience and interests. He laments, "I have always thought loyalty was the first virtue of being a man."

It was also at this stage of his life that he eagerly joined street demonstrations in their outcry against imperialism, feudalism, and fascism.

While he vaguely understood the full implications of yesterday's and today's slogans, he acknowledges that it was his father who made politics a part of the Aquino way of life.

Politics, at least Noynoy's view of it, was simple and naive then.

When his father ran for senator, eventually becoming the country's youngest senator-elect, the Aquino household anxiously worried about a possible defeat. Noynoy could not understand what the fuss was all about. "But who would not want to vote for my dad?" And when the early returns showed his dad at the top slot but appeared to be dislodged a few hours later, all he could think of was, "How could he ever experience defeat when politics meant nothing more than the direct process of voting for the public servant of one's choice?"

Inside him seethed many contrary thoughts especially difficult to quell in the absence of a father in the same household. As competent a single parent as his mother was then, Noynoy's special doubts and needs were resolved in time and answered through a long drawn-out period, over regular visits to his father at Fort Bonifacio.

His high school transcript, confesses an embarrassed Noynoy, carries such a consistent record of miserable grades. There was little motivation for him to excel academically because of his pessimism about the future. Who was to argue with an obstinate adolescent who was convinced about the futility of preparing for a future far too uncertain to be envisioned, least of all, bothered about? Was the rat race worth joining at all? Not even the eloquence of Ninoy Aquino could paint a less bleak picture of the future for his very own son!

As early as then, the son saw how different he was from his father.

"When I plan, I am *segurista*. I want to know the exact steps in reaching a goal, although I know you can't do this with so many things."

On the other hand, his father would say to him, over and over again in so many different ways, "Just because you can't see precisely where you are going does not mean you won't at least try. Otherwise, you will never reach your goal."

It was as an economics student at the Ateneo that Noynoy exerted greater effort at studying. "It was still moving one step at a time, not any long-term planning." A late bloomer, he struggled with his Spanish and Rizal and Philippine history courses that he perceived to have placed too much emphasis on boring data—a manner of learning that he has a built-in aversion for—that could be easily looked up in any book. It was in his junior year while an Council representative that he displayed his potential for leadership.

When he was younger there were moments when Noynoy vainly aspired to be an ordinary citizen. Not that he was ever a prisoner in his own home or that he rebelled against public expectations of Ninoy Aquino's only son. But he has long resigned himself to the fact that he will do his best no matter what destiny has in store for him.

Noynoy does not mean to sound like a chosen disciple. Such stance does not become him, especially when he flashes that charmingly familiar Aquino grin. It is merely his way of saying that for someone like him, it is rather difficult to plan his life independently.

He cites how in 1978, when there was the possibility of his father's release, each member of the family was asked how he or she felt about moving to the States. Noynoy said then that he would help the family get settled abroad for two months, but would want to return home. That sentiment had not changed by the time that possibility became more real when his father then needed heart surgery two years later. Noynoy stayed in the States for a full month after the operation but hurried back to Manila to complete his last year of college. This was despite well-meaning reminders that he may not manage to be reunited with his family in Boston.

There was never any indecisiveness about being back. "I get homesick even after just three days in Hong Kong, so I was eager to be home. This is where I belong."

No, there were no college romances that beckoned. "There were just too many things I wanted to do on both the personal and public levels. This is, after all, where the fight was."

When he did rejoin his family after graduation with no difficulty, he read that as something necessary and urgent. He never worked in the States because he felt the skills he had to offer were more useful to a developing country like the Philippines. "I thought there was such a conflict of interest. I was not an essential individual in the labor market, did not have the skills of an Einstein to offer. Also, I would be depriving another citizen of a job."

Despite his parents' encouragement, he was not willing to enroll in a graduate program because he did not want to be left in the States should the family decide to fly home—a plan of action which was much discussed even then.

Noynoy busied himself in the U.S. doing informal, in-depth studies of the American system of marketing, analyses of the various specialty shops, wholesale and retail outlets, the economics of their well-patronized seasonal sales. He was equally fascinated with current stereo technology.

The time he spent there was well worth it, says Noynoy, if only because "there were many questions in my life begging to be answered." He himself was surprised at the growing experience Boston was for him, and he had been told by his professors at the Ateneo how mature he had become.

His two years in Boston were a unique experience for the family to be together once more. He came to know his father in another light then, as an impatient backseat driver who urged

Noynoy to speed it up on difficult hilly terrain ("My dad drove the way one would if there were fewer cars"), as a dynamic and energetic person who, in wishing to use every minute to the fullest, adopted a gait that really is a walkathon pace ("Walking normally, one would be four steps behind him"), and as a warm and solicitous parent who would engage Noynoy in "man talk over pizza." "*Magkwento ka nga,*" Ninoy would say to the less ebullient Noynoy.

Father and son had disagreements, stuff that Noynoy views now as more a difference in style rather than in substance. He recounts how angry and disappointed his family was with people whose lives Ninoy had literally saved and who were now repaying the favor with a disservice. But Ninoy's display of temper was disappointingly short-lived to Noynoy. "Unlike him, I could not, would not turn the other cheek to be slapped."

His father, he says, had a vast store of knowledge covering many disciplines. Noynoy's own style is to limit himself to particular spheres of interest in which he prefers to acquire more extensive information—karate, cars, dogs, horses, stereos, even ammunition. Probably more thorough and more detailed than actually necessary, he says with a smile.

During the last months in Boston, when many individuals would visit their home to advise his father either to return or not to return to Manila, Noynoy was careful not to add his two cents' worth to the already existing confusion. The words of counsel were as varied as the persons who gave them. Although he himself did not completely agree with the manner in which his father was inclined to return, Noynoy was at least assured that it was a rational, well-thought-out move, not a reckless *bahala na* option. "He never went out of his way to convince us to follow what he does. But as a family, we have always believed in him, in the choices he has made."

Close to the proclamation of martial law, Ninoy had warned his family to leave the country since he sensed such a move was forthcoming. When Cory and the children discovered that he had no intention of joining them in their flight ("I'll stay to fight it out"), they could not entertain thoughts of leaving him alone.

Noynoy makes no attempt to mask his bitterness over the events since 1972. Shaking his head and closing his eyes as if to shut out the bluntness of the pain, he quietly says, "My father and the family did not deserve all these." It was not his immediate family alone, but people who have been in their employ as well. Because of her association with the Aquinos, a former *yaya* of his and Viel's was arrested. So were a photographer, a houseboy who survived the experience with only three teeth left, and even a Hacienda Luisita caretaker who suffered a nervous breakdown and was last heard of asking people to vote for him as senator.

This is all so pathetic to Noynoy, who says it would have been much easier to have suffered reversals in political fortunes. Those would have been at least completely understandable.

It still disgusts him to think of the thorough physical search his mother and his four sisters had to endure, on their regular visits to Bonifacio, much more than what he as a man was subjected to. "Dad's place," he had thoughtlessly referred to it, but in the next breath laughingly corrects himself. His father's prolonged detention could very well have earned Ninoy some degree of ownership of the place.

The one word Noynoy dares to articulate to describe his father's death is painfully unequivocal. A slaughter, he calls it. "Even an animal is treated far better—coaxed to relax, shut its eyes before its moment of death so that its meat may be tender." And granted that Galman was indeed the assassin, Noynoy wonders what magical Superman powers this man possessed for him to have remained unseen by airport security. Full of unanswered questions about the circumstances of his father's death, Noynoy continues, "Was he crazy to think he could get in and get out alive from such a scene? It appears he was more victim than perpetrator. Why, even kamikaze pilots face a 50-50 chance of survival."

His frustration and disappointment mount as he remembers the tight security measures provided his father during his detention. Borrowing from Ninoy's own logic, Noynoy describes how on the trip from the cell in Bonifacio to another building also in Bonifacio for the trials, twenty military men would surround the senator but with their backs to him, lest any surprise attack be sprung on their ward. And inside the vehicle where Ninoy was allowed to ride, he was made to sit at the center, similarly guarded, and the vehicle followed by a fleet of support security vehicles. As a detainee being sent off to the States for surgery, Ninoy shook hands with friends over a sea of heads, those of the security assigned to him.

Straining to see the blessings behind the tragedy, Noynoy tries to mellow his anger by saying that perhaps it was kinder this way. Death, after all, could have come to his father under even more mystifying circumstances in Laur, or during his hunger strike, or in a contrived situation where he could have been fired at as he resisted arrest or continued detention. Shaking his head again, Noynoy says pensively, almost in disbelief until now, "We never thought they would make a martyr out of him." **(NSRC)**

Building a
Vision that Lasts

Noy's war against corruption is now being bolstered by his administration's filing of plunder and graft cases against three senators—Enrile, Estrada, and Revilla—several lawmakers, and Janet Lim Napoles. This is now leading to further investor confidence in the country's economy.

After Marcos transformed the Philippines from being the second richest nation in Asia, next only to Japan, to being the sick man of Asia, the principal complaint of investors was the lack of good governance due to widespread government corruption at the highest levels, especially in the past two administrations.

Under the leadership of Corazon Aquino, the country toppled the Marcos dictatorship and restored democracy. Unfortunately, she had to contend with several coup attempts, including the ones led by Gringo Honasan. But during her presidency, the country rebuilt its democratic institutions and returned to the rule of law.

However, succeeding governments failed to introduce good governance to the country. Erap Estrada was forced to resign and was convicted for plunder. Gloria Macapagal-Arroyo is currently under detention facing trial for plunder. The recent pork barrel scandals mostly happened under GMA's administration.

But PNoy's *Daang Matuwid* is gaining international recognition. The *Wall Street Journal* said: "Still the Philippines' continuing fight against corruption points to the gains that other emerging economies might achieve if they tackle their own problems, whether they be nationalist protectionist policies in Indonesia or a growing dependence on populist subsidies in Thailand."

While he was campaigning for president, PNoy laid out his economic game plan, which later became the Philippine Development Plan. One of its main features is the identification of the four major bottlenecks that have historically been the obstacles to Philippine economic prosperity. One of the four was systemic corruption in all branches of government.

At the start of the Aquino government in 2010, the World Bank estimated that the cost of corruption was as high as 40 percent of the government's annual budget. At that time, I thought the estimate might be a little too high. However, after listening to the Napoles whistleblowers, perhaps 40 percent is too low. Some of the whistleblowers did say that only 15 percent to 20 percent of the pork barrel funds went to actual projects. The rest were distributed to the implementing agencies, the lawmakers, and their chiefs of staff.

Even though the loudest outrage against corruption is from the middle and upper classes, it is the poor that corruption hurts the most by diverting funds meant for development. This undermines the government's ability to provide basic services, which in turn results to greater inequality and injustice, and discourages foreign aid and investment.

Daang Matuwid has focused on cleansing the executive agencies like the Department of Transportation and Communication, Department of Public Works and Highways, Bureau of Internal Revenue, and the Bureau of Customs. The filing of charges against the HERMES group in the Senate and other lawmakers is a clear sign that the anti-corruption drive is also happening in the legislative branch. HERMES is a term coined by the public representing the initials of the family names of six senators allegedly implicated in the PDAF scandal. These are Honasan, Enrile, Revilla, Marcos, Estrada, and Sotto.

There are many signs that we are seeing a brighter future especially for the next generation. The 2013–2014 Global Competitiveness Report of the World Economic Forum shows that the Philippines has dramatically improved from 85th place, when PNoy took over, to 59th out of 148 countries, in just three years. More significantly, for the first time, corruption is no longer the top concern affecting the country's competitiveness.

If this government and succeeding administrations build on the recent progress under PNoy and remain focused on economic growth and on improving the living standards of the population, an HSBC report forecasting the world's top 50 economies in 2050 may just come true. In this report, HSBC places the Philippines as the 16th largest economy in the world and the largest among ASEAN countries.

This is a vision that can be achieved if we, as a people, ensure that that we will continue to have what we now have—a moral leadership at the top level of government and the active support of an outraged public that will demand that its leaders—in all branches of government—live up to the highest level of moral standards.

Daang Matuwid can and must be a way of life for the Filipinos. **(ESC)**

PNoy and a Transformative Senate

The 2013 midterm election was clearly a victory for the change and reform agenda of PNoy. This was not only due to the overwhelming victory of his candidates but also to the fact that even opposition candidates were cautious in stating that they support the President's program of good governance, knowing that they could risk antagonizing the public.

I am hopeful that the nation's political ruling class, often considered as one of the most selfish in Asia, will become an ally in the President's vision of institutionalizing the rule of law and good governance in our country.

There is a need, however, to understand that we have two general classes of politicians in our country today. The first type views winning elections as the end goal of a politician. This is similar to the businessman who considers maximizing profits as the overriding objective of any business.

In both politics and business, the maxim is that the end justifies the means. Therefore, resorting to corruption or intimidation to win elections or to maximize profits is considered as a necessary part of the "political game." This type of politician is what we often refer to as the traditional politician or *trapo*.

An example of this type of politician was Ferdinand Marcos who declared martial law, replaced democracy with a dictatorship, and allowed widespread violation of human rights in his desire to perpetuate his political power. There are also those personalities who run for public office simply because they believe they can win like a Lapid and other celebrities.

However, the PNoy phenomenon has brought a new game-changing character to our political process. More and more politicians, even *trapos*, are becoming aware that good governance and *Daang Matuwid* can actually become winning formulas. Therefore, even most *trapos* will support these advocacies for as long as they believe the public will support PNoy's programs.

The President will, however, need to continually bring his message directly to the public in order to influence public opinion. This was the formula that convinced many senators to support the impeachment of Renato Corona. This was the strategy that resulted in the victories of PNoy-backed candidates in this election.

The second type of politician is a small but growing number of reformist politicians who are true believers in the need for change in our society. To this type of politicians, winning elections is a means and not an end.

While I empathize with this class of politicians, their biggest liability is their seeming inability to win elections. The principal reason seems to be that they believe that their message of change and reform will be enough to win elections. They need to understand that if the people are not aware and do not trust the messenger, their message will not be heeded.

We have a highly personalized society which is not just a Filipino but an Asian trait. Contemporary political history shows that nations around us were able to achieve political and economic breakthroughs under the leadership of highly charismatic personalities like Mahathir of Malaysia, Lee Kuan Yew of Singapore, and Park of South Korea.

Reform advocacy and charisma can be merged in a single personality. We had Corazon Aquino and Jesse Robredo. Now we have PNoy who has a charismatic, transformative, quiet style of leadership.

The next question now is how long will the senators focus on their task of advancing national interest before they become obsessed with the 2016 elections. Remember that the 1987 Constitutional Commission reinstated the Senate with a margin of only one vote, 23 to 22. The belief was that the Senate would equalize and balance the gap between local and national interests. It is disheartening to observe that the majority of Senate bills are local bills and discussions are often focused on investigations.

Transformative leaders know that if they want to gain commitment from followers and achieve high standards of morality, they must themselves be models of principled behavior. Leaders must also be clear about their guiding principles and their vision for the Philippines. **(ESC)**

PNoy in a Different Light

W ho does not know Noynoy Aquino today? He has emerged as the new kid on the block, seen in a different context, in a different light. More than just "the only son of revered parents," he now appears as a knight in shining armor, dead set on his quest to make a difference in our lives by leading by example.

Though PNoy is now a very popular household name or brand, a certain mystique still envelops Pres. Noynoy Aquino's public persona.

Lawyer Rene Saguisag, trusted family friend and Cory Aquino's presidential spokesman, says he only knows of Noynoy from a distance and cannot boast familiarity with him. But Noynoy would always cordially acknowledge Rene. The last time they were together was when they briefly walked toward Cory's final resting place at the Manila Memorial Park in 2010, although that sad rainy day was not the time for any meaningful conversation.

On the other hand, Saguisag remembers a marathon ten-hour conversation with PNoy's father in Boston in 1982. It was actually a monologue, as Ninoy did all the talking—and for someone to outtalk Rene is also a record-breaker of sorts. Ninoy lavished praise on his daughters, especially Ballsy, but he was, Rene recalls, "jurassic and slightly old-fashioned" in his inability to decipher his only son. Yes, Ninoy sounded like an all-too-ordinary father with all-too-ordinary problems. Seeing Noynoy now in the news, Rene describes him as "gusty *at buo ang loob*," like his iconic parents.

Former Tourism Secretary Jose Antonio "Tony" Gonzales is also an old family friend who would drive Ninoy to his many speaking engagements while in Boston and would stay overnight in their home in Newton, Massachusetts. As president of the flourishing Mondragon Industries in Manila then, he knew Noynoy as a quiet and respectful employee assigned to business development for Nike products. It was there where Noynoy worked closely with Tony's son, Anton, and with Rene Saguisag's wife, Dulce, then a successful executive at Mondragon.

Even those who worked closely with Cory in Malacañang say that they had very little personal interaction with Noynoy then. *Philippine Star* columnist William M. "Billy" Esposo, who headed the Cory Aquino Media Bureau during the campaign and the Public Information Agency during Cory's presidency, says he only remembers seeing Noynoy at the Valle Verde Country Club in 1984, when Noynoy, then a college student, delivered a speech.

Neither did trusted Aquino speechwriter Teodoro L. "Teddy Boy" Locsin Jr. see much of Noynoy during Cory's tenure. "He was hardly at the Palace," Locsin says. "He didn't indulge himself in his mother's power, but just kept to himself."

That, Locsin adds, is why Noynoy carries his presidential title lightly, even lighter than his mother did: "He is a man unimpressed by the power that has dropped on his lap at the price of his parent's sacrifices."

Noynoy was never visible as a privileged member of the presidential family. The only time he came into prominence was when he was shot on August 28, 1987, during the coup attempt led by then Colonel (now senator) Gregorio "Gringo" Honasan.

Three of his security escorts were killed in that attack just two blocks away from Malacañang, and Noynoy himself was hit by five bullets, one of which remains lodged in his neck.

On the whole, however, Noynoy did what was not easy to do—to be unobtrusive throughout his mother's presidency. He maintained simple ways, including dining unobtrusively in fast-food restaurants without his security guards.

How then to explain his phenomenal leap to prominence after August 1, 2009?

Gregorio "Yoyong" Magdaraog, an active member of Corvetsfornoy—the campaign group of "Corvets," or "Cory veterans," those who were associated with or worked for the Aquino administration—says he felt suddenly orphaned with the death of Cory Aquino: "It was as if we were left in the hands of an abusive and unwanted governance."

Stage actress and Philippine Educational Theater Association (PETA) president Cecilia "CB" B. Garrucho, who was at the Quirino Grandstand during Noynoy's inaugural, describes the event as a communal high, with the huge crowd coming on its own volition from near and far, rather than herded in buses with a day's allowance, to witness the oath taking of "a servant leader" who allowed the people to hope and dream once more. "I am forever grateful to Noynoy for saying yes to the presidency," CB says. The fact that Noynoy called his first day as president as *"umpisa ng aking kalbaryo,"* she points out, shows that he seriously means to walk the difficult and often lonely road of government service.

Chris Zaens of the Institute for Solidarity in Asia, which is involved in promoting good governance work with local government units (LGUs) and NGOs, can only describe the nation's belief in Noynoy in this way: "parched land longing for water."

Andy Ibarra, a batchmate of Noynoy's at the Ateneo de Manila from grade school to college, was one of the many volunteers for the campaign from their high school batch of 1977 and college batch of 1981. In college, as A.B. Economics students, they were classmates in a subject taught by Gloria Macapagal-Arroyo, whom Andy describes as admittedly an effective teacher, though her students mercilessly made fun of her because of her distinct nasal voice.

Noynoy, Andy recalls, had no airs about him and, like a typical teenager, loved video games and music. He once gave Andy a Burt Bacharach album from his extensive CD collection. It is little surprise then that, at the June 30 people's party at the Quezon City Memorial Circle, Noynoy gamely (some say, bravely) sang Michel Legrand and Norman Gimble's "Watch What Happens" and Freddie Aguilar's "Estudyante Blues" before a swooning audience.

Back in college, Andy says, Noynoy was always just one of the crowd, in jeans and loafers, enjoying a burger or a pizza, as his break from the typical student's cafeteria meal of rice and a viand or two. Because Andy married early, his and bachelor Noynoy's social life no longer coincided after graduation in 1981. Their occasional meetings would be at Ateneo homecomings or at a classmate's birthday, or whenever there was a visiting *balikbayan* classmate.

Another classmate, Angela "Gel" Perfecto-Caguioa, refers to Noynoy as "every Filipino." He is, she says, everyone's devoted son, loving brother, doting uncle, loyal friend—every Filipino's real person, "ordinary, reachable, touchable, textable."

After college, Gel says, her meetings with Noynoy were mostly at wakes (Ninoy's in 1983, and those of parents of classmates, even her father-in-law's). But there was one encounter she cannot forget.

She and her daughter were flying in from Sydney in December 2007 when her husband Ben, driving back to Manila from Baguio with their son and the son's four best friends, met an accident in Tarlac. They were rushed to a hospital in Urdaneta, Pangasinan. Friends and family were soon there too, including Noynoy.

When the distraught Gel got to the hospital, the first person she saw was Noynoy, who was then a senator—and she was miffed, thinking to herself, "Must he use this moment for politics?" And who's to blame Gel for her distrust of politics and politicians, her own classmate included?

Later, she found out that, before her arrival, Noynoy spent time by her husband's bedside, comforting Ben and keeping him company, recalling with pain and difficulty how his own bodyguards died for him in 1987. She was also told that it was Noynoy who ordered Jollibee meals for her family, and that he and his security detail took care of fending off men who came to the hospital, claiming they had rescued Ben and the boys and demanding payment for their services. Looking back now, Gel acknowledges that Noynoy was not intrusive and did not even announce his presence.

On the first anniversary of that accident (in which one of the boys died), Gel sent her former classmate a text message: "Noy, today we remember the accident a year ago and as we continue to struggle with and anguish over the events of that day, we thank God as well for the many miracles of that day. We thank you, Noy, simply for being there with Ben."

Senator Noynoy replied promptly. "Gel, no need to thank me. I was there at the right place at the right time."

Gel says she realized then that he was not the typical drumbeating, PR-obsessed politician, after all. He did not go to the hospital with thoughts of the next election in mind, but was there for his friend who happened to be her husband. When Gel and Ben lined up in the rain to send off Tita Cory on the day of the funeral, they were also there for their friend Noynoy. Days later, she sent him a text message, which he did not reply to, and need not have replied to: "Noy, step into the fight. Now *na*."

Ma. Victoria "Bitchik" Panlilio-Dimalanta, another classmate of Noynoy's, led a rally during the campaign to launch what she called the Goodness Revolution. Having known Noynoy for thirty or so years, she admitted in her speech that he is not perfect, but how could he go wrong when his credo, as quoted by the *Time* magazine cover story (April 26, 2010) on Noynoy the presidential candidate, was: "We are just instruments put in the right position to execute God's will." PNoy is not perfect, Bitchik says, but is perfect as president at this time in our history.

Couple Mike and Monina Valencia campaigned with Noynoy's batchmates and saw for themselves how Noynoy inspired volunteerism in both friends and strangers alike. Monina says: "He inspired hope and answered our desire for change, our call for help."

It is PNoy's good fortune that he has loyal friends and classmates from way back—people with whom he can think out loud and test his ideas. And yes, share a good laugh with at the end of grueling days. **(NSRC)**

The Everyman President

Much of PNoy's charm comes from his image as the Everyman president, a pretty regular guy who cannot sleep through brownouts and is not all that interested in foreign travel, so that his passport has lapsed from non-use.

Journalist Marites Dañguilan Vitug says she was rather aghast to discover that PNoy has not even been to Europe. The truth is, he is happiest being in the Philippines. "*Parang*, if you take me out of the Philippines, I'm like a fish out of water," he told us when we interviewed him for the December 2010 issue of *YES! "Iba talaga pag nasa Pilipinas.* [It's really different here in the Philippines.]"

Content with short trips to Baguio or to one of the islands, he was also this way when the Aquino family first discussed the possibility of Ninoy being sent into exile. The daughters all said they would go as a family. Noynoy was the contrarian, saying he would go and help the family settle down but would prefer to return home. His reason may have been, and he does not deny this now, that there was a girl he could not leave behind, but the prevailing reason, as he told us during the interview, was: "I'm not fond of travel. If I've visited the place and I've seen the sights, that's it. *Okey na 'ko doon.* [I'm okay with that.]"

Book publisher Karina Bolasco is convinced it is not mere media hype or sloganeering when PNoy says, "*Kayo ang aking lakas* [You are my strength]" or "*Kayo ang aking boss* [You are my bosses]." Just knowing him, like many others, from a distance, Karina feels that perhaps

PNoy, who prefers to be just a laid-back, regular guy, is actually his father's son. For how could he have risen to the call of the circumstances and not failed anyone during the campaign, if he did not have it in him at all? That his dad died at fifty, and that the son is now, at fifty, the president of the country, cannot be a mere uncanny coincidence. Perhaps, Karina says, destiny will banish the regular guy in PNoy forever.

Dr. Wilfrido Villacorta, scholar and professor of political science and international relations, says he was initially struck by Noynoy's simplicity and lack of affectation in lifestyle, manner, and speech, despite his pedigreed background. Early on, he saw the potential in Noynoy: "I was lucky to be present when then Thai Prime Minister Abhisit paid him a courtesy call to express his condolences, a few weeks after Tita Cory was laid to rest. Noynoy was very composed and engaged the Prime Minister in a discussion about political and economic issues that faced the region. I told myself, the son of Cory has indeed the makings of a future president."

According to Teddy Boy Locsin, a bishop said of Noynoy the candidate: "I don't care what his qualifications for president are. I just know that he will never hurt his mother's memory." Who needs any more image-building with that? Locsin says that, with Noynoy, the nation has gotten back both Ninoy and Cory, for he is "clean and strong like Cory, strong and single-minded like Ninoy."

Noynoy's own courage is admirable. Locsin recounts: "I saw what he went through when Gringo attacked the Palace, viewed the bodies of his slain guards, watched his mother make herself appear calm and collected and focused on defending the government rather than giving in to her evident impulse to be by her wounded son's side. He never complained and never talked about the bullet that is still lodged inside him."

Any other politician of lesser stock would have capitalized on that condition and turned it into a tearjerker.

"Thank God for surprises and the gift of circumstance," says Maria Asuncion "Mariasun" Azcuna, St. Scholastica's College dean and a close associate of the Aquino family. She is grateful for the time and circumstances that have honed this simple man for his "time in the sun."

Noynoy's simplicity is striking because, even as senator of the land, he never courted special treatment. At the retirement ceremony for Mariasun's husband, Supreme Court Justice Adolf Azcuna, Senator Noynoy tarried late, stayed in the back, and was just an ordinary guest.

Another educator, Alice Pañares, says she was witness to Noynoy's phenomenal growth, his rising to the occasion. Like the rest of the nation, she saw him transformed from a tentative speaker to a statesman, calm, powerful, sincere. But it is, Alice adds, Noynoy's relationship with his nephew Josh that is most revealing of his person. She was touched to see him finding time for Josh in a large crowd of people. It was, to her, a poignant and tender scene. Children do not mask their feelings, and a person that a child like Josh loves and trusts must be a genuine one, Alice muses.

PNoy does have a special relationship with his nieces and nephews, and enjoys spending time with them. The older ones—Jiggy and Jonty Cruz, Miguel Abellada and Kiko Dee—talk of the times when he would ask them about their social life and even give them a little cash for dates. But it is with Kris Aquino's sons, Joshua and Bimby, that Tito Noy spends more time with, taking them to the malls to shop—but always with the caution to be frugal in their choices, as it is their mother who has more money than he has.

Josh spent a lot of time at the Aquino family residence in Times Street, Quezon City, because he had his special tutorials there and was on frequent visits to his Lola Cory during her healthier days. He would announce his presence by banging on his uncle's bedroom door, and when that did not wake him up, he would holler in his ear. If that still did not work, all 200-plus pounds of Josh would shake Noynoy and even jump on his bed. Cory used to say that, when she had a dinner engagement and had to be out of the house, she would ask Noynoy to take Josh to the neighborhood hamburger drive-through to make up for her absence.

Michael Charleston B. Chua, a native of Tarlac and a history professor at De La Salle University, laughs that, for the first time, he is on the side of the administration. An almost incredulous turn of events, he feels. He is committed to a better Philippines that can be enjoyed by his future children. Campaigning for Noynoy with the Yo!Noy UP Diliman group, along with Joshua Duldulao and Kiko Aquino-Dee, made Michael feel like a hero, and he would like to continue that heroism by being a good citizen—being the best teacher he can be, helping others understand the work of the new administration, and however else he can make himself useful.

The history professor says his admiration for the Aquinos, and for Noynoy in particular, goes back to his childhood. The father of his seatmate in Grade 4, Sunny Grace Galleta, was a member of the security force that protected Noynoy during that ambush on Arlegui Street, in the season of coup attempts to overthrow President Cory. Noynoy was a congressman when Michael first met him, at a wedding, and Michael asked him to sign his copy of a book on

EDSA 1 (*Nine Letters: The Story of the 1986 Revolution*, by Cynthia Sta. Maria Baron and Melba Morales Suazo). Besides giving his autograph, Noynoy wrote: "Keep the dream alive in your generation." In 2010, that dream was made real, Michael says with an air of triumph.

Michael also remembers how approachable Noynoy was when he, then a student doing his thesis on the elections, dared venture into the Batasang Pambansa in 2004 to interview the congressman. Through a congressional page, Michael had sent a note regarding his request, introducing himself as a native of Tarlac. Congressman Noynoy, cigarette in hand, was warm and accommodating and articulate during the lengthy interview by the Batasan lobby. Michael says: "He was too simple and humble. I never thought he would be president one day."

Business World columnist Sonny Coloma, head of the Presidential Communications Group, was among the most trusted advisers during the campaign. Like Michael, Sonny witnessed just how patient and approachable the man of the hour is. On February 3, 2010, the final day of the Senate's regular session, Sen. Noynoy Aquino was scheduled to give a press briefing. The room had been set up and reporters were ready. There was considerable delay not only because the senator had been "ambushed" by other members of the media on the Senate floor, but also because as he tried to make his way to the press conference, he was detained by a man over a personal concern.

As Sonny Coloma tells it, the man kept saying that since he knew that the senator and his father were both advocates of the welfare of soldiers, he felt emboldened to approach the senator. Noynoy listened patiently, never raising his voice, even as he kept asking the man to write a brief summary of his concern for his Senate office. The dialogue continued for a long half-hour, in the course of which the senator never lost his equanimity or poise.

Amelia E. Bautista narrates a similar firsthand experience. She worked for the then newly established Benigno S. Aquino, Jr. Foundation as assistant executive director, and she knew Cory as a grade school classmate at St. Scholastica's College of her sister Aleli. However, she had never met Noynoy until January 2010, when he spoke at a presidential forum at De La Salle Zobel, in Alabang, Muntinlupa. Amelia was impressed that, during the jam-packed and rather lively reception, when she introduced herself and her relationship with his mother, Noynoy was intently listening to her, not manifesting any hint of distraction or disinterest. What a true gentleman he was, she says.

Carmina Flores describes PNoy as "simply Pinoy," the epitome of a true Filipino, from his looks to his values to his dreams. Admiring him from a distance, especially for his disdain for the trappings of power, she recalls an impressionable fleeting encounter with President Cory. Carmina was a Grade 6 student when her school bus stopped at a red light at the corner of Vito Cruz and South Superhighway in Manila. To her surprise, the presidential convoy also stopped beside them. President Cory waved to the students, who were all awed by the lack of sirens and fuss. It is, Carmina says, easy to understand why the "no *wangwang* directive" was a masterstroke of the new president. **(NSRC)**

Unselfish, Nonmaterialistic Noy

Was Noynoy ever burdened by the name he carried and the role he was born into as only son?

His close friends and classmates say that he was extra careful about being embroiled in controversies or tarnishing the name he carries. The circumstances of his youth left him wrestling with the choices to be made, like whether to live abroad with his family or stay here. When the family finally went into exile, it was five days before his college graduation, so he could not even join the graduation ceremonies.

His friends and classmates also say that while they learned history together, Noynoy lived history.

Maria Vargas Montelibano, head of PNoy's effective campaign communications team, reminds us of the unusual circumstances he has been subjected to. He was only twelve when his father was incarcerated by Ferdinand Marcos. During the seven years and seven months of Ninoy's incarceration, his family spent their holidays visiting him in prison. Noynoy was eighteen when his father wrote him that wildly known letter where he was passing on the torch to him. The letter said, in part: "Look after your two younger sisters with understanding and affection. Viel and Krissy will need your umbrella of protection for a long time. Krissy is still very young and fate has been most unkind to both of us. Our parting came too soon. Please make up for me. Take care of her as I would have take caren of her with patience and warm affection."

Yet, what could he really do at that stage in his life? He was twenty-three when his father was assassinated. What could have been running in his mind then? He must have felt frustration because, while in exile in Boston, he was always troubled by these thoughts: "If we're doing that which is right, why are we the ones who are in exile? Where's the justice in all of this?"

A longtime next-door neighbor of the Aquinos on Times Street is the Ocson family. Noynoy was comfortable going to their home because theirs was a household of three boys and one girl, while Noynoy belonged to a household of four girls and one boy.

Teng Ocson, one year older than Noynoy, recalls that the smoking habit that Noynoy finds hard to kick may have unwittingly started in the Ocson household. Now it can be told where that "bad" influence came from. While smoking was completely prohibited by Cory, Teng's mother allowed it because she felt it would help curb the weight gain of her sons. So it was to the house next door that Noynoy would go for a smoke, even at 6 a.m., when Teng and his brothers would still be asleep. He did not need to wake them up. He just needed a smoking refuge.

Teng noticed, especially after Ninoy's detention, that Noynoy was extremely careful about the company he kept, not easily trusting anyone. Understandably, he felt close and comfortable only with those who had proven to be true friends. To these friends, he was loyal, but he was also such a tease. When he saw Teng at the Ateneo conversing animatedly with one of his classmates, Irene Marcos, Noynoy yelled out to Teng afterward: *"Ganyan ka, ha! Lumipat ka na, ha!"* [You already switched sides!]

Decades later, the Ocson boys have fond memories of their shared childhoods: the helicopter ride to Hacienda Luisita; Ninoy's gun collection; the side gate that led to the Ocson swimming pool and the Aquino basketball court; Noynoy's promise that they would soon play basketball games in Malacañang; Noynoy's jokes, which Noynoy himself always found funny but everyone else found flat. "We were," Teng recalls, "just boys in high school, uninitiated, *torpe*, not street-smart at all."

Their parents were friends, and when Ninoy was assassinated, Teng's father was especially mournful, and not only because "Ninoy promised me so much when he becomes president . . . ." When Cory became president, Teng reminded his father to approach their neighbor. His father's reply made sense: "But it was Ninoy who made all those promises."

Teng, now a permanent resident in the U.S., has not had a chance to renew ties with his old friend. Like many of Noynoy's other supporters, he wants to reassure the new president: "I just want to talk to him, but not to ask for any favors."

Maria Montelibano, an Aquino relative, describes Noynoy as "Cory and Ninoy incarnate." He thinks like Cory, she says, but the "Ninoy DNA is so strong that there are times I am moved to tears when he acts or sounds like him."

Indeed, as his first SONA on July 26, 2010 showed, PNoy, like his father, speaks in rapid fashion.

PNoy is very deliberate in his actions, carefully weighing the situation before making any decisions. Maria recalls that, a month before election, when the survey results were very encouraging, he asked Maria what might still negate the trend. After she answered that only an act of God would, he instructed his sisters to stop accepting contributions from donors.

He felt that there was enough to sustain a respectable election day operations and that the donors' money could be put to better use. Besides, he added, those Johnny-come-lately contributors would now give only because they could smell victory.

Noynoy's instructions on those financial contributions reflect his lack of interest in money, says his sister Pinky Aquino Abellada. "Noy is very unselfish and nonmaterialistic," she notes. Asked about her favorite human interest Noynoy story, one that would allow the public to know her brother better, she goes back to Cory's last days:

I've said this story a number of times, hope it's not old news. When Mom was in the hospital for the last time and was there longer than we had expected and we knew bills were mounting, Noy told Ballsy one night that he would like to help take care of the bills. He told Ballsy how much withdrawable cash he had, and could immediately get all of it to help with the expenses:

> Noy will give his last peso if someone needed it. Ballsy told him, Mom saved enough for her old age. Also, during Mom's hospitalization, we agreed that one of us would always be with her 24/7, so we originally had two twelve-hour shifts per day—in the last two weeks, we disregarded the schedule Viel prepared and we were there daily—and Noy and Kris would usually take the evening shift. He always came on time or even a little earlier, and there were times when I would relieve him in the mornings. And when I was running late and texted him that I might be to ten to fifteen minutes late, he would always say, "Take your time." He never demanded, even if I knew he hardly slept during his night watch.
>
> When we asked him to go choose what items from Mom's room he wanted after she passed on, he said it should just be for the girls, since he got most

of Dad's stuff, anyway. Now that he's president and we try to maintain the Sunday lunches we used to have when Mom was around, he still manages to take care of his Sunday lunch turn, in spite of all his worries.

When I had a chance to travel to Hong Kong last November, and he was very busy going all over the country, Manolo (Pinky's husband) and I asked him what he wanted. His only request: a *toyo* seasoning no longer sold in the Philippines.

That's why when I told people during the campaign, 'My brother will *not* steal,' I knew what I was saying, because he is unselfish, unmaterialistic, and it is very clear to him what is right and what is wrong—no in-betweens.

Incidentally, Noynoy's personal withdrawable funds are no great shakes. To go by an Aquino family insider story, his sister Kris, long used to megabucks paychecks in her profession, was alternately "*nagulat at naawa*" (surprised and sympathetic) upon discovering the amount he had in his bankbook. Everyone in the family, according to the story, would not have minded sparing him the expense after discovering how "small" his savings were. **(NSRC)**

PNoy's Battle

Despite the continuing negative attacks and the burden of enduring several natural disasters, President Noynoy, in his first three and a half years as president, earned high trust ratings from the Filipino people. After many years of despair, the Aquino presidency gave the Filipino people the gift of hope for their future.

At the beginning of his term in 2010, his message was clear—to transform Philippine society and reintroduce morality to public service. His two major weapons were to institutionalize the rule of law and to set an example of personal integrity. This model of personal behavior would extend to his immediate family, especially his sisters and their families.

He has remained true to this promise. For so many years the realization of a government that would actively fight graft and corruption and where corrupt judges and politicians, tax evaders and money launderers would actively be prosecuted and punished, was just wishful thinking for Filipinos.

Today, after the filing of graft and plunder cases against Enrile, Estrada, Revilla, and other politicians, there is a real sense of hope that this quest for a just society is actually taking place and may even be realized in our lifetime.

But there will be many detractors especially those who will suffer if the struggle against corruption succeeds.

There are those who benefited, in many forms, from the largesse of the past two administrations. They are either facing charges in several scams or have lost influence in society due to loss of positions or access to powers in Malacañang.

There are politicians preparing for 2016 hoping the environment will remain as before where patronage, money, and cheating win elections.

And there are media personalities who somehow believe they have been anointed to set national agendas. But generally, media is simply focused on ratings and since the biggest competitors are entertainment shows, then these radio and television commentators must find ways to be entertaining. Listen to their programs and you will find a mix of gossip, wild commentaries, and games where the public can participate with the lure of a prize.

Our news media is intellectually light years away from serious news media like BBC and Bloomberg. But these detractors must not be a deterrence or distraction from the real struggle against corruption no matter how difficult the challenges are. Perhaps it would be good for the President and his people to remember the words of Thomas Paine during the struggle for freedom:

> These are times that try men's souls. The summer soldier and the sunshine patriot will, in this crisis, shrink from the service of their country; but he that stands it now, deserves the love and thanks of man and woman. Tyranny, like hell, is not easily conquered yet we have this consolation with us, that the harder the conflict, the more glorious the triumph. What we obtain too cheap, we esteem too lightly; it is dearness only that gives everything value. **(ESC)**

PNoy's Battle, Part 2

I n order to attain his goal of changing the behavior of Philippine society, especially the elite, PNoy must generate short-term wins. But the central component of all great leadership is ensuring that all actions remain consistent with the vision.

Visionary leadership requires a director of change. In this role, the president is out in front, establishing goals and encouraging others inside and outside government to follow. The president is the moving force of the system and the initiator of change.

But presidents do need public support or at the very least presidents want to avoid needlessly antagonizing the public. Therefore, presidents want to lead public opinion in support of themselves and their policies. They also want to avoid expending their limited resources on hopeless ventures.

When PNoy took office, he had extremely high approval ratings and very high expectations. But this can have negative consequences. These unusually high expectations could not be met in a single term. And there is always the possibility that these expectations become the ultimate source of public frustration.

Another obstacle in the efforts to gain public support is that, oftentimes, there will be contradictory public expectations. For example, it is a wonder that media commentators and even ordinary residents of Metro Manila can shift their discussion from the devastation of Typhoon Yolanda to traffic problems in a single discussion as if the two were national priorities. For some, easing the traffic congestion is more important than the Mindanao peace process.

Then there are businessmen who want a clean and honest government but will now complain that the BIR commissioner is intent on implementing the tax laws on their business firms. Many businessmen are opposed to crony capitalism only because they are not among the cronies.

But there are times when the President must lead public opinion instead of following it. The President cannot run a country on the basis of public polls or approval ratings alone. The president must listen to the people but he cannot make hard decisions based solely on their effects on his approval ratings or what media will say.

The ideal thing is for the President to make hard decisions and then educate the people on why an unpopular decision was actually necessary. In the end, history will be the final arbiter of PNoy's legacy. At this point, a quote from Churchill serves as a reminder: "You have enemies? Good. That means you've stood up for something, sometime in your life . . . . What is the use of living, if it be not to strive for noble causes, and to make this muddled world a better place for those who will live in it after we are gone." **(ESC)**

Noynoy, Hindi Ka Nag-iisa

*S*inabi po sa akin dati: "Noynoy, simulan mo lang." Sinimulan nga po natin, at ngayon, kitang kita na ang layo na ng ating narating. Ngayon, Pilipino, ituloy natin ang pagkakapit-bisig, sabay natin arugain, pabilisin, at palawakin ang transpormasyon ng lipunan. Ako po si Noynoy Aquino, ipinagmamalaki ko sa buong mundo: Pilipino ako. Napakasarap maging Pilipino sa panahong ito.

(Once, I was told: "Noynoy, just begin the change." So we did, and we can all see how far we have come. Now my countrymen, let us continue to stand arm in arm. Together, let us foster, accelerate, and expand the transformation of society. I am Noynoy Aquino, and I proudly say to the world: I am a Filipino. How wonderful it is to be a Filipino in these times.)

From my point of view, PNoy summarized his main message during the 2013 State of the Nation Address with this concluding paragraph. It evoked memories of People Power and its constant refrain that it is the Filipino people that will decide their own destiny.

PNoy went into detailed facts and figures in reciting his government's accomplishments. For example, he talked of the past three years' budget of P33 billion for the improvement and modernization of 4,518 hospitals, rural health units, and barangay health units.

But beyond those statistics, he gave specific examples, mentioning the Dagupan Medical Center which has successfully completed five kidney transplants in the last year and the Northern Mindanao Medical Center in Cagayan de Oro, which now has the capacity to perform open heart surgery due to upgraded facilities and equipment. There were many other examples of provincial hospitals which Metro Manilans may take for granted but which are major improvements in provincial cities.

In education, he stated that the inherited backlog in books and chairs has been erased and the inherited backlog in classrooms would be fully addressed within the same year. Now the Department of Education (DepEd) is confident that it will have the ability to prepare for the additional needs that the implementation of the K to 12 Program will require.

Then PNoy again gave a specific example of a success story. One textbook used to be priced at P58, but when Br. Armin Luistro became DepEd secretary, the price has gone down to P30. This may not mean much to those who send their children to private schools, but to the average Filipino, these are major successes.

It is these statistics, translated into real accomplishments, that have given PNoy such high ratings of trust and approval especially among those in the C-D-E socioeconomic income levels.

I believe that the private sector is the primary creator of jobs. The SONA included statements addressed to the business community. Among them were the commitment to revise and rationalize existing incentive-giving laws, the revitalization of the Bureau of Customs, the NLEX-SLEX connecting road, and the acceleration of infrastructure projects.

There are critics who said that PNoy did not mention the pork barrel scam. But this is what he said:

> On the topic of Cadavero, PDAF, MRT3 and others; just because the critics are not aware of what we are doing, they assume that we are doing nothing about these issues. If government possesses no data and yet announces who it will investigate, does that not send a message to the suspects to just hide the evidence? This is why we go where the truth takes us. The evidence decides our path.

For those who may not be aware, PDAF (Philippine Development Assistance Fund) is in reference to the alleged P10-billion pork barrel scam implicating five senators—Enrile, Marcos, Estrada, Revilla, and Honasan.

The second message was a recommitment to the rule of law when he said:

The transformation of our society is not just evident in the economy or in statistics. Now, Filipinos know, rich or poor, with or without political connections, when you do wrong, you will pay the consequences. Now justice is truly blind. We will not undermine the orders of our Bosses to hold the corrupt accountable, and to right the wrongs of a system that has long beggared our country.

But there is also a call for Filipinos to ask themselves: "*Ano ang inambag ko sa solusyon?* [What have I contributed to the solution?]" PNoy said: "Government has been fulfilling its obligation to the people, but let us ask ourselves, 'How have I contributed to the solution?' If someone dumps trash into a river, confront them; if you see a building being built obstructing an estuary, report it to the correct authorities. We will only drown in our problem if we do nothing."

This is clearly a call for People Power in transforming our society. It was an Aquino—Ninoy—who offered his life after he said, "The Filipino is worth dying for." And People Power responded by saying, "*Ninoy, hindi ka nag-iisa.* [Ninoy, you are not alone.]"

It was another Aquino—Cory—who asked us to march with her into EDSA and face the tanks of the Marcos dictatorship to win back our freedom. And People Power responded by saying, "*Cory, hindi ka nag-iisa.*"

Now another Aquino, in his SONA, tells us: "The road ahead is long and we never said it would be easy or that we could tread this path free of challenge. But I do not doubt our capacity to overcome any obstacle. We did not achieve our current success by chance. Let us not allow this transformation to be temporary; let us seize this opportunity to make the change permanent."

It is time to do our part and to actively contribute to the change we need in our country. And it is time for People Power to say, "*Noynoy, hindi ka nag-iisa.*" **(ESC)**

One-on-one with Pres. Benigno S. Aquino III

*W*hat was originally scheduled as an hour-long interview with Pres. Benigno S. Aquino III spilled over to another hour, to our surprise, with cues that he could still be available should it be necessary. An indication that the President was enjoying the conversation, Presidential Communications Operations Office Secretary Sonny Coloma was to say afterward. The President was relaxed and gave the assurance at the start of the session that he would try to answer all the questions expressly meant for this book, even as he was previously—and rather apologetically—forewarned that these would range from the political to the personal to the mundane. True to his word, he was candid and honest—and maintained an admirable, unhurried focus on the interviewer and never once allowed his gaze to wander. We were prepared for a simple office set-up, but a videographer, a photographer, and a staff of about a dozen were also present at the Malacañang Music Room on September 16, 2015. And although we had known him decades back from the time when he was anonymously known as Ninoy and Cory Aquino's only son, we confess there was still undeniable awe about PNoy's presidential presence today. *(NSRC)*

Excerpts from the interview of Pres. Benigno S. Aquino III by Elfren Sicangco Cruz (ESC):

ESC: How have your parents influenced you in your personal life and in your presidency?

PNOY: As I was growing up they were both available to render advice for my various problems. Although after the declaration of martial law when my mom became both mother and father, I tended to try and solve my own problems. I didn't want to impose any more burden and hardships on them. In hindsight, that was wrong. I probably should have opened up more to them and asked for more advice. It would have spared me from some heartaches.

How do they shape the way I view the world, the way I absorb and analyze the problems? It all really comes from what I learned from them and to this day, whenever I have my own hardships, I look at what they had to undergo and I'm strengthened by how they confronted the problem and how they overcame the problems that came before them. All the problems that I have now pale in comparison to what they had in their lifetime. That inspires me that no matter how dark the period is, there is light at the end of the tunnel and we will get there somehow.

ESC: So it's really more their life experience rather than specific advice?

PNOY: Yes, it would seem that words are cheap but actions really mean a lot and when they made pronouncements, there was no disconnect between their words and their actions. So anybody can mouth all these platitudes but they actually walked the talk.

ESC: In what ways are you like your father and your mother?

PNOY: My father has always been the leader in any group. There may be the process of consensus building, but it seems a decision has already been reached earlier, so the process leads you to the decision. His dynamism is something I strive for. He would be walking and everybody would be almost jogging just to keep up with him. He also had this fixation about not having enough time to do all the things that he wanted to do. I feel that way at this stage of my life—will I have enough time to do all that I want to do?

My mother was very, very patient and would always try consensus building rather than dictating to everybody or ordering everybody around. I'd like to think that I'm combining both of their talents. They have similarities for that matter. For instance, [while] my father was a voracious reader, my mother inculcated the love of reading in us.

The quest for knowledge was in both of them. In [Fort] Bonifacio, my dad had so much time on his hand, he started reading the Encyclopedia Britannica. He had such a fantastic memory. He'd suddenly ask us a question, like, what is angina pectorus? *(Laughs)* Thought it sounded *bastos* [malicious] at first. It is actually a painful heart condition.

In my youth, the *Hardy Boys* hardbound books were a significant expense based on the allowance that I had. We were never discouraged [from] purchasing books. We were always encouraged in that quest, to satisfy the thirst for knowledge.

ESC: Do you have time to read for leisure?

PNOY: The job entails so much reading. Then you have to do multiple takes on a particular topic. Let me give you a sample. Yesterday, we got documents from [the Department of] Energy. We had to measure it by the inch because of the bulk. I asked the staff, "*Meron ka bang kontrata sa dyaryo bote sa dami nito?*" The brief that comes to me is about several inches thick. So I said, "*Paano naging brief 'to kung two inches?*" Then they say, "Sir, the original documents were three feet tall."

ESC: How long did it take you to read?

PNOY: Should have been only twenty minutes but I made a mistake of opening it the wrong way, so the spine was broken. I had to reattach everything. That took longer than reading.

ESC: If we go back to August 21, 1983, what was your most vivid memory of that day?

PNOY: Of course, as my dad was approaching the Philippines, there was much tension. We were waiting for word that he was rearrested and brought back to Fort Bonifacio and I guess that was the common expectation.

ESC: Where were you then?

PNOY: Boston. I was in the room adjacent to the dining room. And that was where the family TV was, tuned to CNN. And that was where I first heard about it. My dad's name, "Opposition leader Benigno Aquino..." and something like shots being fired and lying in a pool of blood. Enough to really cause you shock and at the same time you were hoping it wasn't true. The way I remember it was, it seemed the world stopped. All your senses weren't functioning until the phone rang. And it was a Filipino-American friend of ours from the West Coast. She had a very tense voice, like she felt the worst has come. I was trying to take the message for my mom.

I think I eavesdropped for the part of that phone conversation she had with my mom. My mom was right beside the phone. So I went up and said, all of these might be exaggerated, might not be true, so my mom asked us all to start praying the rosary.

At about 3 in the morning or thereabouts, Takeo Iguchi, the former Japanese Consul in Manila who had been the friend of my parents in the '60s, called to confirm that he heard the news through a Japanese politician, Shintaro Ishihara [former member of parliament and later governor of Tokyo] who was informed by a Japanese reporter [Kiyoshi Wakamiya] on board the plane with my father. Sometime at that early morning hour, my mom had to talk to Shintaro himself. He said what the reporter told him, that my father was lying in a pool of blood. They believed that my dad had already expired at that time. It became a mad house. There was media attention, so many callers after that. That's when we first met Fr. Catalino Arevalo, SJ who said Mass for all of us the following day. At that time, he was staying in nearby Boston College and he felt compelled to offer his services as a priest. That's how the relationship of the family with Fr. Arevalo started.

If I'm not mistaken, they were all TOYM [Ten Outstanding Young Men] awardees on the same year. My dad, Father Arevalo, and President Ramos. I remember the plaque that had all of their names.

ESC: One of the things that the public has asked is, why is it that the Aquino family never really pursued to the end the parties responsible for the assassination of Ninoy?
PNOY: From the start, my mother felt that there was no justice possible under the martial law regime. Secondly, there were others during the martial law regime and after who were pursuing all of the leads. She didn't want it to be said that the president abused her position and just used the resources of the state to pin the blame on anybody. Unfortunately, key individuals managed to leave after or during the Agrava Commission proceedings. And one has to assume they have been supported and protected in their flight. One or two of the key individuals was supposed to have changed names and just kept on moving from place to place. And of course, at the end of the day, there is a prescription period.

ESC: So you have no intention of pursuing this anymore?
PNOY: There is the prescription period I mentioned. If you haven't brought the person to trial within twenty years, I think you're prohibited from doing so. There have been so many reports that somebody will come up with a tell-all book. Never happened. If they do come up

with that book, it would be self-serving. So it would not really advance our people's quest for the truth.

ESC: The Aquino family may be likened to the Kennedys in their share of triumphs and losses. What to you is the best thing about being an Aquino?

PNOY: My dad has said this, I'll be able to open doors for you. Whether or not those doors remain open is up to you. I should be proud of my legacy or the legacy that I'm a beneficiary of. Throughout generations, certain members of the family were called to the forefront, did their role and stepped aside after doing their role.

I had a colleague in Congress and his staff was telling him, you're not an Aquino, you don't have to fight Malacañang. Let's try to be accommodating to all sides and he said something to the effect that to him, it is choosing the difficult right over the easy wrong. That ought to be what you should do. The staff actually told him, you're not an Aquino. It's not expected of you. To his credit, he stood up for that which is right even if he was punished for that.

I was spared from any harassment myself. *Sa tigas ng ulo ko raw*, any such action would be useless. They pegged me inside a box and because they knew I wouldn't be influenced in any manner. That's another plus. *Parang klarong klaro: ito puti, ito itim.*

ESC: What is the most difficult thing about being an Aquino?

PNOY: Are we not bearing a disproportionate share of the burden? For instance, for me it started when I had all this time in Boston when I began to question—if we are doing that which is right, why are we the ones in exile? Why are the ones doing the wrong living it up here in this building?

During my dad's time, the slogan was, "*Hindi ka nag-iisa.*" With his solitary confinement, *talagang nag-iisa ka*. People were shunning us and what did we do wrong to deserve to be shunned? I guess the easier way to explain it is with this joke. My great grandfather [Servillano Aquino] was in the Katipunan and eventually wound up in Fort Santiago. My grandfather [Benigno Simeon Aquino, Sr.] was left by Quezon when the Commonwealth government went into exile. He also wound up in Fort Santiago. My father wound up in Fort Bonifacio. I guess in every generation, there is somebody winding up in incarceration. Hopefully, by the time it's my turn, it will be just at The Fort.

When I was really, really young, the *yaya*, the driver, everybody would say, "*Wag mo tutularin yung anak ng iba dyan, abusado*" There seemed to be too many dos and don'ts, I didn't really understand at that point. When my dad ran for the Senate, everybody was so tense. I didn't understand why because Superman *ang tatay ko*. Who would not want him?

ESC: What is the real story on how you got your wounds during the coup attempt in 1987? There are so many different versions.

PNOY: I'm not sure if I kept the affidavit but I didn't submit it formally. But my mom told me to put down on paper all the details that I remember. I think it's still in an attaché case that I have. Anyway, I had an argument with my girlfriend at that time. I had to go to their house in Parañaque. Unfortunately, the PSG already had knowledge that there was going to be a coup attempt. They weren't exactly clear when. Somehow that information that there were troop movements never got to me.

I got to talk to Chito Roque through the radio, got diverted to Joker Arroyo's house in Dasmariñas with Jojo Binay who was then Metro Manila Commission Governor. I think Chito Roque was there, though Joker was not there.

ESC: We were in Malacañang then.

PNOY: I decided to come back home with the four security personnel with me. Mom was going on provincial sorties, so remembering my promise to my dad that I will take care of my mother and sisters, I really wanted to come back. It was so vivid that when we left Joker's house, the backup vehicle was swerving so sharply on all the corners. I guess they were so tense.

ESC: You had two vehicles?

PNOY: Yes, I was driving with the civilian PSG agent with the three military escorts in the backup vehicle. It seemed a bit normal until crossing Nagtahan. There were people actually on the streets, many *usiseros* were already in the streets up to the foot of Nagtahan. After we crossed Nagtahan, that was where it became very eerie. Everything was dark, there were no people around. So the plan was to get as close to Malacañang as possible and reunite with my mother and my sisters. I drove to JP Laurel and if we saw the enemy we would fire to disengage them and look for another route. But the road was clear. Upon approaching the junction of Concepcion Avenue and JP Laurel, we saw one soldier with a backpack. *Sabi ko mukhang nandiyan sila.* We didn't know if he was the scout or if he was the trailing guy. So we went to the JP Laurel side. Unfortunately, the guy we saw was someone who got lost. The main contingent was in JP Laurel. They weren't visible because there was a portion that was S shaped, like a bend in the road. They were hidden at the curve. They were on their way out. That's when we bumped into each other. Then we had a dialogue for a few minutes.

ESC: You got out of the car?
PNOY: Well, they stopped us.

ESC: Did they know you were there?
PNOY: I introduced myself. They were facing Sta. Mesa. So they were roughly in the position where the first checkpoint was, who did not know that these were the attackers who were retreating. So as they were retreating, we were trying to go in. The dialogue lasted about 5 to 10 minutes or so. The funny thing was, well, not funny, I would talk and there would be five or six people who would respond. They would say get out of the car, go back to the car, turn on your lights, turn off your lights—confused commands from them. They tried to arrest me. So for about 45 minutes, there was an exchange of about three sets of gunfire.

ESC: And you were in the car all the time?
PNOY: They made me get in. Then there was a lull. Maybe what saved me was my security shielded me. I had a lot of shrapnel hits in the head and the neck. I was told that my head injury was very bloody. Half of my shirt was filled with blood. The left sleeve had a very big hole. Eventually Bodet Honrado [aide-de-camp of President Cory] came around and talked to them. He brought in an armored vehicle and actually rescued us in the presence of the attackers. They themselves were also confused.

Later on, some of those who participated were interviewed. They turned out to be Rangers undergoing training and they were told that this was their test mission. A test mission was a necessary requirement before they graduate. Two months before they were ordered to defend Malacañang against the communists. So they were fooled. Actually some of them were captured with notebooks because they were students. So they were misled by their officers and I'll never forget that guy who was interviewed I think by Jessica Soho. She asked them what they were doing in Malacañang. They said, "*Pinapunta po kami dati para labanan yung Comunista dahil inaatake daw po ang Malacañang.*" How did they do it? "*Hinabol po dito, hinabol dyan, eh kami ho pala ang hinahabol ng rebelde. Sumusunod lang kami dito, kami po pala yung kalaban.*"

At that time, my mom was looking for me in Arlegui. And we actually fooled her. I had to talk to her on the intercom because I was still bleeding. I couldn't give her a plausible explanation why I was bleeding. And then she was told only at 7 the next morning that I actually had been shot.

ESC: Is it true that the one who told her was Bodet and that he was scolded?
PNOY: Bodet told Voltz [General Voltaire Gazmin, commander of the Presidential Security Guards of President Cory] *na baka dapat sabihin na natin.* They both decided to do so but they asked Eldon and Manolo, my brothers-in-law to accompany them. I think it was Eldon who was the spokesperson.

But they were all scolded, "How dare you keep this from me. I'm not only the president, I'm also the mother. Don't you dare ever do this again."

Hindi naman type ni Mommy na naninigaw. Kolehiyala, biglang nag-don't you dare!

ESC: But I heard she raised her voice.
PNOY: If you look at Bodet's pictures, that was the only time he was two to three meters behind my mother, obviously trying to avoid being in her line of vision. My mom actually had an engagement that night, probably in Manila Hotel. So that was one of the first things my mom asked when she saw me after I was discharged. *"Nagkita tayo kagabi, saan ka ba nagpunta?"* Then I had to explain to her.

ESC: What are your thoughts during these last few months of your presidency and as you look toward the future?
PNOY: You know, whenever I go out in public and with all these cellphones and cameras, there's always that demand for pictures—a lot of times pictures and selfies, regardless of the age bracket of the people. Even when people just wave at me, for instance in a motorcade, these tell me there is an appreciation for all the efforts that have been done the past five years. That there's really a marked difference [between] where we came from to where we are now. I guess what I'm aiming to do and I'm still doing at this point in time is to make sure with our economy to maximize the resources to effect the changes that we all sought from way back. I guess it's the continuity I think of. If my dad was the inspiration to get us back to democracy, my mom to lead the fight, then I want to make sure that the achieved democracy works for everybody. And that there really are tangible benefits for all and it will be a self-perpetuating system.

ESC: After you step down on June 30, 2016, what is the first thing you intend to do?

PNOY: Ahh. *(laughs)* Relax. The few times that I stay at Times were enough of a break. I guess I can liken it to going on a vacation. There really is an immense relaxation just being able to sleep overnight in Times. Probably we will have something in Quezon City perhaps but unfortunately our house right now is being remodeled so that is not an option. A lot of times at the end of the day, I just have the thought that I'll be going home soon. So I guess that's the whole point, getting back to some normalcy.

ESC: But you haven't set out any definite plans like Clinton's Clinton Global Initiative or a presidential museum or library?

PNOY: I'm so caught up with today's problems . . . that can wait. And by our laws, I cannot work for a year. So in that year, I will have enough time to plan what the next chapters will be.

ESC: Do you intend to write a book about your years in the presidency?

PNOY: Manolo Quezon [Manuel Luis Quezon III, Undersecretary of the Presidential Communications Development and Strategic Planning Office] and I are discussing certain chapters of the book. We are putting down notes, hopefully to impart some lessons so that others will have an easier time when they are confronted with similar problems. Perhaps case studies on running government.

ESC: That's not about being president?

PNOY: Well, about problems and issues even before the presidency. The Left has all these people who wrote histories from their perspective, but those at the Center and Left of Center, unfortunately, were so caught up with all their activities and they never really put down their experiences. Hopefully, we will not have a need to relearn the lessons that have already been learned. So the book will hopefully address that issue.

ESC: But will you miss Malacañang?

PNOY: *(Laughs)*

ESC: Or is there anything at all about this that you will miss?

PNOY: When I was in the opposition especially, I knew and so many other people knew what had to be done but was never done and right now, if there's anything I will miss, it is the ability to be able to shape the present and the future instantly, somewhat instantly. In the opposition, you were championing something you knew was right, yet you felt like a kid just hitting your head on the wall and not able to achieve anything. Here, I think we've achieved quite a lot and we can all imagine what can be further achieved because [we're] starting from a higher level than where we were in the past.

So will I miss anything? The point about not tolerating that which is wrong but doing corrective action as soon as you are able to will be something that you will never have that direct a role in from the periphery. But at the same time, there has to be a transition. This has to be something that is self-nurturing. There will be others who will carry on.

ESC: When President Cory stepped down, she told us that she wanted to retire. But then events became such that she became the moral force and the moral compass of the society, of the country and she never really retired. In fact, she became more of an activist after she stepped down. Would you be prepared if that role again is needed in the country?

PNOY: I'm not comfortable with the idea that it will just be me or somebody like me who is the indispensable factor in moving our country forward. Although I do believe, if there is a call then as in the past, we will respond to it. But at the same time, I'm very, very conscious also of all the lives that I've affected especially those closest to me. My sisters, my nephews, and nieces, how many of them have really had a normal life especially after 2010?

And it goes beyond that. What about the staff that [have] gone through the ups and downs and how they have reordered their lives to accommodate the direction that I had to undertake? That bears heavily on me. *Ang dami kong dinadamay sa lahat ng kinikilos ko, sa mga desisyon na gagawin ko.*

ESC: But I think in many ways the role was forced on President Cory. I don't think she wanted to but circumstances said she was the only one who could unify.

PNOY: I occupied this office not because I wanted to.

ESC: How would you want to be remembered after you've stepped down as president?

PNOY: I would like to think I was a part of that movement that changed the people's attitude from one of cynicism and defeat to one of perhaps, unbounded optimism—that the Filipino is really capable and special and we can achieve all our dreams. Every time there is a criticism, valid or not, we'd like to think it is an advancement in our people being active in governance, being concerned which is the key to strengthening the democracy and making it really work for everybody. So we welcome that and again, I'd hope that people will say that I had a part in changing that attitude which was so prevalent five years ago.

ESC: How would you like to be remembered not as a president but as an individual?
PNOY: They had a leader that they could trust, that I never lied to anybody.

ESC: In terms of legacy, what do you want people to remember as you step down?
PNOY: Let's go back to the issue of a president that can be trusted. Many possibilities were open to our people, some attained, some became reality. The support and the unity of the citizens have allowed us to overcome all the propaganda, all the falsehood, and we got somewhere. I think that's the most important part, to have demonstrated that these achievements are possible at all. It is not an impossible dream. It is a possibility, a reality actually. The possibilities are now a reality. This reality can be perpetuated.

ESC: Going back to your views or ideologies, were these influenced by any person shaping your worldview, aside from your parents?
PNOY: There were individuals like Teddy Benigno who once said these wise words, "To have the strength of the youth and the wisdom of the aged." In *Les Miserables,* there was Inspector Javert and his sense of right and wrong, the world was black or white. Then he had to confront John Valjean. And of course, his world turned topsy turvy.

Other personalities like Nelson Mandela—I only had one opportunity to see him. And the only thing he told me was, you chose your parents right. And I said, yes, I agree with you. After his twenty-seven years of incarceration and being poisoned after being incarcerated and yet, having no animosity toward anybody.

Both my maternal grandfather [Don Pepe Cojuangco] and my paternal grandmother [Doña Aurora Aquino] were significant influences with their ability to love despite everything. For instance, there was something that truly upset my Lolo. He did not shout nor scold, [he] just showed his disappointment [over] for such a major issue. His moral suasion was such that that was enough, not wanting any negative reinforcement. My paternal grandmother always demonstrated so much love, unconditional, almost unreasonable love.

And maybe today, *pag meron talagang sobrang kabwisitan, kung may* patience *ako, baka nagmumula doon sa dalawa, sa* examples *nila.*

All that you've seen and interacted with have had an influence. It doesn't have to be really somebody in an exalted position. Even the man on the street can impart so much knowledge. The school [Ateneo] I went to sent us on immersion programs in high school. We tutored public elementary school students in grade six. One of them had difficulty reading. To us from a private school, grade six *di pa makabasa*—how's that possible?

So one time I asked my dad, *pano naa*-advance to the next grade *kung* something as basic as reading is not achieved? He told me about the government's limited resources. They can give you an opportunity but whether or not you learn is really up to the individual. That was also my exposure to dedicated public servants like grade school teachers spending their own salary buying encyclopedias, school supplies. They had to even take on second jobs just to make ends meet. There are parents who are really very serious about their children's education and are active participants who will not tolerate their children fooling around.

ESC: After the presidency, what is next for you? Are there more mountains to climb?
PNOY: In the past, there have been attempts of people who were in government to try to study what could have been done better and impart that knowledge. If you were a leader right now, you would be so concerned with the day-to-day matters that sometimes in the Cabinet meetings, we want to study this and that but at the end of the day, we have to do something ***today***. We do not have the luxury of time, of getting the perfect solution that we would [have] if we were perhaps in the academe, after an extensive study. But here, waiting for the perfect answer would be depriving the people of the good they would benefit from right now. It doesn't redound to serving them because they would be kept in a worse off situation.

When Barack Obama was here, he did say what his plans were: get in touch with all of these people that you worked with and are no longer in office and try to come up with a manual to help all those that come after us. How do you handle the insecurities, how do you tackle unforeseen consequences, how to decide in an imperfect environment when the needed information will only come after?

ESC: Do you intend to stay in politics?
PNOY: Move to other areas. Perhaps in public service you affect others' lives in a general manner. I'd want to be more specific, more focused, more direct. Maybe help build the

entrepreneurial abilities of the Filipino. I'm really not sure yet. My body is saying that I should take a break first and I'm sure everybody is saying the same thing. It is a fantasy for us here to return to Hawaii, to at least step on the beach this time. I went to Samal Island actually recently. We were inaugurating part of the Circumference Road. There are many resorts that are opening up there and I said, the first time I was here, I saw the port. Now I see the beach. Now I'm seeing the sea. Next time I come here, I'll be able to get to the sand and wade in the sea. Maybe just to take it a little easy.

ESC: If you were looking at the Philippines ten years from now, let's say 2025, 2030, what would you hope to see?

PNOY: I think we're seeing the beginnings now. We go back to the premise that democracy works for everybody. You are all given these opportunities. For Philhealth, for instance, we now have about 84 to 89 percent coverage from 63 percent, with a wider coverage of diseases and zero billing for the bottom 20 percent.

Some people may say this is too much of a stretch. What was America before World War II and after World War II? Coming out of the Depression to having an economy fully mobilized, so suddenly growing the middle class to empowering the women who had to take over jobs, etcetera.

With credit fueling the economy, we're there. Part of the reason for the traffic is that there is over 20 percent increase on vehicle sales yearly. Motorcycle sales is about PHP1.2M per year. And how long does it take to build the infrastructure to support all of these?

We went to one of the financial executives and his team said they had seminars for people who had just graduated from college who wanted to have their own car or condominium within three years after graduating. When I was studying, it took twenty years to get a secondhand car. Today, there are vehicle models that are below PHP 500,000, even lower.

So with a PHP5,000 amortization, low downpayment, there is the confidence of the young graduates with stable jobs that they will be able to pay. The idea of credit with financial institutions hopefully moving into the direction of ability to pay rather than collateral makes the growth of the economy that much faster.

There is a study that we will be a high-income (they don't call it first world any more) country by 2040, in less than a generation if we keep on this track. We are at the lower end of the medium income right now. There is much confidence in our people and our ability to develop and progress. *Wala nang abante, atras, abante, atras.* Empowered people see all the opportunities offered to them. And it is not merely aspirational but a reality twenty years from now. There are 2019 figures supporting this.

ESC: Do you have a philosophy about running government that you'd like to share with other people who would be taking your place in the future? Or an ideology?

PNOY: One of the greatest qualities of single-term leaders is the ability to decide based on the factors of the problem rather than on what is popular. That frees you from making a popular decision which might have a negative effect prolonging the already negative effects of the situation you are trying to resolve. So what is the underlying philosophy? Personally, I'd like to impart this with the rest of the Cabinet. At the end of the day, can we really say that we put in an honest day's work, that we did everything we could at this point in time? It doesn't mean that you made the perfect decision, it doesn't mean everything has come to fruition. But the point is, is there anything else that you could have done that you didn't do at this particular day to have advanced the cause? If you can say, positively and honestly, that you did everything that could be done, that is good enough. There is always the tendency to choose between what is popular and what is right. Sometimes you really have to make an unpopular decision. But if you know that's right, then you have to be able to stand by it and be able to convince others that this is the right path.

ESC: If you can address the millennials to say why the legacy of Ninoy and Cory Aquino is something they should remember, and not mind the dismissive attitude of some who say it's time to move on, what would you say?

PNOY: This will sound like a broken record: those who cannot remember the past are condemned to repeat it, are the words of George Santayana. He didn't say, "might repeat it," he said, "condemned to repeat it." Now, *may kasabihan tayo, yung hindi marunong lumingon sa pinanggalingan, hindi makakarating sa paroroonan.* There are some committed persons who take it upon themselves to fight for a cause. I'd like to include my father in that mold. *Babalik ka sa tanong, bakit kailangan kargahin ng isang tao sa balikat ang lahat ng problema natin?* How did we get here? All the excesses of martial law could not have happened overnight. The majority allowed the abuses to pile up. We are lucky we had EDSA, a peaceful revolution with no bloodshed. We cannot say that all Filipinos wanted a peaceful revolution, though.

There is another Filipino saying that what we do not value and safeguard, we are bound to lose. So if we do not look at where we came from, it is guaranteed that we will not reach our destination. We have to ensure that the way we were abused in the past should not happen again.

ESC: Have you ever felt any slight resentment that your family has borne so much of this burden of preserving that legacy?

PNOY: The human side says, can our share be lessened? But at the same time, I can see how God prepared us. It seems that for us to progress as a nation, the assassination of Daddy had to happen. We asked then, how do we continue this struggle? It seemed that we lost the light, the unifying force. But it really did give birth to so many others to take up where he left off. There were several, many more trying to achieve the purpose. Then we got to where we had to go. There will be more and more who will lessen the burden of any individual. My only resentment probably is if it all turns out pointless and leads to nowhere, after putting in all your efforts. That would hurt.

ESC: Your father was supposed to be the next president. We all thought he would be the next president. His greatest and challenging moments came and he was not president. Some of President Cory's most memorable speeches were actually made after she became president, when she was there in the rallies, during the terms of FVR, Erap, GMA. So it is very possible, since you have inherited his legacy, it could happen, that your most challenging moment might actually be after you step down. If we take a look at what happened to your parents, it could happen and it could even happen sooner than you think. When that moment comes, how do you think you will react?

PNOY: *(Laughing)* To new challenges? *Marami na rin kaming* challenges *na hinarap dito. Siguro* in 2013, as an example, from Zamboanga to the next month's earthquake to the next month's Yolanda, all happening roughly in the last quarter. *Yung* every time *na may* confidence *kang kaya mo na 'to, bibigyan ka ng mas mabigat na dagok.* Maybe I have the confidence that if it is for the country, I trust that God will take care [of it]. He will take care that I give all that I can, even with my limitations.

ESC: But this will be the time when you will not be president anymore and you will not be required to actually meet these challenges.

PNOY: If there is a need that comes to my attention that I can meet, I think I will be hard-pressed not to address or to give my all to satisfy the challenge. If there is a need to serve at my age as an elder statesman, perhaps not in politics . . . I really don't know what it is. But the willingness to be of help, I guess, is best summed up by both my mom and dad. My mom said words to the effect that if there was something she could have done and chose not to, she would not be able to live with herself. I think that applies to me and the rest of my siblings also.

PNoy Fun Facts

I n college, we had a professor who would literally bring a dozen books each time that he would recommend as worth reading. We used to tease him about being a salesman of National Book Store.

I generally read *The Economist* or *TIME* or specialized magazines for my hobby, shooting, music reproduction, but many times on military history, ancient and medieval warfare. I find it ironic that while reading tires my eyes, when I want to relax, it is reading I go back to.

I'm actually buying a lot of books that I'm storing for the time I will have after June 30. To start catching up on all the reading

I like reading actual books, rather than from an electronic device. I came across an article that said a hard copy allows you to take down notes or to mark passages—an aid to enhancing your memory on the subject. I think I inherited this from my father, not exactly photographic memory, but I would be able to tell the person I assigned a particular task on what page something is, even what part of the page.

Of course, I read *Noli* and *Fili*. It was obligatory. Read it in English, Tagalog and even in the original Spanish which was difficult.

On his fluency in Filipino:

There was the Filipinization drive when we were in grade school and everything was taught in Filipino, even Greek mythology in high school. I was very fortunate to have this teacher, Mrs. Nenita Escasa, who had such command of the language that we bought all the English-Filipino dictionaries and they weren't enough to overwhelm her vocabulary. She insisted we did not talk in Taglish.

I praised Mrs. Escasa in one SONA. I found out she started as an English professor but when martial law was proclaimed practically the entire Filipino Department in Ateneo was incarcerated or had to go underground. They had to look for new teachers and she was one of those asked to join the Filipino Department.

On movies:

I get kidded a lot for my penchant for old westerns, old war films. I like science fiction—many times I really need to take a little time out from the concerns of the world.

I have not watched all the movies of Kris. *Baka naman mag-away pa kami.*

On how he unwinds:

I do shooting once a week. Listening to music is a daily affair. Getting to drive to Tarlac or to Baguio once or twice a year.

I used to listen to everything except heavy classics and rock but the other night I was listening to Black Eyed Peas. My nephew who got me the CD complained that the song I wanted, "Where is the Love," was from 2003—that was why it was so hard to find. Another one I like is "Next Episode" by Dr. Dre.

On memorable places in the Philippines:

I would like to visit as a tourist all the places I have promoted. The Underground River in Palawan where I was for three hours, inclusive of lunch. The Sleeping Giant rock formation in Bukidnon that I saw for fifteen seconds. Even Tagaytay's panoramic view, I saw for two minutes. I have been to Boracay only for an hour and I remember my mom's photo wading in the beach, looking so serene.

Maybe I can drive around the country doing a RORO trip via all the roads which have been built.

On his sister Ballsy:

I liken her to a second mom. All the things that were beyond our abilities when we were younger or did not want to bother with, we'd bother Ate with. The joke among us growing up was if you borrow Php6 from her, you pay when able and only Php5. She even makes you feel *na may utang na loob pa siya* when you pay. She is just so kind, caring, and full of concern.

It was not easy for her to be the eldest. There were many demands and restrictions on her. Before martial law, she had such a hard time getting permission for a party. She would have to bring the senior bodyguard, the family driver, and the mayordoma who kept the strict curfew for her set by our parents, with travel time computed. If Ate ignored it, [the mayordoma] would even go to the dance floor and say it's time.

V.
The Aquino
Legacy

Democracy and Peace

Let me state frankly that I am not always an admirer of Lee Kuan Yew. I do not agree with his views about democracy. I also do not think we can compare Singapore, a city state, to the Philippines, an archipelagic nation with more than 100 million citizens.

In a book he wrote where he again pontificated on his ideas, there is one part that is interesting reading. He has different views on other countries which includes the Philippines. One of his comments is about Philippine culture. He wrote:

"The difference lies in the culture of the Filipino people. It is a soft and forgiving culture. Only in the Philippines could a leader like Ferdinand Marcos who pillaged his country for over 20 years, still be considered for a national burial.

Insignificant amounts of the loot have been recovered, yet his wife and children were allowed to return and engage in politics. They supported the winning presidential and congressional candidates with their considerable resources and reappeared in the political and social limelight after the 1998 election that returned President Joseph Estrada. General Fabian Ver, Marcos's commander-in-chief who had been in charge of security when Aquino was assassinated, had fled the Philippines together with Marcos in

1986. When he died in Bangkok, the Estrada government gave the general military honors at his burial.

Lee Kuan Yew quoted a Philippine newspaper article:

> Ver, Marcos and the rest of the official family plunged the country into two decades of lies, torture and plunder. Over the next decade Marcos's cronies and immediate family would tiptoe back into the country, one by one—always to the public's revulsion and disgust, though they showed that there was nothing that hidden money and thick hides could not withstand.

He then added: "Some Filipinos write and speak with passion, if they could get their elite to share their sentiments and act, what could they not have achieved?"

This is one of the few times I can partially agree with Lee Kuan Yew. However, I do not necessarily agree that we have a "soft" culture. My personal observation is that massive resources are being spent to try and rewrite Philippine history.

But it is true that we are confronted by certain political events that are clearly ironic and even bizarre. Take the case of the Senate hearings on the Bangsamoro Basic Law. The chair is Ferdinand Bongbong Marcos, Jr., son of the late dictator Ferdinand Marcos.

In an interview conducted during the commemoration of that Philippine "Day of Infamy"—the proclamation of martial law—the son vigorously defended the declaration of martial law. There was no hint of apology in both words and tone.

Germany has officially apologized for the Holocaust. Even the Japanese have apologized and paid reparations for their war crimes during the Second World War. But the Marcoses and former senior members of their martial law regime have never even acknowledged their responsibility for the numerous human rights violations and for turning the second most prosperous country in Asia into the "sick man" of Asia.

In order to fully appreciate the irony of the unapologetic Bongbong Marcos chairing the hearings on the Bangsamoro Basic Law, we need to recall an event now known as the Jabidah Massacre which happened in Corregidor in March 18, 1968. This massacre served as the impetus and rallying cry that started the present-day Muslim insurgencies in the southern Philippines.

The Jabidah Massacre was the massacre of several Muslims by the Philippine government. This incident was the offshoot of the dispute revolving around the territory of Sabah, between the Philippines and Malaysia. Marcos had planned a guerrilla-type operation against the Muslims of Malaysia by training local Philippine Muslims to fight in Sabah. However, after the Muslim recruits discovered the true intentions of their group's formation, they refused to go against fellow Muslims. Under the watch of Marcos and Ver, the Philippine government slaughtered the Muslims and tried to keep the whole incident a secret.

The best description of the actual events is in a chapter in the book *Under the Crescent Moon: Rebellion in Mindanao,* written by Marites Danguilan Vitug and Glenda M. Gloria, first published in 2000. Here is one part from that book where they quoted the story of one survivor, Jibin Arula:

> We went to the airport on a weapons carrier truck, accompanied by 13 (non-Muslim) trainees armed with M-16 and carbines. When we reached the airport, our escorts alighted ahead of us. Then Lt. Eduardo Nepomuceno ordered us to get down from the truck and line up. [Nepomuceno was later killed in Corregidor under mysterious circumstances.] As we put down our bags, I heard a series of shots. Like dominoes, my colleagues fell. I got scared. I ran and was shot in my left thigh. I did not know that I was running towards a mountain . . . . By 8 a.m., I was rescued by two fishermen on Caballe Island near Cavite.

When then Senator Ninoy Aquino first publicly exposed the plot leading to the Jabidah Massacre, Marcos and his henchmen denied the killings ever happened, and the expose was condemned as part of a grand plot by the opposition to simply discredit the Marcos administration.

After the massacre, one of its main perpetrators, Rolando Abadilla, became head of Marcos's Military Intelligence Security Group. He gained notoriety by causing the arrest, disappearances, and killings of many political activists during martial law.

It was only in 2013 that the Philippine government, under PNoy, finally and officially acknowledged that the Jabidah Massacre actually took place.

In almost every region of the world, nations are trying to find a peaceful solution to violence caused by ethnic and religious tensions between the majority and the minority populations of their country. This is happening in India, Pakistan, China, Thailand, Myanmar, Ukraine, Syria, Iraq, Kenya, and even in rich countries like France, United Kingdom, and the United States.

Samuel Huntington once wrote a book called *The Clash of Civilizations and the Remaking of World Order*, in which he said that conflicts between the major civilizations—Christian, Islamic, Hindu, Confucian—were inevitable. But I continue to hope that in spite of the ironic twists and turns in Philippine history, this "inevitability" will not happen in the Philippines.

We have a culture that is based on strong family ties and spiritual values. We can be forgiving and tolerant. But history has shown that we, as a people, can rise and confront great challenges with courage, fortitude, and unity.

Democracy, through the People Power Revolution was one of the greatest legacies of Corazon Aquino and the Filipino people of that period. Peace, through a Bangsamoro Basic Law, could very well be one of the greatest legacies of PNoy and this generation of Filipinos. **(ESC)**

The Lady in Yellow

Cory Aquino's wake at La Salle Greenhills in Ortigas Avenue, San Juan City was a homecoming of sorts. Indeed, she was on familiar grounds.

It was not just because of the campus's physical proximity to EDSA, site of two People Power uprisings in which she played a key role. A prominent fixture in the gym that continues to stand proud—today draped in yellow—is the large tally board in Operation Quick Count, the National Citizens' Movement for Free Elections (NAMFREL) project that recorded the final update for the 1986 presidential snap election, its original chalk figures lacquered with a fixative and preserved for posterity as a testimony to a historic moment: Cory Aquino's clear lead in the NAMFREL count. In more recent times, the gym was the venue of prayer rallies in support of Jun Lozada, NBN-ZTE whistleblower, who took refuge in this campus and whose principal supporter and ally was Cory Aquino.

Even before Cory's passing, the familiar yellow ribbons had made their appearance, fluttering from trees, homes, building, vehicles, fences, and road railings. Two text messages had gone the rounds, calling for a show of citizen support for the ailing Cory, who had been hospitalized for loss of appetite since June 23, 2010. One read: "Rekindle the flame of democracy that Cory began. Believe that the Filipino is worth dying for. Tie a yellow ribbon today: Cory, *hindi ka nag-iisa!*" The other text message was also an exhortation: "As a final tribute to Tita Cory, let us display yellow ribbons in cars, homes, offices, fences from a grateful people from every corner of the world!"

Yellow, Cory's symbol of struggle against the dictatorship, had become the poignant expression of her battle with physical disease—colon cancer, the very same illness that her mother, Demetria Sumulong Cojuangco, had been afflicted with. Who could hold back tears at the sight of the façade of the Makati Medical Center draped in yellow to honor its esteemed patient on the ninth floor? There lay a woman who had risen to rescue us from the dark years of martial rule. Why couldn't we similarly come to her rescue now?

Ayala Avenue sprouted yellow again, a nostalgic reminder of countless rallies past. Tied to the road sign of Quezon City's Times Street, the street where Cory and her family lived, was a solitary yellow ribbon. The Cojuangco ancestral home on Palm Avenue in Dasmariñas Village, Makati—the venue of many planning meetings and countless celebrations for Cory's January 25 birthday, Ninoy's November 27 birthday, not to mention more trivial excuses for her family, friends, and former Cabinet members to get together—bore its own yellow ribbons, but looked especially desolate this time around.

It was easy enough to heed the call to display yellow ribbons, though stores were soon running out of stock of that suddenly in-demand commodity. Still, it was painfully difficult to accept the finality of such a gesture. How could one accept that everyone's favorite icon of democracy was vulnerable to mortality? Yes, there may have been chinks in her armor, and she herself accepted that fact. But how to let go when even the most indifferent of citizens begrudgingly concede that she, whose integrity remains intact, is a symbol we are in need of? And we are shamelessly selfish in saying that we earnestly need her as we continue to fight for democracy and a progressive Philippines for all classes of society.

Stages of Grief

The grace, dignity, and courage that characterized Cory Aquino's public life also marked her last days. Cameramen and reporters permanently stationed by the hospital entrance, and vans of television networks parked in the nearby lot, attempted to maintain a reverential distance, so as not to be offensively intrusive, in deference to the lady that the former president had always been.

A climate of rare transparency had been established by the family, from the sudden hospitalization of Cory Aquino during the Christmas holidays of 2007, to the disclosure of her colon cancer, to the various treatments and the need to be physically distant from the former president, especially during the first round of healing Masses that followed. She did not mind appearing in public with the "new fashion accessory" she carried—a slim pouch on a sling that was part of her chemotherapy treatment—now that she was so many pounds lighter. Then came the surgery in early May of 2010 and the hospitalization in June because of the alarming loss of appetite. She could not endure any further treatment for her cancer because of extreme physical weakness.

And so, we all learned to accept, appreciate, and understand the subtext of youngest daughter Kris's tearful statements that she was going on leave from showbiz to stay with her mom round the clock, so as not to feel any regrets. We listened painfully to the latest medical update from Rapa Lopa, executive director of the Benigno S. Aquino, Jr. Foundation, a favorite and trusted Cojuangco nephew, son of Cory's late sister Terry Lopa, who was Cory's faithful companion when she began to emerge in public in 1983. And we shared the agony of her only son, Senator Noynoy, who had to muster the courage to announce that her stage 4 colon cancer had now spread to her liver and kidneys; that her blood pressure was fluctuating; that while she continued to be nourished intravenously, she was also receiving doses of morphine to make her feel more comfortable; and that her stable condition had vacillated to a "guarded" one.

To think that only a week earlier, there was rejoicing over the chicken sandwich that she asked for, the cupcake she ate, the melon slice she seemed to enjoy, and the report that she had managed to walk to the toilet.

A very private affair was the family Mass on a Sunday in late July at the Wack-Wack home of Cory's elder brother, Pete Cojuangco. The Mass celebrant was Fr. Eli Santos, the Don Bosco priest who says Mass regularly at the Jose Cojuangco & Sons Building in Makati, where Cory held office before and after the presidency. According to a family member in attendance, Father Eli recounted that he had asked Cory what special intention she would want him to pray for—her miraculous healing or any other special intentions? She had said: "Nothing, because I have already asked God for so many other miracles in the past."

Pin Cojuangco Guingona, daughter of Cory's younger brother Peping, recounts that her father had been uneasy two days before his sister's passing. He kept turning to Pin, asking her to check on the latest health update. Something was telling him that things were not right. Thus, they paid their last visit to the hospital on the afternoon of July 31, a Friday, after Pin had called her cousins to "clear" such a visit.

Pin speaks with much restraint, sensitive to the Aquino family's request for privacy and solemnity. She says that her cousins are such private persons, except for Noynoy and Kris, who must maintain public personas.

It was Kris who bared her grieving soul on national television, documenting her mother's final stay at the Makati Medical Center, answering the questions that everyone had been too polite to ask. She spoke of the pain of finally seeing her mother in tears.

Kris and her siblings had to go through the stages of grief and letting go. Difficult as it was, after they had reassured their mother that they would take care of one another, the circumstances became lighter for everyone. For the first time, Cory smiled again and had an aura of peace. She kept muttering Ninoy's name and even said she could see Ninoy. The family bade her goodbye, as they were advised, before morphine was administered, because Cory would be asleep and unable to communicate from then on. For her part, Kris thanked her mom for being the shock absorber she had always been, keeping their family life normal even under the most trying circumstances. And Kris apologized for not always having been the daughter her mother wanted.

It was a well-deserved, quiet, and peaceful final end, as the family ("family" had been her last recognizable word) had completed praying the sorrowful mysteries of the rosary. Just as she had promised her mom, the youngest Aquino daughter would not leave Cory alone even in death. It was Kris who made sure her mother looked her best for public viewing, wearing the Paul Cabral gown Cory herself had picked, fancying the gown that former Pres. Joseph Estrada's mother had worn while lying in state. It was Kris who arranged to have the makeup artist (Juan Sarte) prepare her mother for viewing, and who suggested that her mother's ears be adorned with the small pearl earrings that Cory's youngest sister, Passy Teopaco, was wearing while keeping vigil at the mortuary. Cory was known to wear modest-sized earrings, and among the family members, Passy was then wearing the "right" size.

Cory's passing became a time for family reconciliations. Ninoy's sister, Tessie Oreta, had strained relations with Cory's family because of political differences. (Tessie had supported Erap during the impeachment process; Cory had called for his resignation.) But the day after she had a dream in which Ninoy asked her to bring Cory some stargazer flowers, Tessie had visited Cory at the hospital.

Kris did not find any significance in that, as it was well-known that her mother was allergic to flowers. But after her mother's remains had been prepared for public viewing at the Heritage Memorial Park in Taguig, the memorial office places a wreath of stargazers on the casket. That was an uncanny detail that Kris saw as a clear indication from Ninoy that Cory was now with him.

Deep Spirituality

Although the Cory Aquino in repose remained a beautiful woman, it was not the Cory Aquino whose likeness we instantly recognize—evidence of the physical suffering she had to endure in the last month of her life.

Cory had repeatedly said that she was not afraid to die, that she was ready to go any time. She was a woman known for her prayerfulness and deep spirituality. In the most trying times of her presidency and her personal life, she always sought refuge in the Pink Sisters Convent in Quezon City. She always felt strengthened after hearing Mass there, and felt fortunate that there was an Aquino relative among the religious sisters—that gave her a hotline of sorts to heaven. When all else seemed futile, she never lost hope, and she led prayer rallies in different schools.

On the last day of the initial round of novena Masses for Cory's healing at the Greenbelt Chapel, slim pocket-size booklets—bearing on the cover a Cory Aquino painting of a vase of white flowers with touches of pink—were distributed to friends in attendance. In the context of the prevailing circumstances then, the painting seemed to convey a disturbing quiet and desolation.

However, everything in the booklet is hopeful. It carries a prayer originally written by Cory's former appointments secretary, Margie Juico, and edited by Cory's former speechwriter, now Makati Congressman Teodoro Locsin, Jr. This prayer was read at all healing Masses, along with the "Prayer to the Divine Physician."

The booklet's most valuable pagers are those with biblical passage in Cory's distinct penmanship verses and in a 5-7-5 syllable structure. Cory had discovered the haiku when her third daughter, Viel, was in college and had to do some poems for an English class assignment. She wrote some for Viel, who got excellent marks for them. The extra ones that Cory wrote were shared with Viel's classmates who had no homework.

The rosary Cory was said to be constantly clutching in her hand during her hospitalization was a special one, sent to her by no less than Sister Lucia, one of the three children who reported having a Marian apparition in the Portuguese village of Fatima in 1917. Sister Lucia had given it to Cory through Cardinal Jaime Sin. That rosary was a treasured possession, but it was one that Cory generously lent out to sick friends and relatives.

In his homily during the concelebrated Mass on the first day of the wake, Antipolo Bishop Gabriel Reyes related that Mother Teresa of Calcutta had also given her own rosary to Cory, something the Nobel Peace Prize-recipient nun did only with individuals she considered worthy. This was again another unalloyed tribute to Cory. Bishop Reyes wondered where that rosary was now, as he had only heard of the rosary from Sister Lucia.

The rosary that Cory held in the casket was said to be from Fr. Sonny Ramirez, OP. **(NSRC)**

Cory's Legacy
of Leadership

The most remarkable thing about the public outpouring of grief and the long queues of mourners at Cory's passing was that it all happened seventeen years after she stepped down from the presidency. From 1992 to 2009 she held neither a position nor a title.

But for seventeen years, Cory was not just a former president. She was the moral conscience of the Filipino people. She was the only person who could call the people to the streets to express public outrage against the machinations and corruption of even the highest and most powerful politicians.

Fidel V. Ramos won as the handpicked candidate of Cory Aquino in the 1992 elections. But when talks began to circulate that there were moves to amend the Constitution to allow Ramos to run for a second term, it was Cory and her long-time ally Cardinal Sin who called for an anti-Charter change rally. Hundreds of thousands responded by marching to Luneta. That ended any attempt to amend the constitutional limit of a single presidential term.

Then came the scandal-ridden Joseph Estrada presidency. Again, Cory led a series of demonstrations urging the president to resign. After the crucial vote in the Senate where the pro-Estrada forces believed they had won, people were ready for a final confrontation. I remember my son sending a text message that said: "Cory is going to the EDSA shrine to talk and she is going to be in yellow. Let's go."

The "woman in yellow" was the single person who was able to unify all forces, including the military, who brought about the resignation of Erap Estrada.

In 1992 and at the end of the Ramos and Estrada presidencies, there were always calls for her to step back into power. But she refused each time.

The Gloria Macapagal-Arroyo years were a period of struggle and crusading for Cory. But the emotional catharsis that gripped the nation upon her death eventually led to the election of her son Noynoy, bringing about a second Renaissance in Philippine society.

Corazon Aquino was more than just a president. She was also her people's symbol for courageous convictions and morality even amidst a corrupt government. She was the leader the Filipino people turned to every time there was a crisis.

Corazon Aquino showed she had courage when she dared lead the fight against the martial law forces of the Marcos dictatorship. But when she transformed her mission from that of avenging her husband's death to a crusade for the restoration of democracy and human rights to this country, she became the leader of her people and the embodiment of their vision of a nation that they and their children could be proud of. **(ESC)**

In Gratitude, Corazon Aquino

Pres. Corazon Aquino was born on January 25, 1933 in San Juan de Dios Hospital in the city of Manila. She passed away in 2010 after battling cancer for more than a year.

To the Filipino people, she will always be remembered as the inspirational leader in the fight to restore democracy and dignity to our country after decades of dictatorship, cronyism, and human rights violations during the Marcos martial law regime.

To the whole world, she was an icon of democracy and the Mother of People Power. One of the most touching statements after she passed away came from then U.S. Secretary of State Hillary Clinton, who said, "Aquino helped bring democracy back to the Philippines after many years of authoritarian rule with a faith in her country and its people that never wavered . . . . Like millions of people worldwide, Bill (Clinton) and I were inspired by her quiet strength and her unshakable commitment to justice and freedom."

From the assassination of her husband, Ninoy Aquino, on August 21, 1983, to the time she stepped down as the president of the Philippines in 1992, she led her people through many struggles and coup attempts.

Sometimes I am asked what I thought were the core values of Corazon Aquino that made her the icon of democracy the world over. After 1992, instead of living a quiet, peaceful life which she deserved, President Cory continued to publicly speak on many national and international issues. She even led street demonstrations, reminiscent of People Power, to speak out on major issues like corruption and Charter Change.

It is in one of those speeches where she reiterated her values. In October 1996, she was awarded the J. William Fulbright Prize for International Understanding. Here are some of the most memorable lines from that speech:

> Authoritarian government is said to be the Asian formula for success. But we may yet prove that people power can achieve, perhaps more slowly, but more lasting and more widely beneficial effects. Democracy, in the end is the best system for ordinary people. It is the only one that exalts them and unites them in peace across all countries of the world. One can believe in a dictatorship, a few in oligarchy, but only to democracy can the many, in reason, adhere.
>
> I ended my term with less exhilaration but more circumspection than I began it.
>
> I realized that I could have made things easier for myself if I had done the popular things, rather than the painful but better ones in the long run. After all, in the long run, I wouldn't be around to be blamed.
>
> I could have invited the military to share in the government, rather than keeping them out and fighting them off to the disarray of the economy. But I was called to restore a democracy, not divide up a country as spoils.
>
> I could have put pressure on the courts when they favored the enemies of democracy, but I felt that the best protection for freedom must lie in strong and independent courts.
>
> I sued a newspaper for libel but never used my office to advance my cause. I lost the case.
>
> I could have rolled back prices with a single word, but I would have distorted the painful wisdom of free markets which keep, it is alleged, economies on the right track.
>
> I couldn't adopt the ideal solutions proposed by those who had the luxury of a private life. Quite often, often-official actions were dictated by the pressing realities of the moment.

I could have rigged the 1992 elections for my successor. Instead, I directed the chiefs of the military to do the country proud by assuring a fair and free election, whatever the result.

Better still, I could have run myself. The constitutional limitation of a single presidential term did not apply to me; I had taken office under the old Constitution. But that limitation was a cornerstone of the new Constitution I had caused to be drafted and for which I vigorously campaigned. How could I serve as the first example of its moral violation?

June 30, 1992 was, therefore, one of my proudest moments of my life. I was stepping down and handing the presidency to my elected successor. This was what my husband had died for; he had returned precisely to forestall an illegal political succession. This moment is democracy's glory; the peaceful transfer of power without bloodshed, in strict accordance with law.

Many of the thoughts that she articulated after her presidency continue to have relevance today. She had a message for those in business when she gave a speech to the Young Presidents' Organization in 1996. The speech is entitled, "The Ultimate Bottomline: People." She started by saying: "While I find nothing wrong with making a profit—even a large one—as long as it is made fairly and squarely, I am happy to know that you, the younger generation of company presidents and CFOs are interested in going beyond making a buck."

She ended her speech with several questions for the young presidents:

Which brings me to the last point I would like to take up with you today and that is the need for reflection. As you careen your way to success, working as if there were no tomorrow, you must take time to stop and reflect on what you are doing. Ask yourself the hard questions, like what is the relevance of your work to your family, to your employee, and the larger society? What are you working so hard for? How much is enough? When do you have too much? What is the point acquiring so much wealth and power? Have you given back as much as you have taken?

At the Global Forum for Women Political Leaders in 2000, Corazon Aquino said:

> Women are natural candidates for positions of leadership—in business, in the academe, in civil society, in politics. We, who are the keepers of the values of the family and of society, should not leave the important task of leadership in the political sphere to the men alone. It is a job men and women can and should do together, in complementarity, just like they should in the home.

Corazon Aquino talked of what women leaders can do to make a difference in society. She talked of selfless love for and service to the people, of total dedication to a higher cause, of unshakable courage and integrity, and of steadfast faith.

She used these words to describe Mother Teresa and Aung San Suu Kyi. In her humility, she would never use these words to describe herself. In fact, one time she also said, "I am not a hero like Mandela." But the accolades she received and continue to receive tell us that history will always remember her greatness.

A grateful nation will never forget the heroine, dressed in yellow, who became the icon of democracy, the Mother of People Power who fervently prayed for the Filipino people. **(ESC)**

PNoy's Greatest Legacy

In 2014, Thailand's democratically elected Prime Minister Yingluck Shinawatra was driven from Bangkok by anti-government protesters. The elite wanted Shinawatra to resign and be replaced by a "people's council," which was actually a junta. She was insisting on a democratic election to choose the next government. Once Thailand gives up on democracy, there will be political instability which will have negative effects on its economy.

A dozen years ago, the Thais were among the world's biggest consumers of luxury goods. It was the third largest car exporter in Asia. Its per capita income was double that of the Philippines. When Shinawatra was elected in 2011, there was hope that she would be able to address the economic downturn. For a while it appeared that democracy was finally working.

The Bangkok elite accuse Shinawatra of massive corruption and buying the support of the poor with programs like the rice subsidy. While this may be true, the question is whether the opposition's alternative to appoint a junta instead of electing leaders is the solution or the beginning of an era of political instability, economic stagnation, and military interventions.

The Philippines was in a similar situation several decades ago. There were street demonstrations against a corrupt government. The President was forced to flee Malacañang and resign from office. The military had backed the position of the street demonstrators. There was talk of a junta taking over. But Corazon Aquino did not support the proposal and the vice president took over.

For nine years, under Gloria Macapagal-Arroyo, there was political instability due to massive corruption in government and alleged manipulation of electoral results. GMA's popularity ratings were the lowest since Marcos and were, in fact, negative in the last few years. By different international ratings, from credit risk and investment ratings to corruption indexes and business opinion surveys, the Philippines was a failing state.

Again, there were anti-government demonstrations in the streets. There were repeated attempts at military interventions. But the majority of the elite and the masses continued to support democracy.

In the 2010 elections, Noynoy Aquino was elected president. In less than four years, the once failing state has been transformed into one of Asia's brightest economic stars. This is the conclusion of several highly prestigious and internationally recognized institutions and organizations.

On March 2014, the Philippines was judged as having the best investment climate in Asia, ahead of countries like China, Indonesia, Vietnam, Malaysia, Singapore, Hong Kong, Japan, South Korea, and Australia. The study, based on the results of a survey of 334 multinational corporations operating in Asia, was made by London-based Economist Corporate Network, a unit of the *Economist*.

But this should not come as a surprise. In 2013, all three major credit rating agencies—Fitch, Standard and Poor's, Moody's—assessed the Philippine sovereign credit rating as investment grade, the first time in our history. Moody pointed out the country's solid growth, political stability, greater accountability, and a low level of exposure to external shocks. The agency also said that the country's level of economic performance is among the fastest in the Asia-Pacific region and across emerging markets globally.

Ruchir Sharma, the author of *Breakout Nations: In Pursuit of the Next Economic Miracles,* wrote that in the 1960s the Philippines had the second highest per capita income in Asia, next only to Japan. But by the beginning of the twenty-first century, many of its neighbors had overtaken the country due primarily to corruption, political instability, and crony capitalism. But after the election in 2010, he writes:

> Now, at long last, the Philippines looks poised to resume a period of strong growth. The new president, Benigno "Noynoy" Aquino, probably has just enough support and looks likely to generate just enough reform momentum to get the job done . . . . Filipinos saw him as an honest figure who

could deliver on the Aquino mandate for change and they were desperate after nine years of drift and decay under outgoing president Gloria Macapagal Arroyo . . . . Aquino is delegating power to competent technocrats and seems to understand what needs to be done . . . .

After three and a half years of the PNoy presidency, two articles in the January-February issue of the *Foreign Affairs* magazine, published by the New York-based Council on Foreign Relations, gives an extensive analysis of several emerging markets, especially Indonesia and the Philippines. One article says:

> Two of its [ASEAN] members have stood out as particularly promising. Giant Indonesia soared during the last half decade, boasting high growth, low inflation, an extremely low debt to GDP ratio. But it is the Philippines, the region's other archipelago, that is now providing the biggest upside surprise.
>
> The Philippines has momentum behind its reform efforts and a popular president with three years left in his term. This provides a compelling platform for growth moving forward.

Another article, entitled "Why Economic Forecasts Fail," sought to explain why countries like Brazil, Turkey, Egypt, and South Africa—that were considered future tiger economies just five years ago—failed to meet expectations. The same article also asked why countries like Mexico and the Philippines suddenly exceeded expectations and were poised to be the next economic superstars. One paragraph stood out:

> Economists tend to ignore the story of people and politics as too soft and incorporate into forecast models. Instead they study hard numbers such as government spending or interest rates. But numbers cannot capture the energy that a vibrant leader such as Mexico's new president, Enrique Peña Nieto or the Philippines's Benigno Aquino III can unleash by cracking down on monopolists, bribes and dysfunctional bureaucracies.

It is strong, moral leadership combined with good governance and the rule of law that could lead to the dawn of a new Filipino century. This is the greatest legacy that PNoy could leave with his country in 2016. **(ESC)**

Toward an Enduring Legacy

When PNoy banned the use of *wang-wang* on all streets, his real message was that no one is above the law. When he said that his "boss" is the Filipino people, he was advocating a society where the government would treat everyone—the powerful and the powerless, the rich and the poor, the educated and the illiterate—equally in terms of government programs and the dispensing of justice.

From the very beginning of his term, PNoy was envisioning a society where the rule of law is institutionalized. It is important for people to appreciate that the rule of law is an extremely critical foundation for economic progress and has an impact on the lives and work of all people.

Imagine a Philippines where the physical infrastructure—roads, bridges, airports—are safe and in first-class condition because corruption in the government construction process has finally been eliminated. Honest and efficient contractors are now encouraged to bid for government projects because prohibitive bribery and kickback costs have been removed. Finally, roads and bridges that have been budgeted for construction really do exist unlike in some of the previous administrations. Also, high quality materials are used to build safe structures.

Imagine a Philippines where public safety is a major government concern—where the police, military, and judicial officials are equally responsive to the concerns of everyone, without consideration for that person's influence or power and where these same officials are not affiliated with criminal gangs. Imagine if there are effective crime detection, investigation, and resolution mechanisms in place through out the country.

Imagine a Philippines where there is a dynamic private sector—so necessary for economic growth—because there is a level playing field in the enactment and enforcement of laws and regulations that affect business. A nation without crony capitalism means there is an effective and transparent means to settle disputes, property rights are secure, and laws and government regulations are clear.

Imagine a Philippines where educators, government, business, and civil society leaders sincerely believe that education is the most critical pathway to providing even the poorest among us, the opportunity to improve the quality of their lives. Quality education for everyone leads to social stability and economic growth, and eliminates dependence on politicians for economic survival. However, corruption and disregard for laws that regulate education standards lead to a failing school system which ultimately results in poorly educated students except for the children of the elite who can afford to be educated in a few high-quality schools here and abroad.

Imagine a Philippines where an effective system of regulation and its enforcement will resolve the threats to the environment such as pollution, deforestation due to illegal logging, loss of biodiversity, and poor waste management.

Imagine a Philippines where there is equitable access to an effective health care system and public health service is considered not just a public good, but a fundamental human right. It is a nation where public health interventions and services ensure that we have safe, reliable, and affordable medicines, medical treatment and health care delivery systems including clean drinking water. A healthy population is essential for a prosperous and stable society. That is why it is so important to break the cycle of poverty that has been present for so many generations among poor Filipinos.

Imagine a Philippines where the fundamental right to religion is respected. But this right must balance mainstream beliefs with local tradition and promote harmonious linkages between formal and traditional structures of justice. Thus, the rights of indigenous tribes must always be respected and not contravened by any law.

Imagine a Philippines where freedom of expression through the arts is protected as an acknowledgment of how the arts can effectively convey and document the truth about political and social conditions. The rule of law must assure artists of their right to expression as well as protect their intellectual property rights.

Imagine a Philippines where there is both a free and responsible press—free from restrictive laws, harassment, and violent persecution. Media can provide accurate and informative information that can educate the public about their rights and responsibilities and serve as a platform for responsible citizenship.

Imagine a Philippines where human rights are an integral part of the judicial system. The rule of law protects and enforces the fundamental human rights—the right to life and security; freedom of thought, religion, expression and assembly; fundamental labor rights; right to privacy; equal protection of the law; and due process of law.

Many lawyers and legal scholars believe that the rule of law is an end in itself. But for most citizens, it is a means to an end. According to the 2012-13 World Justice Project which was also the basis of the scenarios described above, "The rule of law is the underlying framework that makes prosperous and fair societies possible."

But there will be many obstacles to institutionalizing the rule of law in our nation. The presence of systemic corruption in all branches of government—executive, legislative, judiciary—and in many parts of the private sector—business, media, social groups—is the biggest obstacle.

The second challenge is that the rule of law will change the balance of political power, giving more power to the ordinary people at the expense of the rich and the powerful.

Institutionalizing rule of law requires not only institutional changes, but also political and cultural changes. This vision is possible because in PNoy we have not just a political leader, but a transformative head of state. We also need Filipinos to believe in their own strengths and commitment. We need to forget the cynicism of those who preach that Filipinos are not destined for greatness.

Transforming Philippine society can be the enduring legacy of this administration. Just as eternal vigilance is the price of liberty, a society built on the rule of law will be a continuing crusade. **(ESC)**

VI.
The
Aquino
Girls

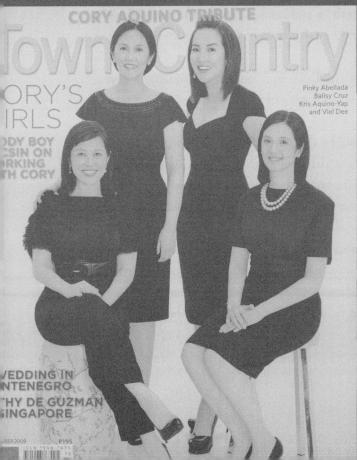

CORY AQUINO TRIBUTE

Town&Country

CORY'S GIRLS

Pinky Abellada
Ballsy Cruz
Kris Aquino-Yap
and Viel Dee

ODY BOY
CESIN ON
ORKING
TH CORY

EDDING IN
NTENEGRO
THY DE GUZMAN
SINGAPORE

P195

YES!

MAR & KORINA

THE NUMBER ONE ENTERTAINMENT MAGAZINE

74 PHOTO

ONLY IN YES!

THE AQUINO FAMILY

Revisits their Times Street home,

The Sixth Child

Nothing ever happens by accident, Cory Aquino liked to say. It did not seem so at the start. It seemed, rather, that she was destined from birth to lead a genteel, charmed life.

She was born on January 25, 1933 to a wealthy and landed family, the sixth of eight children of Jose Cojuangco and Demetria Sumulong Cojuangco, familiarly known as Don Pepe and Doña Metring.

Her older siblings are Ceferino (a stillborn child), Pedro, Josephine Cojuangco Reyes, Teresita Cojuanco Lopa, and Carmen (who died of meningitis before she turned two). Younger siblings are Jose Jr. (Peping), the only surviving sibling, and Maria Paz Cojuangco Teopaco.

Cory went to elementary school at St. Scholastica's College, Manila, a Catholic convent school run by the Missionary Benedictine Sisters of Tutzing, Germany. The school was known for its motto, *Ora et Labora* (pray and work), and the strict discipline and work ethic it instilled in its students. The sisters were reputed to be so strict that they did not even allow black patent shoes.

Carina Tancinco Mañalac, grade school classmate and good friend, remembers the young Cory as quiet, kind, and very shy, with a demure half-smile. She excelled in her favorite subjects, English and math, and was consistent class valedictorian. She was also unassuming, and even wore hand-me-down uniforms, leading no one to suspect her elitist background.

Tide of Time—a coffee-table book on the history of the Jose Cojuangco Sr. family, lovingly researched and written by the eldest Cojuangco granddaughter Marisse Reyes McMurray, and published in 1996—recounts why Cory was driven to excel in school. She felt she was unnoticed as the sixth child in the family, and happily realized that being valedictorian was an effective attention-calling tactic. Her mother was bursting with pride over this distinction. For Cory's graduation speech, her very first public speaking event, Doña Metring sought the assistance of her younger brother Lorenzo Sumulong, who would later become senator. The speech he prepared for Cory was polished and form-perfect. But her teachers decided to revise it to make it more appropriate for a young girl.

At that time, the Cojuangco family lived in a two-story house on Agno Street, off Taft Avenue, a mere two hundred meters from De La Salle College. It was convenient to send the boys to La Salle and the girls to St. Scholastica's. This house was the family's first in Manila. Home to them before this was their maternal grandparents' residence in Sampaloc.

Cory's favorite pastime in her childhood was reading—and reading aloud—whatever printed materials she could lay her hands on, including encyclopedia articles. She even read the newspaper out loud to her maternal grandfather when his eyesight failed him. This may explain the clarity, the cadence, and the pleasant accent with which she speaks.

With the outbreak of the Second World War, Cory moved to Assumption Convent, because St. Scholastica's remained closed. There was no longer an Agno home to return to; it had been razed to the ground by the Japanese. A temporary home was offered by Claudio Sandoval, a good friend of Cory's father. The Cojuangcos stayed with the Sandovals until they found a new home of their own on 2221 Roberts Street in Pasay, a home fondly remembered for its *kaymito, chico,* and *kamias* trees, its tilapia pond, a garden abloom with San Francisco plants and African daisies.

With his defeat in the 1946 congressional elections, Don Pepe retired from politics and seriously considered sending his children to the U.S. for their studies. He was, moreover, keen on exploring potential business opportunities there. This was also an opportunity to make good on his promise to the family that after the difficult war years, they would all travel together. Cory's parents belonged to the old and landed gentry of Tarlac, but they had never gone abroad before.

Cory was thirteen when her family took the eighteen-day journey by boat to the U.S. They lived for a year in Philadelphia, where Cory spent her sophomore year in high school at Ravenhill Academy as an *interna,* like her sisters.

Journalists in search of good copy and memorable human interest details about Cory's childhood are disappointed that it was such a secure and predictable life, spent in a serene and congenial family atmosphere. Still, there are anecdotes worth telling.

When her parents and two elder sisters returned to the Philippines in 1947, Cory, Peping, and Passy were left behind in New York under the guardianship of their mother's youngest sister, Belen Sumulong Bautista. It was Cory who usually prepared the meals because Passy did not know how to cook. But Passy remembers that, one day, the diligent and proper Cory simply refused to get out of bed. Passy kept asking whether she was going to school, and big sister's advice was for Passy to go to bed herself if she wanted to.

On another occasion, both again skipped classes to watch the personal appearance of child actress Margaret O'Brien in a Broadway movie theater. Cory and Passy cajoled their aunt into writing them an excuse slip. The nuns were not pleased, and reprimanded the sisters for always being absent.

Despite such infractions, Cory was a good student. She completed high school at Manhattan's Notre Dame Convent School, and it was here that she came to have the nickname that she carried to her dying day. In high school, she was Cora to everyone, but at home she was Coré—pronounced as two syllables, Co-ré. Her American classmates eventually rechristened her Cory, because that was the only successful pronunciation they could manage.

For college, Cory and elder sister Terry went to Mount St. Vincent's College in Riverdale, New York, a Catholic school for women run by the Sisters of Charity. One of the nuns, Julie Marie Weser, remembers Cory as "quiet and showing few signs of anything so dramatic." Her classmates say she was bookish and a good student, pleasant and smiling, but not the kind of girl who made a big stir. Cory's own self-analysis in her philosophy class then was that she did not have "too many great potentials." **(NSRC)**

Constant Companion

Ballsy's biggest childhood nightmare was losing her mother. She could not bear the mere thought of it and was fervently praying to die before her mother did. But after seeing her mom go through life despite the loss of their father, she thought, "How could I cause her more grief after all that she has gone through?"

With their father in detention, he could never buy them traditional presents. In lieu of gifts, he wrote the letters and poems that live on today. For Cory, he had written a romantic poem, "I Fell in Love with the Same Woman Three Times" (set to music by Jose Mari Chan as tribute to Cory when she was lying in state). Ballsy recounts that when Cory's friends told her they envied her because Ninoy had written the poem for her, Cory bluntly reassured them that, were their husbands in detention, they too would have received something similar: *"Subukan niyong makulong ang asawa n'yo, igagawa din kayo . . . ."*

During the wake for their mother, many people were struck by how much of Cory they saw in Ballsy—her stately and dignified ways, her proper demeanor, her special quiet charm. Why, even the way she walked, some remarked. In the publicly circulated, moving letter written to Ballsy on her eighteenth birthday by her father while he was in detention, he lavished praises on her by describing her as possessing the best traits of her mother.

Called the favorite daughter by her siblings, Ballsy was Cory's constant companion, especially during the presidency, when she served as her mother's private secretary, and in the years that followed, when they worked together at the Jose Cojuangco Building on C.

Palanca Street in Makati. Sharing the same office space and even leaving the office together, they never ran out of stories to tell each other. And as soon as they were both in their own homes, conversations continued over the telephone—about a name that had slipped their minds earlier and was now suddenly remembered, something that just came up since they bade each other goodbye a few hours earlier, or yet another forgotten story to laugh over. It is that kind of *kwentuhan* that Ballsy says she misses most.

Ballsy is truly her mother's daughter, and a characteristic they share is not being *mautos*, preferring to do things on their own, rather than asking someone else to do things for them. For her hospitalizations, for instance, Cory preferred to pack her own things, saying that it was she who knew what she needed—and how to pack the items in their own organizers. She was never demanding even during the last weeks of her hospitalization. As for Ballsy, in the frenzy of a *YES!* pictorial, which required making a few wardrobe changes and wearing high, high heels that she was no longer accustomed to, she repeatedly refused to have anyone carry her shoes for her as she moved from one area of the living room to another. The shoes, incidentally, reminds Ballsy of that embarrassing time on her first date with Eldon, when she wore fashionable heels, only to have one heel come off during the date.

Ballsy corrects the common false public image of her mother as a "weak" person. Those who knew her up close know that Cory Aquino had a mind of her own, had the same dominant personality as Doña Metring Cojuangco, and, for all her gracious ways and fine breeding, was not one to mask her displeasure. Ballsy and her husband Eldon knew when it was time to bail her out during social functions from company she did not particularly relish. Eldon, in particular, knew how Cory detested having people, especially men, put their arms around her shoulders—never mind if it was meant to be an act of gallantry. Almost on cue, Eldon would instinctively rescue her from such a situation.

Ballsy considers it fortunate that Eldon got along well with her mother and her aunt, Terry Lopa. He was their trusted escort during the campaign for the 1986 elections, helping them get on and off provincial stages, even pinning their skirts to keep them from flying. He has blended so well with the Cojuangco cousins that on weekend visits to Hacienda Luisita, Ballsy would have retired for the night, but Eldon would still be in the company of the cousins. He rather enjoyed that extended family camaraderie that he never knew in childhood, since his family moved from one province to another because of his father's job with sugar mills.

Ballsy continues to report for work at the Cojuangco Building, as she works with the Jose Cojuangco family corporation, and is a board member of the Benigno S. Aquino Jr. Foundation. **(NSRC)**

Two NGOs that Really Exist

U pon PNoy's assumption of office in 2010, presidential sister Pinky Aquino Abellada conceptualized the AGAPP Foundation, or Aruga Tungo sa Pag-angat at Pag-asa. The foundation gives free books, teacher training, feeding, livelihood, and parenting support to people, to give them a better quality of life and hope. It was Pinky's way of assisting her brother in the best way she knew how, through a meaningful educational measure. Formally incorporated on August 1, 2010 and drawing special meaning from the significance of the day, President Cory's first death anniversary, AGAPP envisioned building classrooms that our public schools never have enough of.

But the AGAPP classrooms are special in many ways. These were targeted to be preschool classrooms in clear support of the mandate of the Department of Education and Br. Armin Luistro FSC, to provide mandatory preschool education to all children. One can easily spot them in the public school grounds because they are painted in bright and attractive colors. There are typically two classrooms, with an inviting reading nook with carefully selected picture books for K-3 readers, learning materials and manipulatives, and a comfort room.

That AGAPP is devoted exclusively to preschools is a welcome development as it acknowledges the importance of better preparing children for the demands of formal schooling. It is a tremendous boost to the public school educational system (and DepEd's limited resources) when a nongovernment organization tailors its program for a specific target grade level and in a sense "adopts" it by concentrating all its efforts to support, strengthen, and enhance the grade level curriculum.

Pinky gives the latest update with understandable pride—as of July 2013, 601 classrooms have been built nationwide. "An average of one classroom in less than two days" is a record accomplishment, considering that the initial modest goal was 100 each year. It looks like AGAPP's target of 1,000 classrooms by 2016 will easily be met, in fact overshot. There has not been a shortage of donors willing to build classrooms costing from P700,000 to 1 million. Pinky reports that Cebu has had the most projects because of the numerous donors from there.

This attention to the preschooler has gained more impetus with the launch of Save the Children's First Read Program, during the National Children's Book Day on July 16, 2013. Save the Children is a familiar foundation in 120 countries all over the world and is known for its aim of protecting children's rights. "We save children's lives; we fight for their rights; we help them fulfill their potential," the foundation's reason for being, was reiterated by Save the Children Philippine country director Anna Lindenfors.

First Read has become a necessary adjunct program because statistics show that access to early childhood care and development programs is only available to around 33 percent of Filipino children. Viewed with the education statistics on poor completion rates, high dropouts in grades one and two, and an increasing number of struggling readers, it becomes imperative to nurture the development of children way before school age.

The goal of First Read is to boost the development of children from childbirth to four years in 123 barangays in six cities and municipalities in Metro Manila—Caloocan, Malabon, Navotas, Valenzuela, Taguig, and Pateros—and in south Central Mindanao, South Cotabato, and Sarangani Province. The three-year project enjoys generous financial support from the UK-based Prudence Foundation and Pru Life UK Philippines, and aims to reach 96,924 direct beneficiaries composed of 29,520 children and 67,404 adults.

First Read works directly with parents to provide them with the knowledge, skills, and even the books and toys that they themselves will not be able to access, much less purchase for their preschoolers' needs. It is a more responsible and committed parent education program with strong community support which will have a direct impact on preparing their children for literacy and numeracy skills. It is working closely with the Early Childhood Care and Development Council, a government agency under the supervision of the Department of Education.

Another government agency partnering with First Read in this initiative is the National Book Development Board and a first joint effort was scheduled on August 2013 in Valenzuela, also to celebrate Linggo ng Wika.

In his remarks at the launch of the First Read program, British Embassy charge d' affaires Trevor Lewis concluded with a quote from William Shakespeare: "Ignorance is the curse of God; knowledge is the wing wherewith we fly to heaven" (Henry VI).

He also voiced out a timely plea shared by all: "Let's continue to work together to give Filipino children the wings that they need to take them on their own personal journeys to happiness, prosperity and success. Let's make the ability to read the air beneath those wings."

When one thinks of the scandalous and unconscionable alleged P10-billion pork barrel donations (yes, the people's money) to nonexisting foundations, the P700,000 needed for an AGAPP classroom structure sounds like a pittance. And the sheer number of First Read communities that can be supported with a "measly" P1 billion from that bottomless pork barrel fund is staggering. Why do genuine working foundations have it so tough? **(ESC)**

The "Invisible" Third Daughter

Viel, the third daughter and fourth child in the family, relished being the youngest and Daddy's princess for ten years, with everyone duly advised about her doting father's mantra, "What princess wants, princess gets." That was until Kris, the youngest in the family, was born. The dethroned princess, as Viel refers to that stage of her childhood in mock exaggeration, was fleetingly so affected, so upset that she had a severe asthma attack.

There was a gap of nine years and four months, too big to allow for any sibling rivalry. "After the initial stress of being 'dethroned,' I eventually was thrilled to become an *ate* and actually enjoyed having a new baby in the house." By the time Kris entered Poveda for Kindergarten, Ate Viel was already in high school.

She was frail and sickly as a child, had frequent nosebleeds and the same seasonal asthma attacks like her mother. Despite Viel's frail constitution, she remembers that she was more confident then in public speaking, "I was much braver facing big audiences then. I would sing or recite poems during some of Dad's campaign sorties." Her repertoire included a Spanish poem about a little duck, "*Patito, Patito quiel agua de vas*?" She describes this as totally irrelevant to campaigning, but because it was a delight to hear Spanish from a six-year old, it was certainly a charming addition to political speeches. She remembers singing "I could have danced all night," either in campaigns or family gatherings.

She also excelled in her elementary school years at Institucion Teresiana (today known as Saint Pedro Poveda College), always with first or second honors, but slacked off in high school—when it was no longer cool to be nerdy.

The school treated her to gift-wrapped books as a special reward for honors. But to her, the biggest surprise treat was during her Grade 7 graduation as valedictorian, receiving a medal for the first time. How could it not be doubly memorable with the unannounced presence of her dad who arrived in the middle of the ceremonies? Viel recalls how one excited father of her classmate began taking photos of Ninoy. The military personnel with the detainee did not look favorably on that and either confiscated the camera or the film in it.

Even when she was already in college, she did not really know what career she would pursue. The only thing she was sure of was that it would have to do with numbers. The world of finance was where she did end up. Viel finished her General Management course at Boston College while the family was living in Newton. In fact, when her family suddenly flew to the U.S., she was on a vacation with her maternal grandparents along with some cousins. She had just completed her freshman year at the Ateneo and did not expect that her summer vacation would be extended to three years of life in the U.S. It was in Fr. Joseph Galdon, SJ's English class at the Ateneo where her mother helped her with her haiku-writing assignments, a most successful collaboration for which Viel got excellent grades. As her mother proudly recounted years back, Viel even had a few extra haikus to spare for classmates who had not been as successful in their initial attempts.

Not that there was anything to complain about the warm and predictable normalcy of family life there. It was certainly a far cry from the regular routine of leaving school early on special permit every Wednesday at 2 p.m. for the family visit at Fort Bonifacio from 3 to 5 p.m. That was Wednesdays for Viel when she was 11 to 18 years old, throughout her father's seven years and seven months of incarceration. What a vast difference life overseas was, with the Celtics and the Red Sox games she loved to watch either live or on television, and the family trips, like long drives to Knoxville, Tennessee to visit a World's Fair.

It was as Ballsy's roommate at their Newton home that she became close to her eldest sister, whose gentle and serene temperament is most akin to hers. It is a sisterly kinship that continues today.

Her first job was as project analyst in Benguet Management Corporation, for non-mining investments of the company. After two years, she worked as a management trainee at Metrobank but only for five weeks since "suddenly, Mom was in the thick of a presidential campaign." When her mother became president, she considered becoming a teacher but later decided to join Chase Manhattan Bank as a financial analyst. She worked there for ten years and when Jia, her second child, was born, she availed of early retirement to become a full-time mom.

However, just within a month from retiring, she joined Assisi Foundation which was chaired by her father-in-law, Ambassador Howard Dee, putting in half-day work managing the foundation's funds. That half-day arrangement did not last long, for it soon became a full-time involvement in treasury work and its scholarship program. Today, she is vice-chair of the foundation, overseeing the scholarship program and working closely with the president in various programs—many of them involving indigenous people—and traveling to a number of its project sites nationwide. Viel is also an active board member of three other foundations: the Ninoy and Cory Aquino Foundation, Asa Philippines Foundation (a nonprofit microfinance institution), and the Joey Velasco Foundation which highlights socially conscious religious artworks. The latter is named after the late artist who painted the celebrated "Hapag ng Pag-asa" mural that depicted Jesus breaking bread with street children.

"I admire mothers who hold a full-time job and can still cook, drive, and attend to the needs of their children. During these times when kids don't put much value on religion, I admire parents who, by their example, are able to raise children with the right values and are God-fearing individuals." That is, in a sense, what Viel tries to live up to as a working mother. The lessons she has learned from the lives of her father and her mother are precious ones she holds dear and wishes to pass on to her children and the youth along, with honesty, generosity, simplicity, and humility.

Ninoy's love of country was so all-encompassing that early on in her adolescent years, she, along with her siblings, learned to accept that "for Dad, country came before family." It was when her father was incarcerated during martial law when she first realized that her father was no ordinary individual. She knew her family was different from that of her peers' and the best her mom could do was to try to render a semblance of normalcy to the extent possible in their everyday lives.

> "We attended all of Dad's hearings, whether at the military tribunal or at the Supreme Court. I was old enough to understand that he was a political prisoner and charges were trumped up. The martial law years were really trying, especially for a teenager, from Dad's 'disappearance' to Laur, the

forty-day hunger strike, 'smuggling' letters written by Dad from his cell to the outside world, running for a seat in parliament, the sentencing to death by firing squad."

Viel thinks their mom ought to be considered lucky that they were not rebellious children and did not give her more trouble than she already had to bear.

Their extraordinarily arduous journey as a family has bestowed on her mother the strong belief that "faith will enable you to overcome any trial and difficulty that you encounter." This unshakable faith is pure and simple, convincing Viel as a witness to these, that all sufferings on earth will be rewarded in heaven.

To Viel, the proudest thing about being an Aquino is that it is a true privilege. "My father is a hero, my mother is regarded by some as a saint, and my *kuya* has given it all he's got to institute reforms that I never thought could ever happen. Maybe the reforms are not yet institutionalized, but he has planted the seeds in many areas of government that were badly in need of reform."

Watching her brother as president, she has rediscovered him anew, impressing her even more. "I knew PNoy was intelligent but I didn't realize that he's actually also quite a perfectionist. He doesn't settle for *'puwede na.'* I hear him talk about reading volumes of material, studying issues carefully, before making decisions."

Viel never called PNoy "*Kuya*" as they were growing up. She must have shocked him when a few years ago, she began her texts to him with "Hi, KP (Kuya President)." She laughs that he must have thought she was addressing him that way because she had a favor to ask.

Although the only boy, Viel does not recall him receiving preferential treatment from their parents. "He was not spoiled. I don't remember special privileges for him, but he took lessons that the girls didn't, like karate and horseback riding."

Turning pensive about the sacrifices her parents lived and died for, Viel only wishes that we all learn from the lessons of the past. "It's sad when people say Filipinos have short memories. We should learn from the mistakes of the past. It is important to remind the younger generations that we were once under a dictatorship and we should all be grateful that our democracy was restored. It is disturbing that it does not seem out of the question that another Marcos might be elected president of the country."

The private and reticent person that she is, Viel strongly dislikes "living in a fishbowl." Describing herself as "quiet, simple, a follower rather than a leader," one can imagine and appreciate the public self she tries to carry. If she had her way, she'd rather do the things she loves doing puzzles (crossword, sudoku, jigsaw) and watching *teleseryes* and talent shows.

But despite her avowed preference for the quiet life, Viel has not reneged on expectations of her as former presidential daughter and now, presidential sister. She was initially horrified and extremely uncomfortable that she and her sisters became "unlikely cover girls" for *Town and Country* in 2009, right after the passing of President Cory and right before her brother would make public his decision to run for president. These were doubly unsettling, she remembers. On the day of the shoot, she struggled with the designer clothes bearing five-figure price ranges plus the tough choice of choosing one that fits her personality. She even ended up wearing younger sister Kris's 5-inch heeled formal shoes, she recounts in the book *Noynoy's Sisters*.

During the campaign, she knew she had to have her share of public exposure. She was happy her sisters allowed her to volunteer last each time and to be the least visible of them all. She was herself surprised that she managed at least forty "dakilang substitute" appearances in town plazas, public markets, churches, radio stations, among others.

As Viel wrote in "My Cordillera Trek" in *Noynoy's Sisters,* it was fortunate she had her son Kiko with her on a campaign trip to the Cordillera where the Assisi Foundation funded housing projects. It was Kiko, today an assistant professor of political science, who explained Noy's platform in great detail, along with notes and diagrams on the white board. This time, Viel knew better than to be her usual direct, no-nonsense self, speaking in words not politically correct in the course of a campaign. "I didn't have to repeat my faux pas in the early part of the campaign when at an open forum after being told that they were unsatisfied with my answer on Noy's education program, I said, 'I'm not the candidate and I don't think I should be expected to know every detail of his platform.'"

She has learned to psyche herself to circumstances beyond her control, saying that like many other challenges the Aquino family has had to confront over the years, she had to find ways to live with these. It is she who mid-year into 2015, looked forward to October, when public scrutiny and brickbats will be focused on the persons who would have filed their certificates of candidacy—and hopefully, no longer on the presidential family. She warns all and sundry, "Being in a family so deeply involved in politics is something I fervently hope will end on June 30, 2016. My running joke is that if any other sibling or nephew or niece ever decides to run for anything after PNoy's term in 2016, I'm migrating to Japan." **(NSRC)**

Kris Aquino, 12

Because one approaches any further intrusions into the private lives of the Aquino family rather apologetically, fearful of unnecessarily awakening memories or inflicting added pain, it comes as a tremendous relief to have its youngest member, twelve-year-old Kris, reveal with such spontaneity, "If you want to listen, I'll tell you my whole life story."

In complete contrast to her three older sisters who prefer to keep the press at arm's length, Kris admits with little embarrassment, "I enjoy the publicity now." She says she finds the interview especially fun.

She demonstrates how assiduously she follows the media coverage of her family. She is quick to point out the mistakes committed in print. For example, she is Kristina Bernadette, not Kristine as a daily had first reported, misleading Jaime Cardinal Sin into calling her thus. It is Ballsy, without an "ie," and her cousin's name is Rina Teopaco, not Nina. The latter two mistakes were made by *Mr. & Ms.*, she emphasizes. And just because she wears spectacles like her dad (so does everyone else in the family except for Ballsy), why do they say she looks like him? Now no longer complaining, she admits, "I got his nose . . . and his intelligence."

She is just different from the rest of the Aquino daughters—more talkative ("I got that from my dad," she giggles over her second serving of buko sherbet at her Lola Metring's house) and extroverted. Kris was, after all, reared in quite extraordinary circumstances, in quite unusual times. Ninoy, whom Noynoy describes as "liberal in politics, but conservative with the family," insisted on some semblance of normalcy for his children despite his public exposure and the continuous stream of people in their house. The teenagers of the house, Noynoy included, were allowed to go to parties only when accompanied by an entourage of yaya, driver, and bodyguard.

Things changed after that day in September when Ninoy became a member of what is still grimly alluded to as "Class 1082" by his fellow ex-detainees. Kris was all of eighteen months then and perhaps fortunately, did not know what losing a father to detention was like. This lack in her life, she conjectures, was what led her mother to allow her to have a more public life surrounded by a lot of people.

"I never remember him living in our house in Times. My earliest memories of my dad must have been when I was three or four." The family's visits to Fort Bonifacio were especially exciting to this child who looked forward to the little toy her dad would surprise her with—stuff he collected from the cans of powdered milk he had used up. This poignant detail reveals a father who in normal times could certainly whip up a less limited variety of surprises. It is almost strange, too, to hear a daughter say of their father, "Yes, I did get to know him through the times we visited him."

And yet, Kris says, it all came very naturally to have a daddy with them in Boston. A daddy who patiently helped her with her homework especially religion and the Bible, a daddy who never openly expressed pride in her and her all-too-monotonous report card that carried nothing but A's ("A for Aquino" was her father's way of motivating her), a daddy who indulged her passion for shopping and clothes every time she brought home good grades. "He would complain that what I liked were expensive and I would have to argue that I worked hard for it. He was generous about buying me video game cartridges."

What fond and warm memories Kris carries in her exuberant young heart about the three-year period during which the novel experience of enjoying a father was revealed to her!

"He would always want to watch the news," she grumbles because she was the soap opera addict. She would always get into a major debate with her father about what TV program to watch. "He would grab the control and I would complain, debate, and argue, and by that time he would have gotten his fill of the news." But by her reckoning, she won most of those arguments.

"Since we both loved to talk and often no one was there to talk to, we would end up talking to each other," Kris reveals. She laughingly reminisces how Ninoy would often encourage her to be a nun as his sacrifice to God so that she could become his savior. She never quite consented to his grand plan, because she wanted to get married.

Neither her father nor her mother has ever pressured her to be an achiever, but she acknowledges their influence in her interests. "If I enjoy something, I work hard at it. I want to be at the top because if I can do it, why not? I like to read a lot, anything I get my hands on. I also love to write. English is one of my favorite subjects."

If she were not Ninoy's daughter, Kris doubts if she would have been as outspoken or as interested in school as she is. She is no less certain of the influence of her mother, the only parent she has known for most of her life. But she finds it more difficult to be specific about this: "I don't know what it is exactly. I just know that there's part of her that is inside me." Kris confesses that she has not given the matter much thought because it is not the question most frequently asked of her.

Although she considers both her parents strict disciplinarians, not once has she experienced physical punishment. The only time she remembers having had a taste of her father's temper was when she wrote down a telephone message for him from a caller from Geneva. No one could read the message she had scribbled, and Ninoy became very upset. But Kris understands it perfectly now. "He was a very busy man and sometimes got hotheaded."

School has always been a delightful experience for her. She does optional assignments willingly and diligently. And so was disturbed to discover on her first few days at the International School, where she is a seventh grader, that for the first time in her life she was afraid. She could not quite understand why she was feeling that way and was frustrated about it. It took her mother and her sisters to point out to her that she had not physically recovered from the rigors of the Boston-Manila trip—along with the day-long funeral, the ongoing novena masses, the intensity of emotions accompanying their loss. Things were just far from normal and needed coping with, she was told.

Happily enough, she announces that she is herself again these days, enjoying school and the relative anonymity she has on campus ("They don't care who you are there," she says with relief), and eager to excel. She has acclimatized to the school's 250 students per grade, a far cry from her Boston Catholic School's 25 per grade. She still struggles, though, with waking up early enough to make it from Times St. to Makati for the 7:15 morning bell. But once or twice during the week she treats herself to the luxury of sleeping longer by spending the night at her maternal grandmother's house in Dasmariñas Village.

A favorite cousin of hers, Rina Teopaco who studies at Poveda, Kris's former school, lives at the Makati house. When Rina and Kris are together, Noynoy has to turn authoritarian to quiet down their excited tones as they rush to a ringing telephone. Noynoy says with tolerance, almost fatherly indulgence, "They are at that age!" Rina allows herself a cryptic statement: "Kris and I share one thing these days." Despite the aura of mystery, one can easily deduce what the gender of the "one thing" could be.

At school and at times spent with Rina shopping, watching Poveda games, or going to a favorite Pizza Hut, Kris can be a typical girl her age. "Then I don't have much time to think (about things)," she says.

While at her grandmother's, she manages to sunbathe by the pool because she frets that she is much too fair. She does not disguise her emerging teenage vanity, no longer cares to be photographed with her glasses on (a revelation to a slightly shocked Noynoy), and excuses herself to brush her hair before more photos are shot. Her sisters tease her, "Mababasag na ang salamin." Her father used to remark, "In my time, my sisters never spent all that time fixing themselves. Your mother would not even be looking at the mirror at all."

Clearly, Kris is the family pet. When she describes her relationship with her sisters, her first point of reference is that all of them have promised to put her on their payrolls. "It is more a tong," says Noynoy with a chuckle, and she wonders, "What's that?"

Ballsy, she says, is so much like their father in temperament, generous almost to a fault. Ballsy now acts as her mother's secretary and is a solicitous big sister to all her siblings, an inevitability, says Noynoy, because of the disrupted family life since the martial law years. "She helps me with my math," Kris says gratefully.

Pinky, a computer engineer who has recently flown back to the States to comply with her contract with IBM, buys many things for Kris every payday. Through her, Kris got her membership of cable TV programs while in the States.

Hesitating a bit about how to describe her only brother (his being her "best" brother continues to be debatable), Kris is reminded to say, "Yes, he is sometimes good to me," by a glare from him. In the next breath, she confesses, "Sometimes we don't talk for thirty days. He bullies me." But Noynoy makes her recall the many times when she in turn has bullied him into taking her to the movies. The Kris-Noynoy exchange could go on and on. It is Viel, nine years older than Kris, who has reassured her, "Even when you're older you'll still be the baby of the family."

Noy and Kris explain the three older girls' distaste for publicity: "They are no status seekers and prefer to help in a supportive capacity."

Accustomed to addressing large audiences ("I do not stay nervous for long because I like it"), Kris sounds like an entirely different person when she admits, "Yes, my sisters make *utos* me. 'Take out my plate, give me water.'" And how they tease her, she relates, about the scene at the Boston airport as recorded on videotape, *"Hagulgulating na naman si Kris!"*

There was nothing to look forward to on this trip home, she is the first to admit. The mere remembrance of the last days in Boston brings back a flood of unpleasant images. Trying to remain composed even after seeing that scene on television of her father lying in state ("No one else in the family wanted to see it"). Trying hard on the final drive to the airport not to relive the day they drove her dad through the very same path where he had said, "Bye, MIT, bye Harvard, bye St. Ignatius (church)," as they passed those buildings. All he had asked her to take home to him from Boston was a poster, "so he wouldn't ever forget it."

Landing at the Manila International Airport was even more difficult for Kris than leaving Boston. The MIA was, after all, the very same physical space that proved treacherous to her father's homecoming. Gazing beyond the here and now and sounding uncharacteristically uncertain, she remembers how she shuddered at the sight of uniformed military men. She seems to wonder out loud if after this, she can even feel differently toward them.

But this is the only solitary moment when Kris betrays resentment.

Most of the time she is all child, all innocence, flattered that people ask for her autograph, requests which she very willingly obliges with a lengthy dedication ("So time-consuming," says her cousins, grown impatient with waiting for her), looking forward to being allowed to do away with her glasses forever and at age thirteen, finally wear contact lens, and aspiring to become a lawyer or a journalist. Never mind the hazards of today's journalism, adding, "There should be more freedom by my time," she says in a voice ringing with optimism, adding, "I really admire what you people do." One turns around, vainly hoping that some foreign media representative heard Kris Aquino's tribute. **(NSRC)**

Mr. & Ms., October 25, 1983

The Sui Generis
Kris Aquino, 44

NWhat is it that the general public still does not know about Kris Aquino, she who cannot seem to keep any secrets and delights in the drama and theatrics of it all? Reigning as the Queen of All Media and *YES!*'s most beautiful star of 2015, the ultimate celebrity product endorser is followed with such ardor and slavish devotion by a large hero-worshipping populace. It does not hurt that she carries the Aquino name which serves like a charm. Her Cojuangco-Aquino lineage is difficult to match, and having two presidents in the family is difficult to ignore. There are the celebrity's strikingly good looks and irrepressible, spontaneous, and candid comments lapped up by legions of fans. A master of social media, everything one needs to know about her she makes easily accessible on Instagram, her official website, and her Kris Aquino (Official Fan Page) on Facebook. She reportedly has at least two million followers on Instagram alone. Yes, absolutely everything—and then some—you ever wanted to know about Kris would be right there.

One cannot be ambivalent toward Kris who is sharp, intelligent, and articulate—one either loves her or hates her. Some sympathize with her potential ardent suitors who may justifiably worry that every stage of the romance will be shared with the population, and yes, broadcast live. After all, it is not easy to blot out from public memory the saga of a woman who appears to have everything except the good fortune of a relationship that nurtures and lasts.

While she says there is nothing in her life that she has not yet made public, we somehow sense that there is more beneath all the glitz and glamour. For why would a cryptic and mysterious "No comment" suffice from loquacious Kris when asked if she continues to search for love and Mr. Right? Asked if there is anything she wishes to alter were she to relive life all over again, she replies with a laconic "Absolutely nothing." Appearing to have learned from past public unrestrained outpourings, a more responsible and cautious Kris is now mindful of her siblings' advice and sensibilities: "I'm smart enough now to know when to keep my mouth shut. Family unity is something we all value."

Learning from life's lessons, she says, "At least, natuto nang mag-isip." She has turned to lyrics by Stephen Schwartz from the musical *Wicked* to reflect her state of mind and well-being: "But because I knew you, I have been changed for good . . ." To her, having been selected by *YES!* as the most beautiful star for 2015 restored her self-esteem: "I love the affirmation it gave me." She acknowledged that there are many other women more beautiful than she is, but she knows the distinction is for much more than just her physical attributes. She missed the party that would have formally honored her, but who can beat her excuse of attending her brother's last State of the Nation address and the party with family and close friends that followed? Can she help it that her every move makes for wonderful copy?

The path to the essential Kris Aquino is made possible through her siblings (who always hesitate to speak for their kid sister). Noynoy says his blood pressure rises and he is all discomfort when Kris takes the microphone to make public statements about him. He is ready to classify his other sisters into accurate categories, but he hesitates with Kris, whom he calls the sui generis Aquino—truly unique, in a class by herself, defying all traditional categories. It is interesting to see family dynamics at play when they talk about her.

What is beyond dispute is that Kris is the Aquino child who is most similar to the engaging and articulate Ninoy. For one, when they want something done, they want it done now—if not yesterday—no matter the price, no matter the risk, no matter the outcome. They share the same qualities: excellent speaking skills, amazing photographic memory, and that signature charisma.

If Kris is such a success story today, it is because she has worked hard for it. She continues to be so driven, so much that her siblings describe her as a workaholic and have all expressed alarm over her hospital confinements for hypertension, fever, and abdominal woes.

One confinement found her on the cusp of a stroke, jolting her into rethinking her priorities. She was comforted and touched by her family's concern for her, with Noynoy seeing her as soon as he arrived from a provincial trip to Cebu. Even as she promised her siblings and herself to be more prudent about her work-life balance, Kris explains, "Mom said to never expect anything to be handed on a silver platter. Because Kuya Josh has special needs, I need to make sure he's well provided for." She did drop one of two daily shows, *Aquino & Abunda Tonight*. She is well aware of the feast or famine philosophy in the entertainment industry where success and survival are fleeting, where shelf lives are limited. From all indications—BIR reporting her as one of the country's top income taxpayers, her practice of changing her place of residence as frequently and as painlessly as she changes her wardrobe—it is obvious that she is doing a remarkable job of preparing for the future of Josh and Bimby.

Her present all-white three-story residence—bought with cold cash, heeding the advice of bosom buddy and manager Boy Abunda's "Bawal umutang"—has endowed her with a lightness of being that is, yes, almost "unbearable." Tailored to her and her sons' lifestyle needs, it has her dream kitchen with shelves to house her tea set collection, a makeup/exercise room with Hollywood lights on the ground floor, a private second floor for their three bedrooms, and an herb garden for this adjudged best cook in the family. The vintage Amorsolo portrait of Cory, a gift from her dad, and the Ang Kiukok portrait of her mom are proudly displayed there, close to the chartreuse double doors.

Ballsy recalls that even as a kid, Kris was already hardworking and wanted excellent results during her schooldays. That work ethic was ingrained in her just as it was with her siblings: "As children we never thought we could live on whatever inheritance we would get if at all. We all worked hard and didn't rely on whatever our grandparents or parents would leave us. To us, if they left us something, then that would be a bonus." In an interview with *YES!*, Kris quotes her mom bluntly saying to her, "Unlike me, you're not an heiress"—thus, the necessity of working hard. Ballsy knows that Kris is proudest that her stature has allowed her to improve many people's lives." Even as it may appear that Kris may have nothing left to aspire for, Ballsy openly wishes for her to "find a good man for keeps . . ."

Pinky has told Kris in unequivocal terms that the right man for her at this stage of her life and her career would be a challenge. Her stature, her earning capacity, her very public persona, her past relationships, her having the President of the land for a brother, are all but intimidating and formidable obstacles. Couple those with Kris's wish for someone who shares her intellectual wavelength (her own words), is well-read like her or is inclined to read. In a *YES!* interview, she explains in very colloquial language, "Hindi yung parang dumededma lang." Does such a match exist for Kris? In almost the same breath, Kris falls into a sobering reality check and says, "My God, kung my only complaint is wala akong love life, hello! Tigilan ko na, kasi parang ang babaw!"

Pinky says that Kris was born competitive and when challenged, "will attack the problem from all possible angles. She will think aloud and bam-bam-boom, she will have an unending list of must-dos with matching responsible persons if need be, to reach her goal."

The hints of her love for acting were there even in her early years. Her gift for gab has endeared her as a five-star host and anchor. Kris traces this to being the youngest in the family, always surrounded by grown-ups who never indulged in baby talk. At eighteen months, she was speaking in straight sentences—and yes, one might say, has not stopped talking since. She showed an unusually keen interest in show business as a child. As a preteen in Boston, she appeared in school plays. Prior to that, Kris had her public appearances at age six, endearing herself to the audience as she campaigned for her dad then in detention during the LABAN rallies. She could name all the twenty-one candidates in rapid, Ninoy-like fashion, and moved hearts by saying how she missed her dad.

This little girl received extraordinary training for stage appearances early on—and never knew stage fright. Today, decades after, she asks, should I have been scared? Pinky recounts that in 1978, one of the student organizations in UP Diliman invited Pinky to speak for a LABAN campaign. "I was shy then so I made a deal with Kris to do it for me and say all of the names of the 21 candidates led by [our] father." The bribe was to take her to Gift Gate where she could choose any Hello Kitty item. Before the program started, Kris suddenly changed her mind. The alarmed and panicky Ballsy and Pinky asked her what the problem was. Kris answered, "How come they all have leis and I don't?" Her older sisters immediately "borrowed" one of the candidates' leis. Kris did her speech so well that from then on, she was the star campaign speaker.

In her teens, Kris was eager to enter showbiz but her mom required her to complete her studies first. Pinky remembers that when she was in college at the Ateneo and already appearing in movies, Kris would go straight to school with no sleep and fall asleep in class: "Mom, [who was still] President then, was invited months in advance to be commencement speaker the year [Kris] graduated and Mom did not stop reminding her to complete all requirements for her to graduate on time." Thankfully, Kris did.

Pinky wishes to see a more relaxed Kris down the road, instead of one who is constantly trying to catch her breath. Her job may appear easy to the general public, but what is not evident is the tremendous amount of preliminary work that goes behind the scenes. There is sympathy in Pinky's voice as she continues, "As a star, she always has to look like one. She cannot leave the house in comfortable house clothes sans makeup."

Regarding the consequences both welcome and unwelcome during an Aquino presidency, Pinky speaks on how it must be for Kris, who really does not have much of a private life: "It is hard enough to live in an aquarium during an Aquino presidency, but because Kris is in showbiz, she doesn't have the luxury of making herself scarce especially during low times. But luckily we are five siblings trained by Mom so well to rely on one another for support to face our trials (during martial law, Mom showed us the best example). After all, we are all in the same boat and know how the others are feeling."

On how different they are as Aquino siblings and Kris's frequent candid disclosures, Pinky explains the modus vivendi that prevails: "We are five different individuals and sometimes have differing opinions, but we always try to privately express why we think that way on a particular issue to understand the other better. And so far, we have maintained peace and understanding in the family. I think Mom and Dad would be saddest if the five of us are not united." Kris' s siblings have reconciled their innate desire for a more private life and Kris's need to be in the constant glare of publicity, something she and her career welcome: "I guess in showbiz, if they no longer talk about you then that means you are no longer relevant."

Pinky is happy for Kris's status as top endorser and thinks this is because Kris is honest, professional, and nurturing of the relationship she has with the companies that invite her to endorse their products. It is truly serious business for Kris, not a mere generous source of compensation, but lending her name, reputation, and hard work to the product. When she mentions in passing, a newly discovered restaurant or snack item, these become overnight successes. Many restaurants attribute their instant popularity (and long queues) to a Kris rave review. Her daily television show *Kris TV* has such a loyal following, the network's call center usually receives calls on pressing inquiries after every episode. These include the lipstick shade on Kris's lips, or more exposure for her shoes, since her dress covered them in the last episode. Even her haircut becomes a matter of consequence and turns newsworthy.

Kris is much like the CEO of a big company, one that sells the Kris Aquino brand. This is why it is important that she has a roster of people she trusts. Efficient special assistant Alvin Gagui heads the pack, which includes stylists who help Kris with her total look, assistants who help her to do her job well, and staff that ensure her household functions efficiently.

Viel deigns not to speak about her kid sister Kris. How typical, how predictable of her to say, "Less said, less issues for people to talk about." Viel did narrate that when she went through the initiation of being interviewed for a cover story of the Aquino sisters soon after her mom passed away, she was terrified and there was Kris accustomed to it all, easing her into achieving a casual and relaxed look for the photo shoot. Availing of Kris's extensive wardrobe, Viel borrowed the glam high heels for the sisterly poses. And more recently, it was reported that when it was Kris's turn to host the family's weekly Sunday lunch, Viel said she was bringing a guest and could she pay for that share?

Among the siblings, it is Kris born on Valentine's Day in 1971 (does that explain her obsession with hearts—a heart dotting the i in her name, more hearts on her blog, and lovelovelove all over her updates) who had the least time to enjoy her father's company as he was in detention during her growing-up years. Pinky shares, "Kris was the one most deprived of having a dad in childhood so in his last three years, he made it up to her by taking her to movies in Boston and spoiling her in the bookstore." Kris was known to be a voracious reader and has written on her website, "I acquired my love for reading from my dad. He had a rule when we were living in Boston, no limit to how many books I could buy (Barnes & Noble was our favorite) for as long as I read everything we bought. Growing up I was obsessed with the Bobbsey Twins, Nancy Drew, then Encyclopedia Brown, and finally Judy Blume. In high school it was definitely *Sweet Valley High*, then I moved on to Danielle Steel and Sidney Sheldon. In college I loved John Grisham and Jeffrey Archer, as well as Mary Higgins Clark. And now I have remained loyal and obsessed with the works of James Patterson, and Julie Hyzy is my grown-up version of Nancy Drew. I shall try to keep you posted on the books I'm reading, and hopefully we can form a not-so-secret society of Book Lovers!"

Kris was originally scheduled to come back to the Philippines with her father on that fateful homecoming flight. It was fortunate she did not. When the sad news was made known to the family, her mother consoled the crying Kris by reminding her that Mom and her siblings were still around for her. According to Ballsy, "Mom had been Mom and Dad ever since Kris could remember and Mom always had the right things to tell all of us especially during tough and trying times."

What might Kris want to tell her dad today if she were in conversation with him? "THANK YOU. For believing I'd be a star. And seeing in me the talents only time really let me develop." It is interesting to remember that as Kris's fame and popularity was on the rise years back while her brother Noynoy was a neophyte lawmaker, their mother's plea to the media was, "Please stop quoting Kris or me. It is time that Noynoy is given the chance to have the exposure . . . ." What would Ninoy and Cory be thinking of Kris and Noynoy today?

What mountains are there left to climb for Kris whose record of longevity on television is unsurpassed—25 years in the business, 4 years prior of endorsements, 20 years of being visible on daily television? Who has a Kris Aquino business empire that encompasses product endorsements, movie and concert production, entrepreneurial ventures? Can a Ninoy Aquino clone truly steer clear of politics in the future?

Kris says she would like to retire from the entertainment world at 45, remembering her mother's words, "Please know when to walk away." She also feels she has attained a degree of success even during her mother's lifetime, enough for Cory to remark, "My child made it and my child made it big." But knowing Kris, she will surely reinvent herself yet again.

These days, all's well in the world of Kris Aquino. **(NSRC)**

VII.
Up Close
and Personal

Cory, the Young Scholastican

Carina Tancinco Mañalac recalls that during her grade school years at St. Scholastica's College (SSC) with Cory Cojuangco (she was called Corazon or Coré then, as her older sister was known as Teré), she was not particularly close to Core, who belonged to the quiet group that included the class nerds Celine Olaguer, Lita Trinidad, and Aleli Bautista. On the other hand, everyone knew or has "heard" of Carina because she was one of the livelier members of the class.

The war years brought Carina to Boac, Marinduque, her family's hometown. Because her schooling was not disrupted unlike that of her classmates in Manila, she ended up one year ahead of the class when she returned to SSC. When the young Cory asked her why she was suddenly in a different grade, Carina's standard answer was, to the chagrin of her former classmates, "Brains! Brains! You can't stop the progress of bright girls." Cory told her "*Yabang!*" Carina remembers how she and Cory shared a love for reading. (In one of my numerous interviews with Cory, she had said she developed her clear enunciation and public speaking voice because as a young child, she loved reading out aloud from any book, to an actual or an imagined audience.)

Carina said the class knew that Cory belonged to the politically prominent and wealthy Sumulong and Cojuangco clans, but one would never guess that because her uniforms were hand-me-downs from her Ate Tere.

Cory was class valedictorian of her sixth grade class in 1943, always in close and friendly competition with Celine Olaguer who was salutatorian. In other accounts, Cory would say that if Celine did not have to return to her hometown in Bicol, Celine would be the valedictorian, rather than her. The German sisters who taught her described her as "quiet, but exceptionally bright."

Carina lost touch with Cory when they were both starting their young families—she was by then married to journalist Gabby Mañalac. She remembers seeing Cory again during martial law at Mercury Drugstore, buying medicines for the detained Ninoy. They were exchanging pleasantries but Cory quietly warned her, "Carina, don't talk to me, as I am being watched."

When their Scholastican classmates gathered for services at the college chapel after Ninoy's assassination, Carina went up to her to say, "*Ikaw na ang next president.*" Cory reacted the way she usually would to what she thought were Carina's typical outrageous remarks. "*Ayan ka na naman. Wag ka nga loka-loka.*"

Their bantering continued even after Cory became president. She teased Carina, who was her usual irreverent self: "*Oy, presidente na ako. Wag mo na ko tulak-tulakin.*" She invited her Scholastican classmates and friends to Malacañang and even succeeded in having some of them work in her administration, for they were women she trusted. A classmate, Heidi Perez Cruz, was assigned to the Goldenberg Mansion, a nineteenth-century structure that is part of the Palace complex. Celine Olaguer Sarte also found herself, forty-two years after their grade school graduation, "working next door to the conference room of President Corazon C. Aquino . . . an honor and a privilege made possible by a friendship formed in grade school." Another Scholastican, Amelia Bautista, the elder sister of another classmate, Aleli, and who had just retired from a long distinguished career as executive secretary to Procter & Gamble presidents, was with the Benigno S. Aquino, Jr. Foundation for nine years.

Cory did not succeed in inviting Carina to work, despite the President's encouraging words that she could use Carina's aggressiveness and fearlessness in government. Carina, the woman of leisure, had the lame excuse that she could not give up her siestas.

Carina saw Cory more regularly over the years because her husband, business columnist and editor Gabby Mañalac, wrote on Malacañang affairs. One particular column did not please the President, who snubbed Gabby when they would meet and complained to Carina that her husband wrote nasty things about her. Carina defended Gabby by saying he meant well because he cared about her administration. Gabby had suggested that Cory should meet with businessmen to find out their true sentiments, without her Cabinet members. Cory was not appeased with Carina's reassurance. "If that's love, forget it." It took some time before Cory and Gabby were on friendly terms again and she invited him to come to Hacienda Luisita to visit the Aquino Museum and play golf.

She wanted Carina to see the blown-up grade school photo of their SSC class proudly on exhibit at the museum. It was also then when she noticed that Gabby was carrying Carina's heavy purse and how she wished she had "trained" Ninoy to do the same for her. Carina once teased Cory about talks of suitors queuing for her attention, even naming them. And Cory, laughing this off, dismissed it as out of the question because anyway, none of them was from royalty nor nobility. During the eightieth birthday celebration of former Aquino Foundation assistant executive director Amelia Bautista ten years ago, Carina and Cory sat together at the same table. Carina casually asked Cory about a particular yellow fabric she wanted for a pantsuit. Cory said she would send it over as her costurera gets it from her source in Divisoria.

Of course, that sounded like an empty promise, but not when it is Cory doing the promising. The yellow *tela* found its way to Carina's house in Alabang, most likely delivered through Aquino's son-in-law Manolo Abellada whose parents live there, too. Carina was pleasantly surprised, but knew it was in keeping with Cory and her word of honor and known thoughtfulness. Previous to this, too, Carina had in jest complained about not buying the Cory Aquino notecards as she found them pricey—and Cory sent her some soon after. And if you know Carina, she was not just dropping broad hints.

One of the "quiet" classmates that Cory was close to was Aleli Bautista, with whom she was corresponding in the 1950s when they were already both in college, Cory in New York and Aleli in Manila in SSC. Aleli remembers attending Cory's birthday parties at the Cojuangco home on Agno Street, and games of hide and seek there till it was dark. In an earlier interview, she had said, "She was really just one of the girls, even if she was one of the richest . . . . She wasn't snobbish at all, but was kind of shy." She is amazed that despite the passage of time and the fire that razed Sandejas Street in the SSC neighborhood where the Bautista home was, her correspondence with Cory remained intact. She returned these original letters to Cory and has kept for herself only a four-paged chatty one dated July 13, 1951, when they were all in college. Aleli went to the U.S. in 1966 after finishing Music Pedagogy to become a music cataloger at the Catholic University of America until 1996.

Written from London on Claridge Hotel's stationery (Claridge's is today a five-star art deco hotel dating back to 1856), the eighteen-year-old Cory was talking about sailing to London with her parents and her sister—most likely Terry whom everyone knew was Cory's closest friend—on the Queen Elizabeth and having to get visas from different consulates for the rest of the trip that lasted until August 20 when they were scheduled to be back in Manila. On board the ship, there were games and entertainment, but they could only watch the dancing because "there were seven of us girls and only three boys."

The elegant and graceful strokes of Cory's legible penmanship were there, as she talked about summer vacation just beginning, her shopping not for herself but for the *pabilins* of her eldest sister Josephine, watching a play *Who is Sylvia* that starred Robert Fleming, admiring a Sadler's Wells Ballet performance that was superior to the American ballets she had seen, meeting Minister Romero (father of Scholastican Teresita Romero, she pointed out) in the Philippine Legation (the forerunner of today's embassy and consular offices) in London, leaving for Paris and Rome, giving the Philippine Legation's address in Rome as her forwarding address for letters she expected from her friends in Manila. There were far too many tourist spots ("sights of interest," she called them) in London to visit, but "I only hope we shall be able to sleep early tomorrow because in the past three days we have had only six hours of sleep."

She ended the letter with this, "I guess you must be back in school now. Well, I hope you're not having too much homework or anything of the sort which would mar your life in college."

The Bautista sisters, Mely and Laly, continue to be faithful Aquino supporters, regularly attending the private Masses for both Cory and Ninoy at the Manila Memorial Park.

St. Scholastica's College continues to take pride in its most outstanding alumna and the country's first woman president, Corazon Cojuangco Aquino (Grade School 1943) and honored her in March 1986, with the PAX award, the college's highest tribute for its outstanding alumnae. **(NSRC)**

Cooking for the President

Fresh *lumpia*, *pesang dalag*, chicken pork adobo, *inihaw na* spare ribs, bouillabaisse soup, *lechon kawali*, Japanese dishes, monggo soup, and fried fish—these, according to the lady who cooked for Cory Aquino, were some of the President's favorite dishes.

Such a simple menu and as the presidential tastes veer toward the *lutong bahay* (home cooking, but of a Kapampangan home, mind you), it goes without saying that tending the Malacañang kitchen was an easy task.

Yes, the president was the easiest to cook for, swore the former president's caterer, Linda Diaz who, for security reasons, we could not call by her real name during the time of the interview.

President Cory was easy to please, but what made running the kitchen at Malacañang complicated and almost nerve-wracking was the thought of who would be eating with her.

President Cory insisted that what she ate, the rest of her staff must also eat. Of course, out of sheer solicitousness, Linda gave the president an extra special dish, like pasta with blue cheese or a soufflé or even a Caesar's salad, which the regular P40 per head buffet budget could not cover.

Anyway, to cope with the pressure and the demands, Linda had built a second, though much smaller kitchen, in the hospital canteen she ran, which was off-limits to everyone except to her and her three most trusted assistants. Linda's most trying hours were from eight to eleven each morning, when she sweats out in time for her noonday deadline, often losing her temper as zero hour approached.

The actual cooking for seventy-five, even the vegetarian portions for presidential assistant Flerida Ruth Romero, is not nearly as difficult for Linda, as transforming herself from kitchen queen to smiling, fresh-looking hostess who must serve her important wards. But the toughest part is still to come: ensuring that the President's meal was always within sight and negotiating the distance from the university belt to Malacañang—just a few traffic stops away, but that stretch was among the most congested in Manila.

For security reasons, Linda did not personally serve the President in her private dining room where she ate with her daughter and personal secretary, Ballsy, and two nieces on the Guesthouse staff, Marisse Cojuangco Reyes and Gina Lopa Bautista. Linda would give the prepared portions a final check before official food taster Jimmy Castro does his job. Boyish and still trim despite all the tasting he had to do, Jimmy would apologetically perform his routine once more, even with this meal from a trusted source. Only then was the meal ready to be delivered upstairs where a waiter and two reliable maids from the Aquino household would serve it. To serve the meal piping hot, it was normally placed on a large hot plate until the President was ready to eat.

Linda did not always have to remain as nameless and faceless as this.

In fact, a few months after her Guesthouse designation, the *Los Angeles Times* succeeded in interviewing and photographing her, but only after patiently waiting it out at the Manila Hotel for weeks. Tighter security measures have altered all that—so much so that no one could interview Linda without presidential approval and only after vowing to comply with presidential security insistence on no photographs and no revelation of Linda's true identity. Linda says that these may have become mandatory because during the August 28 coup, a tabloid wondered about the easy access to her food-bearing vehicle, with its make and plate number accurately described.

Though Linda worked on a two-month menu cycle which she submits to the Appointments Office, she could not always remain faithful to it because the fresh ingredients needed were not always available in the market. It was Ballsy who chooses the more special menu, presumably a notch or so higher than P40 per head, for her mother's lunch meetings or any other special meetings in Malacañang. An added attraction at such meals, her on-and-off Monday lunch meetings with Palace executives, for instance—as if breaking bread with the chief executive were not distinct privilege enough—were the chocolates or fresh fruits she shared with the group which were usually presents for her as she was known to love both. Meriendas were not served at the Guesthouse, though a standard drink for visiting diplomats was Linda's blended mango juice, a trade secret she learned from the Hyatt.

Of course, Cory was often quick with praises. She would compliment Linda on how her Japanese dishes got better each time, and would express girlish delight whenever she noticed a new dish on the caterer's growing repertoire. This had motivated Linda to further her knowledge by taking a hotel and restaurant management course at the University of the Philippines and additional cooking courses with culinary wizards Sylvia Reynoso, Grace Mercado, and Salud de Castro, under whom the Marcos daughters took lessons prior to their respective marriages. She even read up on low-calorie cooking, in an attempt at healthier meals. She was so motivated to excel that even when she choose to unwind by frequenting her favorite restaurant, like Gasparelli in the Makati Greenbelt area, she was always watching out for new ways of improving her art.

Linda knew what a thankless job hers often was, especially on days when she was once more reminded that it was not possible to please everyone. For harder to please were some of the other individuals who partake of her Guesthouse buffet daily, but then she and these dissatisfied others were often reminded that Linda's primary responsibility was to prepare meals for the President and everyone else was *sabit lang* (incidental).

While Linda's stature in the catering world has been boosted because of her presidential link, there were others who questioned her credentials. The question was often whispered about: What does the president value more, one's loyalty or one's cooking ability? The answer is obvious.

In the first place, even in her personal choice of a caterer for the Guesthouse, President Cory appeared to have applied the very same yardstick she was known to use in selecting members of her official family. Competence, trustworthiness, and loyalty of the tried-and-tested variety, preferably manifested from as far back as Ninoy Aquino's years in detention.

Linda has every reason to flaunt all those qualities. Her family hails from Tarlac, her father had been a long-time *katiwala* (overseer) of Don Benigno Aquino Sr., and she herself landed a first job right after college as secretary to Esting Teopaco, husband of the president's younger sister Passy, in the family-owned Tarlac Development Corporation, the sister company of the Central Azucarera de Tarlac. She was always on loan to wonderboy Ninoy during campaign season.

Having been known to the Aquinos as a child, Linda was offered by Ninoy, in typical patriarchal fashion, a personal scholarship in nursing school so she could be a family nurse of the Aquinos. The offer was declined, because Linda's father said he could finance his daughter's college years.

In the sixties, Linda joined the Jose Cojuangco & Sons as purchasing executive, a job she held until she opted for early retirement after twenty years of service in 1980. It was during this period when she met her husband, also a Cojuangco trusted employee.

Even during Linda's early years as struggling entrepreneur and operator of a 24-hour hospital canteen serving several thousands a day, she did not lose touch with the Cojuangco and Aquino clans. During her trips to the U.S., she would hand carry things for Ninoy. It was she and his own personal secretary whom Ninoy wrote to please discreetly claim his two pieces of unaccompanied luggage prior to the August homecoming and to leave these as discreetly in the custody of Terry Lopa, another sister of the president. With much sadness, Linda recalls the thousands of sandwiches she prepared for the original August 7 homecoming and then all those yellow ribbons of the 21st. Though Linda was frequently sought to prepare meals for those endless meetings of opposition groups in the anti-dictatorship struggle (the convenors and the PDP-Laban were regular *suki* for whom she had great sympathy and did not mind cooking her low-budget best for), she could not confine herself to her pots and pans. She dutifully joined the rallies and even became one of her Ate Cory's crusaders. So visible was she then that she proudly landed in one of the photographs in the People Power book edited by Monina Mercado, her role in the struggle properly documented.

During the early days of the Aquino administration, while they were still temporarily camping out at the Cojuangco Building in Makati, Linda was asked to see the President. To her surprise, she was requested to begin lunches for the president and the forty members of her staff. And though times seemed to have so drastically changed for the underdog opposition, the budget still stuck at P20 per head. But the distinct honor of being summoned for such a task remotely connected to nation-building made working on a limited budget a pleasure. Linda continued to provide meals even when the staff moved to the Guesthouse, her first difficult task having been the preparation of its neglected and unused kitchen for the transfer of the official family two days hence. The boxed lunches and plastic flatware continued to be delivered day after day, for cooking could not be done in the Guesthouse kitchen, which was inadequately built for institutional cooking. But Linda grew less and less comfortable about having the head of the state and even former Executive Secretary Joker Arroyo, she breathlessly adds, demonstrating how well aware she was of Guesthouse hierarchy, struggle with the plastic spoons and forks which require fragile handling. Three major changes occurred as the Guesthouse occupants settled down—the President was finally given her own private dining area adjoining her office upstairs; boxed lunches and the chafing dishes provided in the first floor area were replaced with a more gracious buffet-style dining; and, the budget increased to P40 and now covered a soup, two main dishes, rice, dessert, coffee, and tea.

Once, a newly perfected meat loaf dish which Linda prepared in her own kitchen seemed to have given twenty-three of seventy clients a stomachache the next day. The president liked it so much that she even sent some home for Kris to taste. To date, she has not been able to trace the cause of this, even going to the supermarket where she bought the ground beef. She wrote out personal letters of apology to each of the twenty-three persons so affected and was greatly reassured when the President told her through Ballsy that something else must have caused the stomach upset.

It was a gentle reminder that she gets from the president when the feedback was not glowing, as when she reminded Linda that she seemed to have had, for three successive days now, soups with cornstarch.

Busy and for the most part flustered as she was, she has never considered buying any cooked item from any source, for she thought it risky to do so. That she must be able to continue to vouch for what she cooked is almost the credo of this lady. She has no kitchen secrets to share apart from swearing by fresh meat from Aranez and Garcia's on E. Rodriguez, Golden Fry cooking oil, corn oil for tempura, Knorr seasoning, Golden Swan soy sauce, and Cloverbloom butter. And the surprising revelation from someone as gifted in the kitchen as she is, "You can consider me bookish, for I believe in following the recipe to the letter. I believe that cooking is an exact science."

Oh, Linda nearly forgot, the president enjoyed dishes that need the many different kinds of Filipino *sawsawan* (condiments), *suka* (vinegar), and *toyo* (soy sauce) especially. **(NSRC)**

Recipes of the Smart and Famous

During the early years of Cory Cojuangco's marriage to the politician Ninoy Aquino, it did not faze her at all that all the cooking she knew was learned while she had to cope as a student in the States. There, she and her sister Terry enjoyed meals prepared by their mother, who stayed to keep watch over them for three years. Over the holidays they, as thoughtful guests, would help out in the kitchen at an aunt's place. The well-loved traditional Filipino staple was one that had to be mastered, if only to assuage the longing for Filipino food.

There was no pressing need to cook while her husband began his colorful career as the wonder boy of Philippine politics, as mayor of Concepcion, Tarlac. From the house next door where Ninoy's mother lived came regular rations made even more special because of Ninoy's aunt's fresh lumpia of green papaya lavishly sprinkled with peanuts, and another favorite of Ninoy's, nilagang manok. And when the young couple had to entertain guests, it was easy to order the well-known tocino and pancit canton from the town's carinderia.

Even then, Cory slowly became initiated into the strange world of politics, becoming fully aware of her husband's way with people and his special way with words. One day, one of the town's women went up to Cory and volunteered to show this inexperienced cook, apparently as she had promised the young mayor, how to prepare the corned beef that he had told her he loved so much. Cory thought it was so kind of this woman to spend the time with her, until she realized there was nothing new to be learned, for it was sautéed corned beef, straight from the can. "Leave it to Ninoy's politicking to have complimented that woman on her corned beef!" Cory laughed.

In Manila, the young couple frequented the popular Chinese restaurant in Binondo, SeeKee, for its crabs and kutsay, Panciteria China for the corn soup, and Carvajal of the good old days when a respectable meal could be had for P6, Cory remembered. That was not an exaggeration, for Ninoy's monthly salary then as a public servant was P200. The Aquino children fondly remember what a treat it was to be eating out, something they preferred over the movies that followed after the meal, which they could not stay awake for.

Callos, as Cory would cook it, is best eaten the following day.

Hong Kong was a place Cory and Ninoy associated with good food rather than shopping. They frequented Hong Kong for the Shanghai hairy crabs which make their yearly appearance in October, and at all other times for the Peking Duck, which Ninoy loved, excessive fat content and all. The last time they made a food trip to Hong Kong was in 1981, when they were already based in Boston. They had to fly to Tokyo for a wedding and could not resist making the side trip. This was the first for them since 1972, and it was difficult getting used to the difference in restaurant prices, nine years after. It was during the martial law years, when Ninoy was incarcerated, that they viewed cooking differently, an art to be mastered, an art that took one's mind off the era's harsh realities. She, together with other spouses similarly situated, like Pacita Roces, Cecile Mitra, and Marilou Velez, took Chinese cooking and a series of cooking lessons with Maur Aquino-Lichauco, Ninoy's sister and well-known cooking whiz.

When Ninoy was detained at Bonifacio, Cory and her children were allowed bonus visits during special occasions.

These lessons served Cory well, for she felt confident about preparing special party dishes, heeding well Maur's advice never to substitute the specified ingredients for anything healthier or more economical.

Even while under detention, Ninoy did not have any particular favorites. He could eat anything and everything quite heartily, paying little attention to any dietary restrictions. And because Cory had provided him with a small refrigerator, he could store his special food requests—boiled chicken and lettuce for him to make sandwiches with; ready waffle mixes which he surprised his children with during their Sunday visits, something he became quite adept at whipping up on the waffle maker he asked for; cans of Libby's corned beef; and spicy sardines in oil or tomato sauce. Since Ninoy loved onions, relish, and mayonnaise, he kept a generous supply of these. "I guess cooking helped him pass the time away," Cory remarked.

The Aquinos celebrated birthdays and all other special occasions provided a good excuse for bonus visits with Ninoy in Bonifacio, if permission from higher authorities was granted. Lechon was always available and other special dishes which would not spoil easily in the amphitheater, the usual venue for those milestones. Once, Maur Lichauco, knowing of her brother's weakness for Japanese fare, sent Ninoy and company all the ingredients for instant sukiyaki that even a non-cook should have no problems with. It was successful, except for the fact that all the ingredients were tossed in exactly as they were received, even those carefully and neatly held together by rubber bands.

During their three-year stay in Boston, with their Newton home never empty of guests who came and went, Cory and her daughters found themselves forever busy in the kitchen. The standing rule was to wash one's own plate, which even Ninoy did, but that did not hold when there was company. Suddenly, there were far too many plates to wash. There was the dependable dishwasher, but unfortunately Cory only allowed her goblets to be washed manually, to the dismay of both Ballsy and Pinky. But the killer chore of all was having to wash the greasy and grimy pots and pans. Ninoy helped the situation somehow by taking care of preparing his own coffee.

It was because of the exigencies of living—and entertaining—in Boston that Cory went on to experiment rather successfully with quiches, Peking Duck (this was the easiest for her because of the dry Boston air and her convection oven), chicken and liver pate, (after discovering a use for the bounty of apples they had from an apple-picking trip,) and a survival meal of Swedish meatballs (especially concocted for the time when the Cojuangcos came en masse to Boston for the surgery of matriarch Doña Metring and there were twenty-one of them in the Aquino home in Newton).

It was not long before Cory struck entertaining patterns to live by. Since their family was not big on breakfasts, it was not a mere polite question when they asked their guests, "What would you like for breakfast?" Guests were pressed to elaborate more than the expected, "Anything that you yourselves had," because that meant absolutely no breakfast. Cory learned to stock up on frozen fresh juices and a variety of breakfasts in the pantry, that she received the highest compliment from the late senator Lorenzo Tañada who remarked on the different breakfasts she served each morning. American dinner guests were not as difficult to please, for they are accustomed to a one-dish meal along with a soup and a salad. Filipino guests, accustomed to a buffet, were the ones who tried and taxed her culinary know-how. A real treat for Cory and the kids was eating out, even just at McDonald's.

Cory had fond memories of Ninoy's favorites, both inexpensive items there—boiled corned beef served with mustard, horseradish, boiled potatoes, and boiled cabbage which is served as a one-dish meal, and also delicious sandwich filling for his brown bag lunches at Harvard—as well as the more expensive Maine lobsters, which Ninoy personally bought whenever there was company. Ninoy loved lobsters and bargains, so he enjoyed buying those at special prices. Lobsters with uneven claws (call them seconds or irregulars, but they were no less alive nor delicious than "normal" ones) were his favorite buys and so were lobster heads that no one cared for. From these heads, Cory would remove all the red stuff and sauté them in garlic and butter to make a mock *taba ng talangka*. This was a most painstaking process, almost physically cruel in the difficult Boston winters, that only those who contributed to the production process were privileged to savor the delicacy.

Ninoy could not resist all the other bargains he saw along the way, including a tall can of cat food for 25 cents. He didn't care that the family didn't even have a cat. He simply instructed them to look for someone with a cat that they could give this to.

The recipes Cory had chosen as her husband's favorites were those she had recorded in longhand in a cheery looking red checkered recipe book. She decided she needed to keep Maur's recipes and all others she had tried and tested, which were written on pieces of paper found here and there, when life began to normalize in Boston. Peking Duck is much too easy for her she had not even bothered to include it in this growing collection of favorite recipes. So easy that for Ninoy's last birthday, she prepared six ducks for roasting.

What she had in the book was the recipe for po-ping or Mandarin pancakes, the thin pancake one uses to wrap the Peking duck with, copied from a *Time-Life* cookbook. The ink had somewhat faded and when she had started to write in additional favorites after stopping for many years, she laughed at how much her handwriting had changed and became bigger and less studied after the presidency. Her latest entries, which sounded special and yet easy enough to do, were from some back issues of *FOOD* and an Assumption cookbook.

Cory was thoughtful about specifying that recipes of her choice were not her original ones, but borrowed from two individuals. Noodles with mushroom sauce was a Sue Zalamea recipe, a dish sent to Ninoy during detention which he particularly enjoyed. Callos and food for the gods were recipes of Maur Aquino-Lichauco. The third recipe had been especially handy for all the gift-giving that Ninoy the politician had had to do.

"You'd think *na napakagaling ko*," she chuckled. **(NSRC)**

FOOD FOR THE GODS

1/2 pound butter, softened

1/2 cup white sugar

1/2 cup brown sugar, firmly packed

2 whole eggs

2 tablespoons honey

1 cup flour

1 teaspoon baking soda

1/4 teaspoon salt

1 can broken (not chopped) walnuts

1 box dates, chopped coarsely

- Cream together butter, white sugar, brown sugar, eggs, and honey. Mix together flour, baking soda, and salt.
- Add dry ingredients to butter mixture. Stir in walnuts and dates.
- Spread in a well-greased 8 x 12-inch rectangular pan lined with wax paper. Sprinkle with brown sugar and bake at 350°F for 10 minutes, then 300°F for 40 minutes or until baked.

NOODLES WITH MUSHROOM SOUP

water

salt

sesame oil

fresh egg noodles

cornstarch mixture

1 tablespoon sugar

pepper

soy sauce (to taste)

1 head garlic, cut into small pieces

1/2 cup onions, diced

1 piece ginger

1 cup pork, cut into small cubes, mixed with cornstarch

2 tablespoons shrimps, cut into small pieces

1 piece bamboo shoot, cut into cubes

3 pieces mushrooms, cut into cubes

1 can of mushroom sauce

- Boil water, add salt and oil. Put egg noodles and allow to boil until noodles are cooked. Run cold water over the noodles and put the noodles in a strainer until cooled. Fry cooled noodles in hot pan with a little oil.
- Prepare the cornstarch mixture by mixing the cornstarch, sugar, pepper, and soy sauce.
- To prepare sauce, sauté garlic and onions in oil. Add the ginger, pork, shrimps, bamboo shoots, mushrooms, mushroom sauce, and soy sauce and cornstarch mixture.
- Pour sauce over noodles and serve.

CALLOS

2 kilos tripe	siling labuyo
1 kilo beef pata	peppercorns
1 kilo pork hocks	1 tablespoon garlic
vinegar	3 cups onions
calamansi	2 cups or 1/3 kilo ham (diced thinly)
water	3 pieces chorizo
1 bunch of leeks	2 pieces red bell peppers (diced)
12 leaves, parsley	4 1/2 cups tomato sauce
1 1/2 kilos carrots	1 1/2 cups broth
5 tomatoes (whole)	2 1/2 cups chick peas
1/2 cup white wine	salt
1/4 cup rum	pepper
1 teaspoon paprika	sugar
1/2 cup olive oil	

- Clean the tripe, beef pata, and pork hocks thoroughly using vinegar and calamansi. Brush and rinse thoroughly till all the slime and dirt are removed.
- Boil the meats together in a pot of water. Add the leeks, parsely, carrots, tomatoes, white wine, rum, paprika, and olive oil.
- Put the siling labuyo and the peppercorns in a piece of cheese cloth. Dip the cheesecloth into the pot. Cook over high fire until the mixture boils. Then allow to simmer until the meats are soft. Leave the mixture overnight. Cover the casserole tightly with cheesecloth.
- The following day, sauté garlic and onions in olive oil. Add ham and chorizos, bell peppers, and the carrots boiled with the meats the previous day. Then add the tomato sauce, broth, and chick peas. Simmer for 30 minutes. Add salt, pepper, sugar, and fresh siling labuyo. This dish is best eaten the following day.

Celebrating Christmas, Aquino Style

What was a typical Christmas like for an atypical family like Ninoy and Cory Aquino's family? What were the special traditions the children grew up with? How have celebrations remained constant through the inconstant circumstances of their lives?

In the family home on 25 Times Street in Quezon City, the enduring and unforgettable memories of Christmas past brim over. And flowing with these Christmas reminiscences are family stories and the typical sibling bantering, highlighting the reality that, for all that's admirable and awe-inspiring about the Aquino family, they bear many heartwarming faces that ordinary mortals recognize and can relate to.

When President Cory was still around, the festivities officially began in early December with a party for the family's personal staff. The party was held in the large garden that Ballsy and Pinky share in Greenmeadows Subdivision, Quezon City, where their houses stand back to back in the same compound. (Viel lives a few streets away, within walking distance, while Kris lives four villages away in one of the Valle Verde subdivisions.) This tradition was inspired by the annual party of the Presidential Security Guards that Cory always attended during her Malacañang years. And when it turned into a family practice, Cory would always be the first one to arrive and the last one to leave.

Viel Aquino Dee is not exaggerating when she says the Aquinos' clannish Christmas is replete with eating—nothing really new or different in the context of Christmas in the

Philippines. And how can it be otherwise with the culinary talent in their midst, their aunt Maur Aquino Lichauco?

December 24, Christmas Eve, is when the entire Aquino clan comes together for an early Christmas reunion at lunchtime. The date also happens to be the death anniversary of Ninoy's mother, Aurora Aquino, and Ninoy's brother Paul likes to think that his mother chose that day to die so that the clan would have a mandatory gathering each Christmas. Ninoy's siblings would take turns hosting the lunchtime reunion.

After lunch, the Cojuangco Aquinos start to get ready for their Christmas Eve dinner on Times Street. Corazon Cojuangco Aquino, at the helm of the celebration, would prepare the staple comfort food: fresh corned beef with cabbage and spaghetti with generously sized meatballs. There would also be her legendary pâté and caviar pies, with one that had no onions, made especially for Kris. Ballsy would bring roast turkey, based on the family recipe of Caridad Cruz, the mother of her husband Eldon. Ballsy's cook had mastered the art of preparing this famous roast. Since Kris had discovered the Manila source of Cebu lechon she always brought this. Viel and Pinky proudly boast: "And we just bring our appetites!"

The fresh corned beef was Ninoy's favorite. Kris says she got tired of it while in Boston so that, until today, she goes for the canned variety. But the rest of the Aquinos apparently don't share Kris's preference. There was a time when Cory, wanting to vary her Christmas spread, decided to drop the fresh corned beef. What loud howls of complaint she received, not only from her grandchildren, but also from the special guests the Aquinos have had during the years after the presidency—the Jesuit priests Catalino Arevalo, Nemesio Que, and the twenty or so scholastics from the Loyola House of Studies in the Ateneo campus. These scholastics, by the way, make the event doubly special with their caroling, the recollection of which still makes Ballsy misty-eyed.

Father Arevalo—or Father Rev, as the longtime family friend and spiritual adviser is affectionately referred to by the Aquino children—literally walked into their lives when they needed him most, moments after the news of their father's assassination broke in the international media. The Aquinos were living in the capital city of Boston, Massachusetts, U.S.A., when they heard the news. Pinky remembers their mother saying how much she wished there was a priest in their midst right then, so that they could have a Mass for the dead. Then the doorbell rang. It was the Jesuit priest at the door, wanting to console and be of assistance. He happened to be in Boston College, right across the street from the Aquino home, at the time.

Since then, year after year, Father Rev has been the constant celebrator of the Masses for Ninoy's family—on August 21, Ninoy's death anniversary; November 27, Ninoy's birthday; and December 24, Christmas Eve. (This is separate from the lunchtime Mass that the bigger Aquino clan holds to commemorate the death anniversary of Aurora Aquino.) Once, when the Jesuit fell ill, Cory told him: "Father, you have to outlive me, because you are going to give the homily when I die." When Cory died, Father Rev found that homily his most challenging assignment. He had to consult a Carmelite nun, and up to the eleventh hour, he couldn't do it. But it turned out to be a well-remembered homily, one that many consider a masterpiece.

Today, Pinky likes to tease Father Rev: "Aren't you sorry you rang that doorbell? You walked in twenty-six years ago and have not been able to walk out."

Usually also in attendance at the December 24 dinner are Maur and Esting Lichauco, and Viel's parents-in-law, Ambassador and Mrs. Howard Dee, who were very close to Cory. Howard Dee, former ambassador to the Vatican, is on the board of the Benigno S. Aquino Jr. Foundation. His son, Dodo, Viel's husband, is the only Dee child in the country.

This Times Street celebration begins with Holy Mass at 6 p.m. Kris says that, given her notoriety in the family for tardiness, the information and reminder given by her mom, who was known for her strict punctuality, was 5 p.m., a full hour before. So she used to kid her mom, asking if the time given her for that event and for all other appointments were for real, or just meant for Kris, to allow her lead time.

It was not the traditional midnight *noche buena,* but an early dinner, so that by 10 p.m., the party was over. This was also to allow Jesuits to join their community for the midnight Mass. The Aquino children would also then be free to join the family gatherings of their husbands. Cory was always mindful of not unfairly monopolizing her children's families.

After the guests leave—but before the family members disperse—Cory, her five children and their spouses, and the eight grandchildren have to have their mandatory family photo. The special backdrop is the one-of-a-kind Christmas tree and décor set up each year by Tami Filler Leung of Tamilee Decors, which specializes in themed Christmas ornaments for export to the U.S. and the United Kingdom. Year after year since 1992, Tami had been creating this for President Cory as a token of her appreciation for the support and encouragement Tami received when her export business was in its infancy. As an added thoughtful gesture, Tamilee takes care of the usual headache of dismantling and packing away the tree and the décor, and not just to be recycled for the Aquino's next Christmas, for a new look is always conjured up and fashioned.

The next day, on Christmas Day itself, the family goes to the Cojuangco clan reunion at the former residence of Don Pepe and Doña Metring Cojuangco, Cory's parents. The sprawling residence on Palm Avenue, just off the Santuario de San Antonio Parish Church and the Dasmariñas Village gate, is actually part of South Forbes. The Cojuangco reunion, which covers lunch and *merienda,* and could precariously run close to dinnertime, is as grand and boisterous as the reunion on the Aquino side. It used to be organized by Cory's youngest sister, Passy Teopaco, until it became unmanageable with the growth of the clan to about a hundred members, and a more equitable rotating system had to be adopted.

If truth be told, there has not really been a typical Christmas for the family. Noynoy categorizes and chronicles Christmas celebrations through the different venues and stages of their lives: Times Street, Fort Bonifacio, Boston, Arlegui, Times Street, and now, most likely, Greenmeadows? **(NSRC)**

When Eldon Met Ballsy

The very first time Eldon Cruz met Ballsy Aquino at her classmate's party, she was wearing a yellow printed top, long before yellow became the color of our campaign for democracy. Or was that when he first took notice of her? Ballsy vaguely remembers the occasion but recalls that they first met at a party of the daughter of Don Chino Roces. He met her again when he was invited to speak on the money market in a career forum at the Assumption Convent where Ballsy was a college senior. She did not attend the session, but only saw him after the talk because Eldon's friend who was with him was dating her groupmate. It was not until they were both working as money traders at Yuchengco companies (he at the IFC Money Market, she with the Phil Pacific subsidiary) that they began to seriously date. Their first date was on October 14, 1976.

When he told his parents whom he was wooing, his father, Regino Cruz, an engineer specializing in sugar technology, and his mother Caridad Concepcion tried to discourage him by saying the family was much too wealthy and political for their standards. But he was young and in love and no such talk could lead him to any change of heart.

Eldon's father knew the Cojuangco family because he had worked at Hacienda Luisita before moving on to other sugar centrals. This was because Don Pepe Cojuangco, Ballsy's maternal grandfather, had told him, after years of employment at Luisita, that the company setup did not allow much room for upward mobility for managers so it was advisable that he move to other companies. His father's career brought the family of four boys and an only girl (with unusual first names like his, Eldon says because of their common surname—Loreli, Alec, Giselo, Nonilo) to Cebu and Silay.

When his parents met Ballsy, they understood why their son had been so smitten. Ballsy was so simple, so down to earth, so charming.

When the Aquinos left for the U.S. in haste for Ninoy's heart surgery, Ballsy and Eldon did not have time for a proper goodbye. Eldon remembers that when he was returning from a business trip to Cagayan de Oro, his travel companion and colleague teased him about a plane that was flying out of the airport as their own plane was taxiing down. That was Ballsy leaving, he jested.

It turned out not to be an entirely false joke for upon his arrival, the Aquinos's longtime family driver, Teody, came to him with a letter from Ballsy explaining the unexpected family trip. And there was Eldon, terribly disappointed about the abrupt parting, as he was even ready with the traditional Cagayan de Oro ham as *pasalubong* for the Aquinos.

Eldon had the rare privilege as visiting non-family member in the Aquino home in Newton, Massachusetts to see Ninoy and Cory go through everyday living. He lived in the basement of the house. He visited for six weeks in 1980 and then for about a month in 1982. He was humbled seeing Cory cleaning the bathrooms in the house and admired how she could whip up breakfast for Ninoy's sudden guests of forty showing up at the door. The standard household joke was sociable Ninoy gently persuading friends and all to come to their home to stay or for a meal, lest "*Magagalit si Cory.*"

Eldon never had a one-on-one with Ninoy, who also never asked him any leading questions that would make him uneasy. Awed by Ninoy's intelligence, he was content to drive Ninoy to Harvard or be in the company of his continuous stream of visitors from an official from the Sultanate of Sulu to the late Senator Francisco "Soc" Rodrigo, a fellow freedom fighter. During that car ride, he remembers them belting out old sentimental Filipino songs.

The closest he got to receiving advice from his future father-in-law about a relationship with a woman was when he was driving and Ballsy argued with him about the correct route to take. Both of them were convinced they were right and when Eldon was proven right, Ninoy consoled him by saying, "*Ganyan talaga ang mga babae. Mahirap . . . .*"

Eldon thought of moving to the U.S. to be closer to Ballsy. He was in fact seriously considering working abroad. He was young, reckless and adventurous, and would do anything in the name of love. He "sold" ("returned" is the more accurate term, he corrects himself) his car back to his father in June 1980 so he would have enough cash for the U.S. trip.

Ninoy knew of Ballsy and Eldon's plan to marry in 1983. And despite Ninoy's assassination on August 21 of that year, Cory agreed that the wedding should push through, though Eldon does not forget that on the day of the wedding on December 10, Cory's asthma attacks recurred.

During the years of the rallies and the Cory Aquino campaign for the 1986 presidential elections, Eldon was the only son-in-law. He was part of Cory's close-in group, in lieu of Ballsy who was home with their first child. Eldon's job was to ensure Cory had everything she needed. On windy days when Cory was seated on stage wearing a skirt, his job was to pin the skirt to her seat so that it would not be blown by the wind. He cannot live down the one instance when she stood up and realized she was still pinned down. There was also the memorable visit to Aklan when their accommodations meant sleeping in a hospital's operating room.

What is it like being a presidential in-law? In the early years of marriage and during the Cory presidency, Eldon was harshly criticized for having nothing to his name except his links to the powers that be. There were rumors of land grabbing, all because he was seen playing golf with then Agrarian Reform Secretary Popoy Juico. He was so disturbed that he came close to resigning and was ready to accept a job in Hong Kong. He was talked out of it with the reminder that that was his share of sacrifices for the country, certainly not much, considering what his in-laws have had to go through. Today, he is managing director of the Tranzen Group, Inc.

He has learned to cope with the limelight even now that he is a presidential in-law twice over. Nothing has changed in his relationship with his brother-in-law now living in Malacañang, but "of course, I accord him the respect his office commands." He says public opinion is harsher and more immediate with social media but one just has to be circumspect about one's behavior, conscious about preserving the family name and legacy. Remembering that often told anecdote about the first Aquino grandson, Jiggy, asking his Lola Cory about candies in a jar before taking the liberty of helping himself to some, "*Sa gobyerno ba ito or sa atin?*" PNoy is lucky, he says, in having four first ladies.

Now he can joke that they, the in-laws, are not the focus nor the sought-after celebrities anyway, but their spouses. Age tempers you, he says. "Had I collected a peso each for every photo I had been asked to take (of an Aquino with a starstruck fan), I'd be rich." The much publicized incident on the Cebu-bound Cebu Pacific plane involving Chinese tourists and

Eldon initially portrayed him as the aggressor until Ballsy herself clarified what happened. Eldon explains that that was impossible because he is so fearful of plane rides that he clutches a rosary in prayer for the duration of every trip. Admittedly, Eldon concedes that Ballsy is the best person to speak on the matter because she, like her mother, is always calm and unruffled.

After thirty-two years of marriage, Eldon has learned to understand the intricacies of politics, though it is outweighed by sadness because of the circumstances the family underwent. More importantly, Eldon says the girl he married has not changed. She has remained the down-to-earth woman in the yellow printed dress. Describing her as a typical Cojuangco rather than an Aquino, he explains that a Cojuangco has to be drawn out, to be persuaded to speak. During Cojuangco clan reunions, no one wants to emcee the program. In complete contrast, during Aquino gatherings, there is a surfeit of superstars who take to the center stage like fish to water. But he admires both branches of the family for not flaunting neither wealth nor power.

These days too, even when they have the resources, Ballsy who still does unbelievably detailed and meticulous household accounting though not required of her, cannot be convinced to travel business class, considering it a needless luxury.

It is not so easy planning trips for their family of four as both sons are now grown and employed. Still, Baguio is a favorite refuge with the simple joys of quiet and a massage at the Baguio Country Club and John Hay. Those short trips, especially trips out of the country, are necessary breaks for them, since they do not need their personal security overseas. Not that they have anything to complain about their assigned security who have been professional in their jobs.

They enjoy their private family gatherings on Sundays which Ballsy, Pinky, and Viel take turns hosting in their homes. (Kris is usually busy working on weekends.) When it is PNoy's turn and he has the time to host, it would usually be in a restaurant. And like any typical family, they eat and gossip and mercilessly tease one another.

Eldon joins the family countdown of 375 days (at the time of the interview) until their living in a glass house will cease. Or will it, really? (NSRC)

Manolo Abellada: Aquino Son-in-law

Manolo Abellada never dreamt he would actually meet the senator he had always idolized even when he was still in high school. But there he was, one of a new batch of youthful recruits of IBM—which included Ninoy Aquino's second daughter Pinky—invited to a family lunch gathering at the Aquino home. Manolo just sat there, mesmerized and enthralled, listening to the senator. For what conversation did the charismatic senator not dominate even without trying?

Manolo thought he was a mere passive participant but learned later from Pinky that Ninoy had teased her, "*Yung singkit na' yun, may gusto sa'yo.*" Pinky and Manolo met in 1979 when both were systems engineers at IBM. Pinky was an economics graduate from UP, while Manolo was a business management graduate from the Ateneo.

Both were bright young stars at the company and were part of an elite group sent to Hong Kong for more intensive training, along with other colleagues from different countries. He concedes though that while he and his friends were enjoying all that the city offered, Pinky was definitely more diligent and belonged to the top quartile of the batch. She was already the charmer, the talkative, and intelligent Pinky we know today.

Theirs was to be a long-distance relationship, one nurtured through a faithful exchange of letters. Pinky was working in the U.S. with IBM in Boston while the family was living in Newton. Pinky would be teased about the constant stream of letters and postcards from the

Philippines, with Ninoy probably reading the postcards and announcing to Pinky, the mail from "Abasolo," a name he playfully made up for Manolo.

When the family returned to Manila in 1983, Ninoy asked that Pinky remain in the U.S. to continue on with her job, saying that he had sacrificed so much for his daughter's career to come true. Pinky returned to Manila in December 1984.

"I'm not a public person and as far as socials are concerned, you do have choices." Often, Manolo says, his presence does not make a big difference. He also points out that he does not have a Jekyll/Hyde persona, so that what you see is what you get. He now enjoys slowing down ("I'm less resilient now"), taking things easy, being closer to the children even as he laughs that they are at an age when they have their own schedules. At home, he is the maintenance go-to person, attending to his family's frequent network complaints. At work, he is president of PMSI, a company engaged in satellite TV.

He would like to spend more time in their country home in Caliraya, Laguna which is not too far from the city and where the air is always cool. It brings him back to his youthful dream of being a farmer and his love for animals. That kind of quiet life is something his kids do not as yet appreciate, he laughs.

Although he has always known Cory Aquino to be a caring person and someone who always made him feel comfortable, Manolo was still tense and awkward that day in September 1985 when he formally asked for Pinky's hand in marriage. Cory, always practical, suggested a morning wedding rather than the evening wedding Manolo had always dreamt of. He managed to convince her about an evening event.

Their two children, Miguel and Nina, both hold corporate jobs today. And Miguel is engaged to be married to Stephanie Yap. It gives their father so much pride to see them as people for others, conscious about protecting the family name and integrity, and not overly concerned about materialism. Of what use is wealth if one is neither happy nor enjoying peace? He wishes for them the same marital joys he has experienced with Pinky, who has told them, "I love your dad more deeply now because as a youth you feel your love is immeasurable. But through the years, it becomes a deeper kind of love, a love that has withstood so many trials."

Manolo's own mother pays Pinky the highest tribute when she reminds her son to always be thankful for life's blessings and for his wife, "the gift of the Lord."

The bond among these family members who have lived through so much pain and joy is strong and enduring. He describes Ballsy as the very compassionate *ate*; Viel as shy, soft-spoken, and amiable; and Kris as the admirable workaholic who is passionate and professional about her work. PNoy has drawn the respect of the immediate family members for maintaining his ground on issues he feels strongly about. He remains focused, is not easily swayed, does not want to be sidetracked, and refuses to compromise. It is, after all, the general welfare of the citizenry that he is most concerned about.

At family gatherings—with everyone in attendance, they are all of sixteen—hosted in the Abellada home, he and PNoy usually browse through Manolo's music and video collection. They share a love for music of the seventies and eighties.

What does he remember best about Cory Aquino? They had the rare opportunity to live with her in Arlegui as a newly married couple, the way Ballsy and Eldon, and Viel and Dodo did, too. Despite a life marked by many sacrifices, there was no regret or bitterness to be sensed. President Cory was never undignified, always motherly and concerned about members of her family. She often engaged Eldon and Manolo in after-dinner conversations.

When it was Cory's turn to live with Ballsy in the last months of her life, it was her family's turn to dote on her. She was prevailed upon to move from her Times Street residence to Ballsy's home when her chemotherapy began in March 2008. Her daughters took turns sleeping with her.

When Cory was first diagnosed with cancer, her family suggested that she goes abroad for a second opinion and possible alternative treatments. She refused, not wanting to be a burden, for she was all too aware that the lives of her children's families would also be disrupted.

It was then when Manolo began the ongoing project of digitizing all her photos to better preserve them. It was something he enjoys doing for her, the family, and for posterity's sake. The files are housed in a dehumidified area. That to him is the least he can do for an extraordinary woman he had the rare privilege of getting to know up close. **(NSRC)**

Dodo Dee:
aka Mr. Viel Aquino

Martial law had been declared when Richard Joseph (Dodo) Dee completed sixth grade in Xavier School. Fearing for his family's safety, his father, Howard Q. Dee, brought his family to Canada. But Dodo always felt an affinity for the Philippines and knew he would eventually return home. He was certain even then that he would not spend his professional life in Canada. After completing his commerce degree at the University of British Columbia in Vancouver in 1983, he joined Unilab, the largest pharmaceutical company in the Philippines. He began as a stock boy and mailing room clerk before he went for his MBA at the University of Pennsylvania.

It almost seemed logical that he would work there because the Dees have a special affinity with the Unilab Corporation. Howard Dee's sister was married to the company founder, Jose Y. Campos, now deceased. Mr. Dee had been appointed the first professional president of Unilab from 1965 to 1972, and was a member of the board until he stepped down in the seventies.

Today, it is Dodo who sits on the board and is senior vice president, overseeing business development and operations. This takes him on punishing travel schedules as Unilab is present in several countries in the region.

Although Dodo never met Ninoy Aquino, his father was an admirer of Ninoy. Howard Dee was a passionate nationalist who was active in the anti-dictatorship struggle through his involvement with social development, as founding chair of the Philippine Business for Social Progress and the Church. While protest gatherings were forbidden by the regime, who could question the prayer assemblies during Marian Year that the elder Dee organized with Cardinal Sin? When Cory Aquino became president, Howard Dee was appointed Philippine Ambassador to the Holy See and Malta from 1986 to 1990.

Dodo first met the Aquinos' third daughter Victoria Eliza (Viel) when he interviewed her for a job in Percom, the Apple distribution company where he was working. How was that for an initial encounter and Viel not accepting the job after all? Then, perhaps because of their parents' association in government, he was asked to help Viel and her cousins plan out a trip to Europe. He laughs that Viel said all Dodo ever did was to send her a guidebook, nothing more.

When he got to know her better after his MBA—a friendship renewed during a small dinner at the Arlegui presidential home—he was surprised to discover what a "grounded and religious" person Viel was. And given the circumstances of her family background, Dodo never felt her to be a person of influence. Neither was she someone who dwelt on the past. They began dating in 1989 and he particularly remembers a day he was on his way to visit Viel, a day when Malacañang was barricaded because of the military coups. He still found a way to get to Arlegui when he chanced upon their family friend, Foreign Affairs Secretary Raul Manglapus, on his way to Arlegui. He hitched a ride and managed a visit, though was warned that it was not safe to be in the neighborhood.

Viel is known to be the most private and reserved of the Aquino siblings. She and Dodo wanted a very intimate wedding, telling President Cory then that she was allowed a quota of ten guests. The president said that was impossible for her and advised them in jest to just elope. Dodo and Viel had a total of 150 guests—a larger number than what they would have preferred—and a reception in the Arlegui residence after a ceremony at the nearby Abbey of Our Lady of Montserrat, San Beda College, Mendiola.

Dodo's best memories of President Cory revolve around her making life as normal as possible for the family. She really went out of her way to make people feel at ease in her company. Early in her presidency, one of her female security felt the need to make a clean breast of her previous service record, even if there was nothing irregular about it. But because of the President's sincerity and gentle ways, she simply broke down and confessed to President Cory that it bothered her that she was one of the guards who did a strip-search on her during her visits to Ninoy.

When she passed away, the family took great comfort in what seemed like Cory's gesture of leaving them in the hands, in the care, of the people. Many came saying she was a great friend to them.

Cory's faith was so deep, a lesson from the martial law years when she "lost" all her friends who feared being associated with the Aquinos. She would always say that it was only God who stayed by her side. According to Dodo, that must be why she made it a point to reach out to people in deep crises, when they seem bereft of friends. It was moving for him to see her reach out to former Comelec Chair Ben Abalos when he faced charges of electoral fraud.

Nothing seemed to faze her, recounted former Philippine Constabulary head Gen. Ramon Montaño during her wake. During the tense days of the military coups, she would confer with the military officers in Arlegui and then suddenly excuse herself to serve them some refreshments. That shift in mood and temper was incredible, Montaño recalls.

It is with justified fatherly pride when Dodo speaks about his two children who are both self-driven. How can they not be, with the values that their parents and both sets of grandparents exemplify, the strong motivation to fulfill service for others and for country, and to give back to others? Admittedly, these are values that cannot be taught but lived by example.

His son, Kiko, who thought nothing of commuting to UP as a college student, is now an assistant professor of political science and statistics of the university, after completing graduate studies at the London School of Economics. Also carrying Joseph as his second name like his father, and also an only son, both have a special devotion to the humble and simple life that Joseph the carpenter led. Kiko aspires to work on his doctoral program in the future. While not interested in politics, Kiko is concerned about the country's development and hopes that a new breed of leaders will emerge from today's generation. To him, it needs to go beyond being an Aquino. When his grandfather, Howard Dee, was named convenor of the distinguished Peace Council on the Bangsamoro Basic Law, Kiko had the opportunity to collaborate with him by acting as his executive assistant and participating in discussions and presentations during the Malacañang meetings. What a special moment that must have been for both grandfather and grandson.

Similarly, Jia knows what she would like to be. Her father narrates that even as a young student in Poveda, she expressed wanting to be more challenged in her academic life. On her own, she applied at the Philippine Science High School and was accepted. For her freshman year in UP, she was accepted as a university scholar. Now a sophomore, she has chosen molecular biology as her field of specialization, keenly interested in doing research.

"I feel so honored to have witnessed history and to be a small part of it," Dodo says of the Aquino experience under two presidential terms. He has a collection of Teddy Boy Locsin anecdotes, which say it all for the Cory Aquino administration—from Locsin feeling like a Sir Galahad in her Cabinet, to seeing how the U.S. secret service agents wept as she rehearsed her speech (so how can such a speech fail? Locsin had asked then) with the teleprompter before Congress, and how that speech may be described as most expensive as it earned the Philippines $350 million in aid.

As trustee of the Assisi Foundation which his father chairs and where Viel is co-chair along with Ernie Garilao, Dodo draws much satisfaction from helping communities that made much progress with the intervention of nongovernment organizations in facilitating government contacts. "We do not ask favors for ourselves from government, but for the underprivileged who perhaps may need urgent medical aid or other forms of assistance." He cites the Cervantes, Kalinga products that needed the proper boost. The Javier municipality in Leyte, a former fourth class municipality that has since made remarkable progress under the leadership of Mayor Leonardo Javier, was another beneficiary of the Assisi Foundation. There are eight other poorest municipalities in the country benefitting from the foundation's assistance in preparing and implementing their five-year development goals.

Within Unilab, Dodo is enthused about the company's long-term plan to preserve, document, and propagate the Philippines' rich biodiversity. It is envisioned to lead the general public to a better appreciation of the country's natural wealth.

A colleague at work has introduced him to vintage audio equipment which is akin to his IT interest. These days, Dodo relaxes while collecting old LPs, enjoying them on vintage equipment.

How Dodo relishes the joys of family life—traveling with Viel and the children, movies with his parents and his children (yes, all three generations together, movie buffs all), having intellectual conversations on politics, school, and national developments, and the comfort of being quiet in a room together, not needing any words.

And it does not matter to Dodo that sometimes, he is still introduced as Mr. Viel Aquino. **(NSRC)**

Special Bonds

If the siblings were forewarned in the past not to tell Ate Ballsy anything that they did not want their mother to know within the next twenty minutes, or that they wished to tell Cory themselves, they are now warned not to tell the irrepressible Kris anything she could thoughtlessly announce on national television.

Noynoy is Kris's usual "victim," for she would—without any malice, of course—talk about giving him advice from head to toe, styling his wardrobe, even commenting on prospects of marriage for him. And because she unfailing invokes her mom's memory and her eternal pledge to help Noy, it is difficult to fault her. In a public response to her outpouring about him and his public and personal affairs, Noynoy once asserted that he is, after all, still her big brother, several years her senior.

And he has since learned his lesson. To all her regular lengthy and detailed text messages about this and that, sent in five parts, Noy answers safely and succinctly: "OK. Thanks." When asked if her brother scolded her for saying too much on television, her impish reply was: "Isn't it, I have shut up?"

Once, for a *YES!* pictorial, Kris sent Noynoy a hairdresser to give what she deemed a respectable trim, and she had him fitted by Manila's best tailors to streamline his wardrobe. From one side of the dining room, she affectionately yelled out to him, reminding him that he had not thanked her at all. Noy's answer: "But I have not received anything yet. *Hindi pa naman tapos*."

Kris is extra cautious about mentioning the brands of her wardrobe choices for her brother, having learned her lesson after the pair of signature leather shoes she once gave him. He needed a new pair, but when he saw the price tag that had inadvertently been left attached, he was appalled and became reluctant to use the shoes.

Noynoy and Kris's son Joshua share a special bond. The uncle worries that one day, his nephew Josh may realize the finality of the loss of his Lola Cory. Noynoy recalls that, during the wake, Josh never wanted to view the remains, but just kept tapping and holding the casket a safe distance from its open glass portion, as if to announce to his *lola* that he was around.

Noy also remains as the ideal disciplinarian when Josh proved too difficult even for his *lola* to manage. One time, during a family Christmas portrait, when Josh insisted on posing behind his Tito Noy and to put his hands on his uncle's shoulders, the uncle complained, "Just put, not push with your hands, Josh."

The boy is very affectionate with his uncle. Their special bond pleases Kris and assuages many of her typical maternal fears about her son's special needs. She has put him on a strict diet to make him healthier and bring down his weight, which is heavy for his 6-foot-1 height. Fortunately, she says, he loves salads and vegetables, but when his mother is not around, such as on Sunday family lunches, he is tempted to try everything taboo on his food list. Unfortunately, we are all spoilers, Kris sighs.

She reveals that her mom was especially fond of Josh because she found him so good-looking and so affectionate.

"I guess the one who is the most needy is the one you'd want to take care of," is how Kris explains the obvious favoritism. Lola Cory would attend all of Josh's school programs and was a regular substitute for Kris at school meetings, so that she knew his teachers so well.

The day before Cory passed away, the students at Joshua's school, The Multiple Intelligence School in Katipunan, went to their teacher to say that they had seen the woman they had written get-well cards to. That is the only reported Cory sighting, and it is attributed to Cory's solicitousness over Josh—just a final check to make sure he was faring well. **(NSRC)**

Not-So-Merry Christmases

Childhood Christmases for the Aquino children were serene, as their father was only then still a politician on the rise, though already one in a great hurry. Life was simple and uncomplicated then, and Santa Claus always paid the children a visit. Ballsy, who seemed in the know, would warn her siblings to go to sleep at once, because Santa was already ready at the neighbor's place, but would not leave presents for those who were still wide awake. Pinky recalls how they would force themselves to sleep. The next morning, there was always the certainty of getting gifts from Santa.

Ninoy was probably already an elected official at this time, because Pinky recalls that she, a young child then, was made to stand on a table and hand out Christmas gifts to the tenants in Tarlac. She could not understand why she was not on the receiving end, especially since she would be celebrating her birthday on December 27.

The Christmas presents of those days still bring back fond memories. Pinky's favorite present was a cash register toy, which she had first seen in her mother's treasure trove of presents in storage, and which she had openly coveted. Ballsy's was a vanity set (a *kikay* kit, she calls it, using today's lingo) that bestowed long nails on her! It included high heels that fascinated her. Also quite memorable was a charm bracelet, which she got when she was just five or six. "I had such a happy childhood," Ballsy says, "and I was amazed that Santa knew exactly what I wanted."

Cory was not a spoiler and only gave her children exactly what they asked for. Noynoy recalls shopping with his mother at Farmer's Market in Cubao, carrying with him his hard-earned savings, just enough to buy the item he had been saving for. He could not fathom the maternal logic, why Cory would not let him buy the item, as he had after all saved up for it. On Christmas Day, he discovered that it was the very gift that his *ninang*, Terry Lopa, Cory's older sister had wrapped up for him.

On the other hand, Viel, who has legendary austere ways, wonders out loud why she has no recollections of any such memorable present from her childhood. Her daughter Jia, like her mother, has inherited her mother's lack of interest in material gifts. Jia always tries to look for a beneficiary she can share her Christmas cash gifts with. That is why her mom's sisters tease her, "If we give you anything, *ipamimigay mo lang naman!*"

Noynoy—who's simply Noy to his family—remembers another painful lesson learned one holiday season when his father noticed that his only son was hoarding a bag of his favorite candies and savoring them surreptitiously, all by himself. His father took the bag and broke Noy's heart by distributing the sweets equally among his sisters and sundry guests, even those who did not care for any. Ninoy reminded his son that it was never good to be selfish, and pointed to Noy's Lolo Pepe Cojuangco as someone who always showed the example of sharing through actions, not mere words.

Even then, their mother was always the parent, the continuing point of references in their conversations, because hers was the constant presence in their lives. Kris says she knows that just as parents should have no favorite child, so must the children not have a favorite parent. With typical candor, she says that, although she is called Daddy's girl, she is really "Mom's girl." Mom was the only parent for her, as she hardly knew her father during her childhood. How she clung to her mom, even wondering why her father had to enter the scene, seeming to be a rival for her mom's attention!

Kris was only one year old when martial law was declared, so she did not even know why weekends were spent in Fort Bonifacio visiting the detained head of their family. She did realize soon enough that her maternal grandparents seemed to be compensating for the abnormalcy of their childhood with their special solicitousness and generosity toward her. Thus, she fondly remembers her favorite loot, all fulfilled wishes on her Christmas list: *Sesame Street*'s gumball machine from Mr. Hooper's store, a Speak & Spell, and a Math Wizard game set, all state-of-the-art toys at the time.

During this challenging period of their family life, the Aquinos spent eight not-so-merry

Christmases and New Year's Days in the small Fort Bonifacio cell with their father—and the Japanese spitz he loved. They now label that period as their *John en Marsha* years, because the cramped sleeping space on the floor that they had to share was reminiscent of scenes in the TV sitcom. Amenities may have been spartan, but family warmth and love were much in evidence. Togetherness was what mattered, Viel remembers fondly. Sleeping bags and wall-to-wall mattresses, which Cory brought in, were laid out on the floor of Ninoy's cell. The kids slept on these bags and mattresses, except for Noy who, being the only boy, had the privilege of sleeping on his dad's cot.

Ninoy would be so excited about these two overnight visits every year, and would prepare his signature chicken sandwich with lots of onions.

Christmas is Christmas anywhere, even in prison. The Santa Claus ruse had to be continued for the benefit of Kris. Cory arranged with the guards to have Santa Claus knock on the door at the stroke of midnight to deliver the gifts for the young girl. Kris remembers with gratitude how kindly the guards cooperated to make Santa's visit so believable for her.

Was it New Year's Eve when, Noy remembers, the kids all turned red and giddy after trying to empty a wine bottle that his dad was going to use to put some clandestine letters in? This family of nondrinkers drank away—Ninoy was flushed, Cory was dizzy, Viel was dancing, Noy was laughing, and Pinky fell asleep. Everyone nursed a headache the next day.

New Year was also the occasion when their father would remind them to follow the folk belief of jumping high at midnight to ensure an increase in their physical height. But he made an exception of Kris. Propping her up, he would tell her not to jump: "*Wag na lang, para princess na lang kita.*"

Come to think of it, Pinky says, she and her siblings never complained nor questioned why their Christmases were in Fort Bonifacio: "I guess it is because Mom made it appear so normal, as she had so much strength. I never felt *kawawa*." Ballsy says the martial law years taught them to look at the bright side of things. She cannot forget how happy her parents were then, together in Fort Bonifacio.

Conversation ultimately and inevitably centers on Christmas of 2007, when something seemed amiss with their mother. She seemed specially drawn and tired. This was also noticed by Popoy and Margie Juico, close family friends who live a few minutes away from Times Street and had joined the family Mass that year.

Did Cory perhaps wear herself out with her Christmas ritual of getting ready for a dinner for fifty, pushing and lifting the pieces of furniture for the Christmas Eve dinner, choosing to wrap all her presents personally—and enjoying it, too—then signing the 5,000 Christmas cards bearing the family photo? Her aide Mel had told the family that Cory wanted to get the house in order that afternoon. The family had just finished the customary traditional shot by the Christmas tree—no professional shoot, just our cameras, Viel says—when Cory, who was holding Baby James, her youngest grandchild, passed the child on to the eldest grandson Jiggy, as she suddenly felt dizzy and short of breath. Her blood pressure rose abnormally. That Christmas was spent at the Medical City.

Cory's persistent cough and progressive weight loss, especially noticeable during Kris's birthday on February 14, 2008, led to the discovery of the advanced colon cancer in March and the public announcement in April. Although Cory left the Times Street house and moved in with her daughter Ballsy at this time, she insisted on the usual Christmas celebration on Times Street in 2008. It was to be her last Christmas. Her daughters recall the poignant homily of Father Rev, profusely thanking Cory for all that she had done, making it seem like it would be a last celebration with her, something many of them dreaded. Cory herself was asked to say a few words, and Viel remembers how her mother kept thanking her five children.

Pinky echoes what her mom used to say after their father's death in 1983, that the "firsts" in family milestones would be the most difficult times to initially hurdle.

The first time the siblings had to clear the bedroom in Ballsy's home that had served as their mother's temporary quarter for seventeen months, in order to restore it to a den once more, was particularly painful. There were far too many reminders of their mother— her toothbrush, for instance, and the special toothpaste and mouthwash—that clearing the room immediately helped Ballsy in her own grieving.

The very first visit to Cory's Times Street bedroom after she passed away, only became possible when the siblings agreed that at least three of them had to be physically present. The emptiness and the memories were impossible to bear without each other's company— and only for two hours at most. Among the priceless items sorted out, to be housed in the Aquino Museum at the Hacienda Luisita in Tarlac, were the numerous rosaries and the yellow wardrobe. They distributed their mother's personal effects among themselves.

Pinky says it comforts her when she uses her mother's bag, just imagining that Cory is holding her daughter's hand and continues to be a source of strength in the many decisions to be made: "She just had the answers to everything. How we miss that now . . . ."

In the course of clearing their mom's personal effects, the Aquino siblings were hoping they would find the letters that their mother said she meant to write for each of them after her cancer was diagnosed. So far, the search has been in vain—but they have not lost hope.

The Aquinos are looking beyond their comfortable worlds every December. It is the special spirit of Christmas that Pinky always welcomes and finds reassuring. "It's no longer the gifts, it's really celebrating Jesus's birthday," she says. "*Di ba,* people are kinder to one another? People are more positive. It is really a season to be nicer to one another."

Noynoy wants government to be responsive to the needs of its citizens, from eradication of poverty to an improved educational system, to dealing with an unmanageable population size. In the face of recent natural disasters that have shown unforgivable lapses in governance, Viel envisions a country that will rise again, proud of its heritage and its progress.

Christmas is a time for the Aquino Children to come together and celebrate another year of family love and comradeship. Each Chrsitmas is a chance to strengthen them for the coming year, just as the Christmases of the past have always done. **(NSRC)**

Third-Generation Aquinos

Eldest grandson thirty-year-old Jiggy Aquino Cruz confesses that he does feel the pressure of being an Aquino, being the eldest grandchild and growing up hearing his Lola Cory repeatedly saying that the family must take care of the Aquino name. "I had to set an example for my younger brother and younger cousins."

There is undeniable pride in his lineage, attendant pressure and all. "My two grandparents are heroes, my uncle is the current president doing such an amazing job, my tita is one of the most successful and influential people in the entertainment industry, my mom and my other titas couldn't be more sincere and simple. I'm proud that I have such great influences around me."

He is especially ecstatic about having his uncle as president. "It's really, really, really cool. I'm such a proud nephew. In this day and age, the word 'politician' can have negative connotations, but my Tito Noy proves that wrong. His 'tuwid na daan' platform set the bar for all political leaders in the Philippines."

He likes and admires his Tito Noy best for his love for the family, for whom he will *always* make time. Despite his busy schedule, when the family needs him, he will be present. But while Jiggy and his cousins would joke around with their "cool uncle" before, today they are somehow inhibited in deference to his office. Jiggy exclaims, "He's like the number one guy in the land!"

Chapter VII: Up Close and Personal

Jiggy grew up hearing stories about his Lolo Ninoy, someone he wishes he had the chance to meet. From the many stories he had heard, he might as well have met him. There may be his acts of heroism, but what Jiggy is most impressed and awestruck about is the Amorsolo portrait of his Lola that he gave her as a special present. "That was such an awesome gift. If I'm not mistaken, it was worth two months of his salary then. At that time, it was such a unique gift to give someone. My Lolo was indeed the charmer."

At present, he works at Nestle Philippines Inc., as business manager for Nescafé Dolce Gusto. He sees himself growing professionally in corporate life, possibly married and with children, busy with family life and "managing my parents as doting grandparents."

Describing himself as an all-around nice guy who is easy to get along with, he also confesses that he is nice to a fault as his friends and relatives also point out, often to the point of being too trusting, too gullible. He admits he does not quite know how to say "No."

He loves reading and collecting comic books, even attending comic book conventions in the U.S. He also faithfully follows basketball, baseball, and American football.

How he wishes that Lola Cory was still around. "She played a significant role in raising me, along with my parents who are really the primary influences in my life." Jiggy cannot forget that she always teased him about the reason he was turning out to be such a good boy: because "I was lucky to be blessed by Mother Teresa."

Reader, Writer, Lover of Comedy

Jonty Cruz finds that even before people get to meet him personally, there is already a set of expectations by the mere fact that he is an Aquino descendant. Not that it bothers him because it is "a welcome challenge and an honor to live up to the name." To him, "it's a true joy to be a part of this family, from my parents, uncles and aunts, and my cousins."

What are his best memories of his grandparents? He remembers visiting his Lola frequently during summers and school holidays in her office at Jose Cojuangco & Sons in Makati, tagging along with his mom when she would go to work. Certainly not the usual setting for grandma visits, but that was what made it much more special. His best introduction to his Lolo Ninoy came from watching his *Face the Nation* guest appearance on television over and over again. Jonty feels he got to know him more, leaving him inspired and awed. "The odds were clearly against him during that biased interview but he showed immense wit, intelligence, courage, and fortitude."

The Aquino Grandchildren

Name: Justin Benigno Aquino Cruz
Nickname: Jiggy
Date of Birth: October 6, 1985

Name: Eldon Giulio Aquino Cruz
Nickname: Jonty
Date of Birth: November 22, 1988

Name: Miguel Gerardo Aquino Abellada
Nickname: Miguel/Abe
Date of Birth: February 7, 1987

Name: Anna Corazon Abellada
Nickname: Nina
Date of Birth: January 23, 1989

Name: Francis Joseph Dee
Nickname: Kiko
Date of Birth: November 11, 1991

Name: Jacinta Patricia Dee
Nickname: Jia
Date of Birth: March 17, 1996

Name: Joshua Phillip Joseph Anthony Aquino
Nickname: Josh
Date of Birth: June 4, 1995

Name: James Aquino Yap
Nickname: Bimby
Date of Birth: April 19, 2007

An avid reader, Jonty says his love for reading grew from knowing that his Lolo Ninoy had been a voracious reader. "I never met my Lolo . . . but I felt that maybe I can get to know him better if I also read books."

He quotes the British-Austrian philosopher Ludwig Wittgenstein that his English teacher introduced the class to: "The limit of my language means the limit of my world." His favorite authors are Michael Chabon, Alison Bass, and B.J. Novak.

How proud Ninoy would have been today to know that his grandson Jonty has been lured to the world of writing and is editor of "Young Star," a dedicated section of the *Philippine Star*, and contributing editor for *Esquire* Magazine. It is a profession that Jonty takes seriously, for his future career plans are "to still be in publishing and/or media and create content that really matters." Elaborating on this, he sees the industry's potential to inform and lend perspective. In *Esquire,* for instance, he is extremely proud of what it has accomplished. "It's important to not only feature the zeitgeist but also discuss and deconstruct it."

He has always enjoyed writing and loved English class at the Ateneo. It was only when he met his boss, Erwin Romulo (editor-in-chief of *Esquire*) when he seriously focused on it and "developed myself as a writer." Jonty loves writing speculative and satirical essays but hesitates to call himself a writer, saying he is more editor than writer. "I enjoy writing but would never insult my idols and this industry by saying that I'm a writer."

Jonty draws inspiration from his uncle president: "It's really awe-inspiring seeing him face so many challenges and never lose faith in his pursuit of positive change for the country. He's still the same man who puts as much effort in being president as he does being a good role model for his family." And because PNoy has remained the same generous and caring Tito Noy to them, Jonty feels and acts no differently toward him despite the official title.

Jonty's favorite things to do are reading books, magazines, and comics; watching shows and movies; and reading up on U.S. politics. He and his brother Jiggy have an extensive comic book collection, with Jiggy having many more than his own estimated 500. Jiggy loved comics even before he did: "I would read his comics (sometimes without his permission) and immediately fell in love with it."

Jonty describes himself as talkative, a joker, and hopefully, "never boring." He does confess the one thing he likes least about himself is that he complains a lot—a given for anyone in the industry where one has to have an opinion on everything and anything, where a discussion is taking place all the time.

His three big wishes are to meet the highly popular comedian and now late-show host Stephen Colbert, to work for a comic book company, and "to be rich enough to take my parents abroad for vacation." With these writers and comedians—again, it's Stephen Colbert, Tina Fey, and Brian K. Vaughan—whom he cites as the major influences in his life, it is not a surprise when he says, "I like that I can make people laugh and have fun." As a very young boy, he remembers watching *Saturday Night Live* and *Conan O'Brien* late at night in his parents' bedroom. It left such an impression on him, leading him to appreciate comedy as "a true craft and art."

Miguel's Self-Imposed Expectations

iguel Abellada describes himself as a "low-maintenance person, pretty much a cocktail of the traits" of his parents, Pinky and Manolo. From time to time, whenever he has to decide on a course of action, he draws confidence from recalling what Mom and Dad would have done in similar circumstances.

Another major influence in his life is his Tito Noy. "It surprises me to this day how many habits, beliefs, and traits I have also inherited from him, probably because of how much time we've spent together. But what I admire the most would have to be the fact that he sees things as either black or white, and not gray." As someone who admits that he finds it hard to say "No," how Miguel wishes that he would also have the conviction and the courage to "take the heat while fighting for what I believe is right."

And of course, Lola Cory looms as a significant figure in his life. "Making her proud was always [more] important than making my own parents proud. I guess her stamp of approval weighed a lot more! Haha! If someday I would get even half of her emotional strength and unwavering willpower, I'd be a very happy man."

Miguel cannot forget how his Lola Cory even went into the court at Araneta Coliseum in 2005 to hug him when the Ateneo basketball team he was playing for won the UAAP Juniors Championship. That, to him, felt truly special, along with Sunday meriendas with her and her special homemade treat of liver pate and grilled cheese sandwiches.

He also likes to share a funny anecdote about how his Lola imposed this rule on Kris as a young girl. In a clothing store, Kris was limited to one item, but in a bookstore, she could get as many books as she desired. This is akin to what he remembers as his Lolo Ninoy's motto in life, "*Paramihan lang ng nabasa.*"

His favorite Lolo Ninoy anecdote is his love for bargains so that he would buy cat food at marked-down prices even though the family had no cats in the household.

While there may be definite expectations about being an Aquino grandson, he says these are self-imposed. "Personally, I want to be able to live up to what is expected of me." He has uppermost in his mind the inherited "clean name that we have all protected over the years." He is fully aware that the family is open to public scrutiny. But he is proudest of the fact that they are so close-knit as a family. Call him old-fashioned, as he is the first to say, but weekends for him are strictly for the family.

This way of life (or coping) is no different from the way they were before 2010. Having an uncle as president has only incurred the mandatory security detail and of course, "being more mindful of how we act." Apart from that, nothing else has changed "because we never really involve ourselves with his job." His Tito Noy also has not changed one bit.

Today, Miguel works as district sales manager at Unilever Philippines. "I sell shampoo and laundry detergent for a living." His outgoing personality, his total ease in meeting new people, and his strong sense of competitiveness which fuel his drive to excel, make him compatible to the pace of corporate life. To unwind, he enjoys eating out, playing basketball, growing his sneakers collection, and traveling.

At twenty-eight, Miguel has begun to take a serious look at the future, especially in the light of his forthcoming marriage to longtime girlfriend Stephanie Yap for whom he orchestrated a most memorably romantic proposal in Phnom Penh where she was assigned. He aspires to be a responsible provider for his future family and enjoy the simple joys of a happy marriage and parenting, like the mundane routine of taking his kids to school.

He cannot help but be equally concerned about the country, that it continues to progress and have a citizenry more supportive of one another, rather than preoccupied with "trying to bring each other down."

Cory Aquino's Namesake

Eldest granddaughter Anna Corazon Aquino Abellada, or Nina, is fully aware of the implications of being the namesake of her grandmother. She considers it a great privilege to be told time and again that Cory Aquino was an extraordinary role model because of her "simplicity and her courage to always stand up to protect our rights." Growing up, getting to know about her Aquino grandparents was inspiring. "More than any title, my lolo and lola led very simple lives and their actions showed how much service they wanted to do for others."

Today, Nina sees that again in her Tito Noy and his siblings. "My mom and my aunts serve as a constant reminder for me to always think of how you can make a difference, big or small, everyday." That has motivated her to ensure that she does her family proud in whatever she does.

Her Lola Cory has left her with many fond memories. She reminisces, "Her thoughtfulness was beyond measure. Once I was asked to accompany Lola on a weekend visit to Macau to celebrate the feast day of our Lady of Fatima. Lola's schedule was packed that whole weekend and we weren't given the time to visit the main sites. Lola knew that I was always one who would get a souvenir from every place I would visit—be it a photo or a local item. On our last day, despite her busy schedule, Lola made a request for me. She asked the organizers if they could allot an hour before heading to the airport so that I could visit some of the major sites of Macau. To this day, I still keep a photo we took in the Ruins of St. Paul. I consider that particular trip to Macau as one of my most memorable trips."

To Nina, her lola remains the best example of grace under pressure. "She lets her actions speak louder than her words."

Lola Cory would tell her stories about the grandfather she never met. She began to be introduced to Lolo Ninoy as the fun and charismatic person whose company everyone enjoyed. He was passionate about his work, especially in his unrelenting struggle for freedom and democracy in the last years of his life. A big asset of his was that he made friends easily and would be in close contact with them. On many occasions here and abroad, Nina's lola "would always be pleasantly surprised to discover all the many friends [her lolo] would bump into." All her lola could say in total amazement was, *"Kaibigan mo din yan?"*

Having her uncle as president has made Nina more supportive of all his efforts to look for ways to make a positive impact to the Filipinos. "You also celebrate triumphant moments for the country more. Seeing where we are today makes me proud of what Tito Noy has done." She admires his hard work and relentlessness "until he knows he has done his best." She is aware that the triumphs grew out of collective efforts, but knowing that he led the change means much to her.

Nina is even happier over the fact that Tito Noy remains the same to her, still has the time to listen and laugh at her jokes, or give advice or just be a sounding board. Nothing much has changed as he would still be just a text, a phone call, or a visit away. "I feel I have two dads because Tito Noy still checks on me regularly."

She laments the hurt and common occurrence of "having to see some of your family members, in spite of their good intentions for the country, go through negative criticism from the media at times."

Like her brother Miguel, Nina works with Unilever Philippines as senior assistant brand manager. She enjoys marketing and creating marketing campaigns but sees herself in the future as a part-time volunteer for an NGO focusing on social entrepreneurship, perhaps running training classes. She is eager to use her skills to help others in the long term. She knows how important it is for our country to experience equality among its citizens.

She would want to someday have her own family and continue the Aquino family traditions that keep the family ties strong and binding.

When not at work, Nina watches movies and TV series, especially enjoying romantic comedies and thrillers. She tries to visit new places with friends, a good way to catch up on one another while in pursuit of new adventures.

Nina describes herself as very approachable and dependable and easy to get along with, but unfortunately, can stress over the most trivial and the inconsequential.

Nina credits her parents too for shaping her into the young woman she is today. She admires her mother for "her determination to drive change and to show how to be a better version of yourself each day." Her father is someone so generous and so approachable one can turn to him for anything at any time.

Kiko Dee, the Professor

hen Kiko describes his personality as deliberately uninteresting, that one can get a glimpse of his hobbies by watching the TV show *Big Bang Theory*, and that he wishes he had a true, working Green Lantern ring to endow him with incredible powers, one knows that one has an interesting enigma to demystify.

The children of Viel and Dodo Dee are the first Aquino grandchildren not to go to the Ateneo for college. There is the well-loved, heartwarming anecdote of Kiko preferring to go to school in a public jeepney, posing a challenge for his assigned security.

Kiko is now twenty-four, newly graduated from the London School of Economics and is assistant professor at the Department of Political Science in UP Diliman. He might as well be one of the characters in *Big Bang Theory*, a humorous sit-com that features Mensa-fied best friends and roommates who are physicists that discuss all there is to know about quantum physics but are at a total loss when it comes to social interactions, especially boy-girl relationships. Kiko says he is interested in things that most would find boring or unimportant.

He is intent on doing a doctoral program, continuing his academic life at the university, and editing a book on Filipino voters behavior. Clearly, the influence of a grandfather, a grandmother, and an uncle who have "undeniably done something concrete to improve the lives of their countrymen" is so strong, that he himself strives to do his best in his own realm.

He grew up in an environment that valued learning and education. As a young child, Kiko and his mom had a nightly routine before bedtime. "We would read children's books or the children's Bible. This continued until I could read on my own."

In his desire to share with others what he has learned, Kiko volunteered in 2014 to teach research methods at the Pamulaan Center for Indigenous Peoples Education in Davao, administered by the Assisi Foundation, which his paternal grandfather chairs and where his mother is vice-president.

What Kiko appreciates seeing in the presidency at close range is the knowledge that a "human being and not some abstract political figure is making all of these important decisions." To him, the presidency is not an enviable but rather a terrible job. "Every Filipino is your boss, so by definition, everyone displeased with you is a failure on your part." When asked, Kiko says that the only thing different now about his uncle is that "we stand up when he enters the room." Sounding like his mother Viel, he wishes that there would be no more family members in public office.

His best memory of Lola Cory is she teaching Kiko to pray for his enemies, if "I have to have any in the first place." And how to love. Perhaps then, the acronym NGSB that he has adopted (no girlfriend since birth) may not be true for long.

Kiko cites other significant influences in his life and at the same time reveals his diverse interests. There is Scottish comic book writer Grant Morrison known for his "nonlinear narratives and countercultural leanings"; professional wrestler Bryan Danielson; and Dr. Lydia Casambre, a retired political science professor and scholar for whom Kiko pays the highest tribute by calling her his "life peg."

Coping with 20 Kilopascals

The fact that Jia Dee can banter about coping with 20 kilopascals (for the uninformed like me, that is the metric unit of measure for pressure) when dealing with the expectations of being an Aquino is truly refreshing. This, together with the fact that her friends make a lot of bodyguard jokes ("Jia, *baka barilin ako 'pag kinausap kita!*"), or that she sees family gatherings alternate between political debriefings and regular kuwentuhan sessions, or that with her Tito Noy, she finds it such a waste of time for the country if she talks trivia with him. All these hint that the very private Jia has learned to deal with the personal circumstances of her life.

The truth is, the only pressure for her is to do her best and to get good grades. A sophomore in BS molecular biology and biotechnology at UP Diliman, after graduating from the Philippine Science High School, Jia somehow does not feel right "claiming" the legacy of the Aquino family. "It is not mine to be proud of as I myself haven't done anything but have the incredible fortune of being in the bloodline. Nonetheless, I'm very grateful."

She feels especially blessed that her maternal and paternal grandparents are both selfless and her parents, practical. With such influences, she strives to live with an "open mind and a giving heart."

She is also well aware of what comes with that good fortune. While she concedes that everybody has the right to scrutinize and criticize her family as "transparency and freedom of speech are paramount," she still smarts and hurts because after all, it is still her family that is the brunt of those comments.

She appreciates her Tito Noy's sharp sense of humor that has not changed and his constancy about openly caring for the family.

Jia is full of dreams that she hopes she can turn to reality, among them to be a successful genetic engineer or novelist (or both—and why not?) and perhaps, if she has the time, to carry on a relationship. She visualizes her career to focus on scientific research and writing, but definitely not politics, she emphasizes.

Her most ardent wishes are to end world hunger, for the Philippines to achieve 100 percent literacy, and to achieve the stamina and strength of American mixed-martial artist, Ronda Rousey.

Jia describes her personality type on the Myers-Briggs Indicator as ENTP (Extraverted, Intuitive, Thinking, Perceiving) though her brother Kiko says she is a utilitarian. According to Jia, her paternal grandmother always says that she has beauty and brains. Of course, she would like to wholeheartedly believe her Lola Betty.

Jia remembers her Lola Cory always playing Text & Twist on her PC and in the process, teaching her obscure words like "lien." She has learned to adopt this technique her lola used: "Whenever she got stuck on a level, she'd pause and search the dictionary for every possible combination of letters before resuming the game." Jia says she does the same routine today as she discovers more obscure words.

And a Ninoy Aquino anecdote? Jia minces no words and is perhaps horrified at a question that is self-evident, that needed not even be asked at all: "Nothing beats the one where he dies to bring back democracy."

The True Loves of Kris: Josh Aquino and Bimby Yap

 osh has what his mom Kris calls a "treasure chest" of memories of his Lola Cory. They had spent most afternoons together, since he had his tutorials in her Times home. They also had dinner together at least thrice a week, and Cory had attended *all* of Josh's school activities and programs.

Josh enjoyed the special treat of always being with his Lola on her trips to Tarlac. All these times together was precious. Kris says with much gratitude, "I was blessed because while establishing my career, Mom really stepped in to nurture Josh."

Josh's special kinship and bond with his Tito Noy is well known. His uncle remembers how Josh would wake him up by throwing his weight on him—and that certainly roused him to wakefulness. He says he loves his Tito because he always gives him Cherry Lifesavers and lets him drive the golf cart.

Though there is a wide age gap between Josh and Bimby. (affectionately called Kuya and Bimb by their mom), they enjoy memorable times together with their mom. Their travels have been chronicled in full detail by media. Kris says they have been all over the country, from north to south, and overseas to—the U.S., Mexico, France, U.K., Italy, Israel, U.A.E., Japan, Korea, H.K., Thailand, and Malaysia—and had four Disney cruises. They have extensively traveled that the two boys, enjoying their new (and nth) home, prefer for now to just stay home. Sounding blasé, both beg their mom to hold off on more travels in the meantime.

The brothers have two separate bedrooms in their new home, furnished to their specifications. Josh has the mural map of the world painted on one wall, travel being the motif of his room. He does not have the TV set that Bimby has, but a large screen desktop where he does his readings and surfing. Josh is taking special classes in occupational, speech, group and life skills therapies. All of 6'2", he is in top physical form as he follows a regimen of daily swimming and portion eating, having developed a disciplined lifestyle for weight control that even his own mother marvels at.

Both have shot commercials with their celebrity mom, bringing to mind their grandmother's reminder to Kris when Bimby was just being "discovered" as a great model for ads: "Please make sure that Josh is also included in your shoots." Both love YouTube features and have special movie favorites. Josh loves *Inside Out*, while Bimby goes for the superhero movies.

Another shared favorite is Japanese food. Josh is fond of fruits, while Bimby has fish preferences: fried bangus, tilapia, lapulapu, and galunggong. Both are musically inclined, with Josh on his electric baby grand piano and Bimby on the drums.

Josh is very generous, kindhearted, and loving, never forgetting to set aside from his travel allowance an amount for the *pasalubongs* he wants to bring home.

Bimby may be considered the male Kris, as he is very talkative and is a born entertainer. He regales, even surprises everyone with the adult-like questions he asks: Why does his mother have two sons who have different dads? Why must Kris work so hard when they are already "rich"? And his mother does not water down her answers, from "I was impulsive, I didn't think clearly and carefully," to her desire to be prepared with nest eggs for the two boys.

Aware of his lineage, Bimby has been reminded often enough by his mother that all these trappings of power are fleeting and must not be relied on nor expected.

It is Bimby's growing relationship with his father, basketball icon James Yap, that led Kris to the recent realization that even as she pours heart and soul to be the supermom she aspires to be, she cannot be both father and mother to her sons. She sees that Bimby has needs that only a father can fulfill. That gives her a tinge of regret about Josh not knowing his father, celebrated actor Phillip Salvador, at all.

Bimby already has a 2013 box office hit to his name, *My Little Bossings*. With much amusement, the grown-ups who work with him in his school like to secretly call him their working student, as he has a busy schedule of shoots for pictorials or public appearances. Both brothers have such a busy appointments calendar that when they were invited to pose for a reading promotions poster with their cousins, they expressed regrets because of prior commitments!

Bimby is a Grade 3 student and it is said that the requirement his mother made at the school was for him to speak Filipino as fluently as the President. And of course, the legions of Kris followers must have heard it when she announced on her TV show that Bimby was asked to mop the floor as part of the classroom routine—and that he did with gusto and certainly,with more flair, the trouper that he is.

A sensitive piece of writing on a yellow ruled sheet by Bimby hangs on Kris's makeup mirror. Kris says in a *YES! interview* that Bimby himself put it there the night before the shoot. Entitled "My Fears," he wrote: "My greatest fear is to see Mama kiss a boy. My other fear includes zombies and ghosts. I am also scared to die young. Another thing I don't like are strict teachers. Lastly, I am scared to have a new yaya. I hate my fears but I will tell God to take away my greatest fear." His Yaya Gerbel has been his nanny from birth. **(NSRC)**

The Lighter Side of the Aquinos

What is your best memory of your father and mother?

Ballsy: Dad—always on the move, very hyper. Mom—cool and calm, a woman of deep faith.

Pinky: Dad—his big smile, fantastic memory, and courage. Mom—her strong faith, sincerity, and courage.

PNoy: We were never discouraged from buying books.

Viel: Dad was a great storyteller and always had his audience listening to his every word. Mom's appearance at the U.S. Congress in 1986 and I was fortunate enough to have been the daughter who accompanied her on that trip.

Kris: Watching the evening news in Boston with Dad explaining world events to me. For Mom, watching her cook, getting recipes from her, and now recreating them (spaghetti, adobo, roast beef, Swedish meatballs, baked prawns).

What is your favorite perk of being an Aquino?

Ballsy: I don't know if it is a perk but being the daughter of Ninoy and Cory makes me feel *lamang na ako.*

Pinky: Feeling the love and respect of people here and abroad.

Viel: I feel that most people treat us kindly. Without seeking special treatment, when I get recognized as being an Aquino, I usually get better service.

Kris: No fear of any breach of trust regarding governance or public life/public service.

What do you like least about being an Aquino?

Ballsy: No privacy.

Pinky: Loss of privacy.

Viel: Since our brother is the president, I feel like the whole country's problems are our problems too.

Kris: Nothing. I love my family.

Who is your role model?

Ballsy: In many ways, it would be Mom. But there are many people, unknown to many, who work hard to give the less privileged a better life and I truly look up to them.

Pinky: Mom. When I am not sure what to do, I ask myself what Mom would have done in a similar situation.

Viel: Mom.

Kris: My mom, my Ate, for their patience and kindness.

What are your hopes for the future?

Ballsy: I hope that all Filipinos will be able to go to school and that poverty will be eradicated. For the-not-so distant future, I hope that those who lose in the elections will not blame cheating for their loss, but instead accept their defeat. I also hope that people will be more positive and help improve lives and situations rather than dwell on the negative.

Pinky: I hope the country continues to grow economically so that our country will become first world.

PNoy: What has happened the past five years is just a taste, just a stepping stone, toward greater heights.

Viel: Eradication of corruption and poverty.

Kris: To raise my sons with the same unconditional love and support my mom gave me.

What is the weirdest quirk your family has?

Ballsy: NOBODY drinks alcohol.

Pinky: We talk in codes especially when on the phone (training from martial law years when all our visits to Dad in military prison were monitored through one-way mirrors, visible cameras and guards, and our home phones were bugged). Enjoying a 3 to 4-hour lunch on a Sunday and just catching up.

PNoy: In the Aquino clan, everyone speaks in a loud voice, even those having one-on-one conversations. They only keep quiet when my grandfather or my father is speaking.

Viel: We refer to each other by various nicknames, not just the names that we are known by.

Kris: It's not a quirk but I think a strength: we know that nothing is permanent.

What's the last book you really loved?

Ballsy: The bio of Antonio Chan. What an amazing life he had! Very inspiring.

Pinky: *Your Best Life Now* by Joel Osteen. I read this about eight years ago but to this day, I practice many of the things I learned from the book.

PNoy: Techno thrillers by Matthew Reilly, Dan Brown, Tom Clancy.

Viel: Have recently enjoyed reading books passed on to me by my daughter Jia, from teen-lit books like *Eleanor and Parký* and *The Fault in Our Stars,* to school-prescribed reading material like *The Giver* and *Memoirs of a Geisha.*

Kris: *Who Do You Love* by Jennifer Weiner (Read it in one day. Reading is my passion, my relaxation, and my escape.)

What "most likely to" superlative would you be most honored to receive?

Pinky: Most likely to be a loving lola. I see how my kids had such a wonderful relationship with Mom and have so many loving experiences with her that I wish for that.

Kris: The ultimate stage mother to Bimb.

Who is the most energetic Aquino sibling?

Ballsy: Pinky and Kris would be tied for most energetic.

Pinky: Most hyper would be Kris and myself, most shy would be Viel.

PNoy: Si Pinky siguro. Si Kris naman very workaholic.

Viel: Pinky and Kris are both hyper.

Kris: Pinky and me.

The most demure/shy/quiet?

Ballsy: Viel

Pinky: Viel

PNoy: Si Viel normally quiet. Pag nagsalita, napaka lalim talaga. Napakamalaman. Ate Ballsy is our second mom, keeps us on an even keel. Kris is sui generis.

Viel: I'm definitely the shyest and most quiet but not quite demure.

Kris: Ate. Shy/quiet: Viel.

Who is the best cook?

Ballsy: Kris

Pinky: Kris

PNoy: All of them have their specialties. Pinky has a Caesar salad dressing, but Mom is the best cook.

Viel: Kris. Actually, it's embarrassing to admit but I don't cook at all.

Kris: Me.

Best "eater"?

Ballsy: We all are eaters.

Pinky: PNoy.

PNoy: I love to eat what they bake.

Viel: We all have good appetites!

Favorite place in the world?

Ballsy: Kung nasaan ang aking pamilya.

Pinky: Our home.

PNoy: I feel like a fish out of water outside the Philippines. I am not really a travel bug.

Viel: Osaka or Tokyo.

Kris: Apart from our beaches (Amanpulo, Boracay, Coron), it would have to be Japan.

Favorite pastime?

Ballsy: Needlework or simple artwork to relax, and shopping for nonessentials but feeling good about my purchases.

Pinky: Paper crafts.

PNoy: Shooting and listening to music.

Viel: Doing puzzles.

Kris: Travel if there's enough free time from work, cooking if I need to unwind.

Embarrassing moment related to being an Aquino?

Pinky: Honestly? None.

Viel: Would rather not think of this.

Kris: It takes a lot to get me embarrassed.

Favorite pet peeve?

Ballsy: People who take advantage of other people's kindness, generosity.

Pinky: People who always see the glass half-empty.

PNoy: Those who only know you during elections. Those who have nothing to say but criticisms.

Viel: People who feel and act like they are above others.

Kris: I'm actually very patient already and quite zen about life.

Most annoying habit?

Ballsy: Mañana habit.

Pinky: Too much clutter.

Viel: Procrastination and not keeping things in order (desk at work is really a mess).

Kris: None.

Best habit?

Ballsy: Praying five rosaries daily.

Pinky: Trying to make at least 10 thousand steps daily.

Viel: Judicious use of funds (both personal and foundation's funds).

Kris: Gratitude and generosity.

Who would be your dream dinner guest?

Ballsy: Mother Mary.

Pinky: Mom and Dad so that I can see their proud faces when we talk about PNoy. Would love to see how Dad will react to meeting his grandchildren for the first time and how Mom will reunite with them. Wow!

PNoy: They no longer exist—Mandela, Napoleon, Stalin, Hitler, *kung maayos sana kausap*—To find out why they chose the paths they did.

Viel: Can't think of any.

Kris: James Patterson (I've read 95 percent of all his books, I am a FAN.)

VIII.
Some of the
President's Men

On Being the Presidential Adviser

xcerpts from the interview with Sec. Sonny Coloma, Presidential Communications Operations Office

What are your principal responsibilities as a Cabinet member/presidential adviser?
As head of the Presidential Communications Operations Office (PCOO), I am performing the functions of a press secretary. I also serve as spokesperson of the President and in so doing, I answer any and all questions from the media on the President's decisions, policies, and actions. I also conduct regular press briefings.

My office supervises all government media organizations: Philippine Information Agency, People's Television Network, Philippine Broadcasting Service (Radyo ng Bayan), National Printing Office, and APO Production Unit.

What is a typical day like for you?
My typical waking time is between 4:30 a.m. and 5 a.m. I start my day with twenty minutes of meditation. (I learned the techniques of Transcendental Meditation in 2009.) Then I open my laptop and read the online version of the daily broadsheets so I would know the main news of the day and get an eyeball view of the editorial commentary. As early as 5:30 a.m., I could

be doing a radio or TV interview by phone patch. Overnight, I would have received several questions sent via SMS by Palace reporters and foreign correspondents, so I start replying to each of these. Breakfast happens between 6:30 and 7:30 a.m. On special days, my wife and I hear mass at 6:20 to 7:00 a.m. in our nearby parish church. Three times a week, I do an exercise routine: either walking in the swimming pool or stretching guided by a physical therapist.

I leave for work at around 9 a.m. and head for either Malacañan Palace or Quezon City, where many of the offices I supervise are located.

On Tuesdays and Thursdays, my regular press briefing days, I prepare with my staff answers to questions received from the members of the Malacañan Press Corps. The first wave of questions (received overnight and early morning) is from the radio and TV reporters; the second wave comes mainly from the print media organizations.

The rest of the day may be spent attending Cabinet cluster meetings, or being called to the President's private office for meetings of the communications team to discuss messaging.

Aside from the scheduled Cabinet meetings, how much time or on what occasions are you in direct contact with the President?

On more than twenty occasions during the past five years, I was a member of the President's official delegation to overseas state visits, working visits, or participation in the ASEAN meetings. This means being with him aboard the plane and in lunch or dinner events associated with the visit or summit. The lengthiest was the twelve-day Europe-US trip in September 2014, followed by the six-day U.S.-Canada trip in May 2015. There are also numerous in-country trips where I also joined the President.

Moreover, there are frequent meetings between the President and the communications team (say, at least twice a week) that he calls on an unscheduled basis.

How accessible is the President to you or your office?

I am ready to receive his voice call or text message anytime.

How would you describe the President's work style or management style?

"Magaan na boss si Presidente" is what I usually tell friends, who express surprise seeing me in, say, parish fellowship or high school classmates' impromptu reunions, or in the golf course. He is not a micro-manager who would look over a Cabinet member's shoulder. He is probably

the first president who, after appointing his Cabinet members, allowed them to form their own management teams in their respective departments. Hence, he would occasionally remind us in Cabinet meetings that there is no reason or excuse for any one of us to say he or she could not execute properly or effectively. (In the two previous occasions when I served in the government, I observed that the Presidents appointed undersecretaries who were not necessarily known to the Cabinet secretary.)

He is very thorough in studying and analyzing recommendations for decisions or actions that he must approve. Early on, Cabinet members realized that it is imperative for them to be fully prepared to explain what they present or recommend during Cabinet meetings or even Cabinet cluster meetings where key decisions are vetted. As a professor, I appreciate the rigor that he imposes on depth of analysis.

But he is also one who would occasionally inject humor, banter, and music while presiding in a meeting called to tackle serious matters of state. He would take out his phone and read jokes sent by friends or focus attention on someone who may have been noticeably reserved or quiet during the meeting. Or he may even play a tune while speechwriters are revising a draft.

What is the most interesting part of your job?
The variety and diversity of the portfolio of my Office is quite interesting. It includes all forms of media (print, broadcast, social or news). It has nationwide coverage reaching the grassroots.

What is most challenging?
Dealing directly with media and replying to questions, either face to face during the regular press briefings, or even by phone or text messages, are by far the most challenging aspect of my job. I always remember the toothpaste analogy. Every word that I say is like toothpaste: once it's out of the tube, there's no way you can push or force it back in. It requires intense focus and concentration on nuances of language and on possible "angles" or "spin" possibilities. This is where Stephen Covey's maxim, "Begin with the end in mind" comes into play vividly. The way a question is framed is often linked to the headline that's contemplated by the editorial desk. Hence, the reply must be framed in a way that minimizes the possibilities for "spin" or distortion.

Above all, it is a daunting and serious responsibility to be speaking for the President of the Philippines. I am reminded that even in off-hours, people still see me not just as an alter ego of the President but also as one who directly speaks for him.

Is your relationship with the President both personal and professional?

It's professional. But when we are on overseas or out-of-town trips, there are many opportunities for personal, off-the-cuff type interactions where his friendly and convivial character emerges.

How did you get recruited into the presidential team? What would you consider your best preparation for this job?

I served with Pres. Corazon Aquino from 1989 to 1991 in various positions, the latest of which was as head of the Presidential Management Staff and Cabinet secretary. Hence, I was known to the Aquino family, especially to the President's eldest sister who was their mother's private secretary. But I met and became acquainted with then senator Noynoy Aquino only in January 2010 when the campaign was about to start. I joined the Noynoy Aquino Media Bureau after it was organized in December 2009.

Being a professor is the best preparation for my present job. I am accustomed to dealing with complex and complicated issues—and distilling the essence so that these may be framed and communicated in plain, person-on-the-street language. My experience as a student activist during the First Quarter Storm also enabled me to learn how to speak Filipino fluently. Few people would guess I am Ilocano by blood. As early as I was in Grade Six, I became exposed to working in a printing press.

Knowing how to meditate is also a vital aid. It has helped me maintain focus and composure amidst a highly stressful work situation (especially when interacting with media).

What do you do to unwind from the demands of your job?

Playing golf affords me quality time for relaxation and exercise in a cool and pleasant setting, while having conversation and light banter with friends.

When I reach home, I "tune out" from the news. Watching sports and Korean drama episodes are my favorite pastimes at home.

Weekends are reserved for family lunch, dinner, or out-of-town trips.

What might you consider your contributions to the position? If you were to describe yourself in three words, what would these be?

Helping maintain the President's public approval ratings at all-time high levels is probably the ultimate measure of the effectiveness of our communications team. Strengthening the

Philippine Information Agency as a public institution comes next. During my watch, PIA (which has 16 regional offices and 71 provincial offices) was recognized by the Philippine Quality Award and has become an ISO-certified organization. Being able to maintain professional and cordial relations with the Palace press corps and with all major media organizations is also an essential contribution.

Believer.

Enabler.

Communicator.

What do the last few months of the presidency look to you?

"Finish strong" is my mantra for the homestretch phase. It feels good to have served with the President from start to finish. It is a rare opportunity and privilege to have earned a ringside seat where one was not just a witness but also a participant.

I am looking forward to our hosting of the APEC economic leaders' meeting in November. We will be hosting as well more than 3,000 journalists and media people from twenty countries. Preparing a transition report is also an important priority. Passing on some kind of a guide map or road map on doing things in a better way is a vital project.

What are your plans after June 30, 2016?

Return to being a full-time professor at the Asian Institute of Management. Resume work as management consultant. Play golf more than once a week. Travel more frequently with family.

What are your favorite or most memorable PNoy anecdotes or stories?

When I congratulated him via text message on the morning after he delivered his final SONA, this was his reply: "Sonny, you will never hear me say I did this or that, it will always be 'We.'"

After learning that the Supreme Court had upheld President Arroyo's appointment of Renato Corona as Chief Justice in April 2010 just before the elections, our Media Bureau prepared a strongly worded statement in his behalf. We also arranged for him to be interviewed by a TV crew for the primetime news as he was arriving from an out-of-town sortie. When I watched the evening news, I was surprised that there was no news about his reaction to the Supreme Court decision. I called up Maria Montelibano and inquired if the TV crew had arrived at the airport in time, and she said yes. "So how come there's no news about him?" I asked. I found out that the President had said, "Let's read and understand the decision first. When the Supreme Court decides, we need to understand its decision." I realized that this Filipino who would probably become President had great respect for the Supreme Court as one of the pillars of our democracy, even if its decision contradicted his personal view.

After learning of the Supreme Court's DAP ruling, he exhibited the same degree of circumspection. He patiently read and studied the main ruling as well as all of the concurring and dissenting opinions. Thus, it was not until July 15, or two weeks later, that he finally spoke against the ruling—and only after fully absorbing and analyzing the landmark decision.

During the aftermath of the Mamasapano incident that played out in media headlines for more than two months (January to March 2015), I was asked by the Palace reporters: "How is the President taking all of these?" My answer: "With equanimity and objectivity." Despite the high emotions and the nearly hysterical media hype, the President remained composed and unfazed. He said it was important to stay focused on ferreting out the truth.

In the Service of Two Aquino Presidents

T he youthful recollections of Aquino niece Maria Vargas Montelibano about their many clan gatherings always had images of her Tito Ninoy as the life of the party. He was the task master for all his nephews and nieces who were coaxed to perform a song, poem, or dance each time. Tita Cory was always the supportive wife, prim and proper, in direct contrast to the boisterous and rowdy Aquino clan.

Ninoy stood tall and was always the uncle hero of the family. They all knew how he volunteered to be a *Manila Times* correspondent for the Korean War and his dangerous mission to convince Huk leader Luis Taruc to come down from the hills. And how these awed them. Each time he ran in an election, they were recruited to give flowers to the sick and the aged in the hospital, or participate in dances in the town halls in Tarlac, their manageable ways of campaigning. They went all out in support, enjoying themselves in the process.

Ninoy was also looked up to for good counsel. Maria's mother Erlinda, a sister of Ninoy (through his father's first marriage to Maria Urquico), sought his advice when her daughter Maria got married. Her mother complained to him and wanted his help for an annulment as she was very concerned about the "Bacolod bad boy" reputation of her new son-in-law. Ninoy spoke to Maria, who would have neither change of heart nor mind. "When I told him my getting married was my own decision, he said he will convince my mother to accept my decision." But his words also bore the firm warning that Maria should be prepared to accept the consequences and that she would have to "sleep in [her] own bed."

It has not been a bed of thorns that she has had to sleep on, as Maria remains happily married to Inquirer.net columnist Jose Ma. "Boy" Montelibano for forty-six years now. Meanwhile, as her marriage and family life flourished, so did her career in television, the profession of her choice, a passion for her, a field where she excels.

Maria has always wanted to be a TV director. At twelve years old, she became a summer apprentice for Fr. James Reuter, SJ's TV shows. She continued on for three summers. "But I never imagined my work to be intertwined with the history of our country." Especially not after her own martial law experience.

When martial law was declared in 1972 and the broadcasting network ABS-CBN shut down, Maria lost her job as staff director. She became a freelance producer and director for television, directing shows on GMA 7 and RPN 9. By then, Maria had realized what her expertise could do so eloquently: "the power of capturing on audio or video an event and then sharing this truth with others."

This was proven yet again in a highly dramatic manner on August 21, 1983. When her grandmother and Ninoy's mother, Doña Aurora Aquino decided not to clean or change Ninoy's clothes after his assassination—so the world "should see what they did to my son"—Maria captured on film that bloodied and bruised face in the coffin in Times Street and released it so everyone could see the brutality. Maria's production team covered the historic funeral march, too. Again, these videos were shared with the public.

With the assassination of Ninoy, Maria began to tell herself that one cannot accept things as they are. She thought, "This isn't over, we must fight back." That was when she began to document what was happening in the streets—the regular yellow confetti rallies at Ayala, the meetings, and the speeches. "What better way to show what was happening and awaken others than to show [them] on video?" Reaching out to the larger public was important because the government-controlled press did not have any coverage of the opposition's mass action.

She recalls the tedious and laborious process of film production then. During the campaign of Cory Aquino, she would cover the rallies and speeches, edit these and dub ten copies on Betamax or VHS format. These would go to Maria's handpicked businessmen friends and leaders of the opposition who would again dub five copies and send to other contacts, who in turn would do the same. Taking pride in what she and her team managed to accomplish given the constraints, she says with amusement, "There were no YouTube, no multiple dubbing facilities, no Internet then. So each video material was done manually." And painstakingly, too.

In March 1986, President Cory, who was familiar with Maria's work as a director, asked her to direct her first presidential provincial trip to Davao. She said the EDSA Revolution was in Manila and people in the provinces needed to know what happened and also get to know her. She wanted each trip documented and shown on television. Then Executive Secretary Joker Arroyo instructed Maria to reorganize the old government agency called Radio, TV & Movies, which did all the presidential documentation and movies in Malacañang. The "movies" portion was dropped and Radio TV Malacañang was born, headed by Maria as its executive director.

It was a special privilege for Maria to see up close her Tita Cory become the kind of president she had been. Maria recalls that at the beginning of her term, she would always say, "I wonder what Ninoy would do in this situation?" But during two challenging occasions, Maria suddenly realized and appreciated that President Cory had become her own person. One was when she had to let go of then DILG Secretary Nene Pimentel on the OIC issue, despite his being among her close friends. The other was the relief of then Defense Secretary Juan Ponce Enrile after a coup d'état. Many of her advisers told her not to do so, but she did what she believed had to be done.

To Maria, there were two memorable highlights of the Cory Aquino presidency. "I would get a lump in my throat each time she would get standing ovations for her speeches in the presidential visits abroad." Two of these were her address to the U.S. Congress in 1986 and her 1989 visit to France for its bicentennial celebration.

Maria also remembers that Tita Cory had a lip twitch whenever she was displeased with a situation. Or she would simply resume her paperwork or read the newspaper to show her displeasure with a person. "Since I always spoke my mind and oftentimes was out of line, I would get that treatment," Maria recalls fondly.

Cory was a pillar of strength for Maria. Seeing Cory's life was filled with prayers, especially during the presidency, this gave Maria the faith that no matter what obstacles the Malacañang years posed, the coup d'etats included, the presidency would survive. "She was so close to God that I felt confident . . . ." Maria says that Tita Cory's most profound influence on her was her "learning to pray." Her own sense of spirituality and service to others has been deepened so that since 2001, she and her husband Boy have immersed themselves in Gawad Kalinga and the service of building communities for the less privileged. She draws inspiration from Pope

Francis and his book, *Open Mind, Faithful Heart: Reflections on Following Jesus.*

Her Tito Ninoy emerged the martyr hero after his death, "galvanizing the Filipino people to rise and fight the dictatorial regime of Marcos. In that sense, he fulfilled his main mission."

His life story and that of Cory Aquino may not be known to today's millennials, as August 21, 1983 was thirty-two years ago, more than a generation back. It is significant for them to know that Ninoy Aquino's death aroused heightened patriotism in the Filipino.

Maria continues to be driven in her work and is extremely proud of her Aquino heritage. She vows to continue to work to provide and open more opportunities for the less fortunate.

She likes to emphasize that her very charismatic Tito Ninoy was considered the politician par excellence but was transformed into ways more meaningful. He was *"tunay na politico,"* to mean how he could regale the crowd with his stories, talk authoritatively in rapid fire fashion on any topic, leaving the audience in awe. Those were the days when the word *"trapo"* was not part of our vocabulary, adds Maria. It was not a word that had to be resorted to.

With Ninoy's spiritual transformation in prison, Maria recounts that her uncle was still charismatic but more authentic and certainly beyond politics.

Her Tita Cory always remained "the pillar of quiet strength, of what was decent, simple, and good in politics." She became the nemesis of Marcos because they were diametrically opposed. The Marcos name was associated with corruption, human rights abuses, and dirty politics.

Both Ninoy and Cory were authentic individuals and Maria bears witness to the simple lives they led. How Maria misses them both.

To Maria, it is a unique privilege to serve in Malacañang for two Aquino presidents, an aunt in 1986 and a first cousin since 2010. "Slowly, I began to realize how privileged I was to be part of history up close, to be a relative and serving two presidents who both only had the mantra of making the lives of the Filipino better."

She was the communications director of Noynoy's campaign, was appointed national events director by Sec. Sonny Coloma of the PCOO, and executive director of the EDSA People Power Commission.

When PNoy assumed the presidency, Maria had remarked that her Tito Ninoy would have been very proud of his only son. "What more can a father ask for, that his only son fulfill his dream, and finish the work that he had started?" Truly, Ninoy Aquino did not die in vain. **(NSRC)**

A Most Trusted Assistant

Rafael "Rapa" Cojuangco Lopa, son of Cory Aquino's sister Terry and Ricardo A. Lopa, was much more than a mere nephew to President Cory. He remembers that he was only four years old when he began to be "starstruck" with his Uncle Ninoy who was then running for the Senate. Ninoy's charismatic and engaging presence would always be felt in any room he stepped into. One could not help but take notice of this. In contrast, his Auntie Cory was always the quiet and attentive wife, mother, and aunt. It was she that Rapa saw more often than Ninoy back then at the Cojuangcos' weekly Friday reunions at the Palm Avenue home of his maternal grandparents, Jose and Demetria Sumulong Cojuangco.

Rapa was a college junior at the Ateneo when Ninoy Aquino was assassinated. After graduation, he immediately joined Sariling Sikap, Inc. (SSI), an NGO headed by the late Dr. Antonio L. Ledesma. This was short lived as he took a leave to join the Cory Aquino campaign for the 1986 snap elections, helping in the distribution of campaign collaterals. He resumed work with SSI as a community organizer when his aunt became president. He worked with fisher folks, small farmers, landless laborers, and indigenous peoples, helping them organize cooperatives to enhance their livelihood. After "the ultimate sacrifice of Uncle Ninoy in 1983 and the courageous response of Auntie Cory to challenge the dictatorship and embrace the challenges" of the presidency, Rapa felt he had to do his share in the way he could, humble though it may be. He was also inspired and motivated (call it the Jesuit "brainwash," he jests) by the Ateneo mantra to be a man for others. He knew he had to "immerse [himself] in the realities of our broken society."

In 1993, while he was executive director of SSI and a young father of two, Rapa received a call from his second cousin Tonyboy Cojuangco, then PLDT president and chief executive officer. Tonyboy broached the idea of helping his aunt, who had completed her term of office, to manage the Benigno S. Aquino, Jr. Foundation (BSAF) established soon after the 1983 assassination. She had wanted to continue to serve the marginalized through NGOs and through the foundation. The call was timely: it came as he was considering other employment options because his growing family was finding it difficult to live on his NGO compensation. That was not a decision he struggled with, Rapa remembers. "It was a no brainer. Who in his right mind would not like to work for her?"

In August 1993, Rapa began to work for Cory as her executive assistant in BSAF which she chaired. Thus began a profoundly meaningful experience for Rapa. If truth be told, he was initially intimidated by the very idea of working for a former president and a living icon of democracy. He felt inadequate, but she always encouraged and trusted him. She valued his NGO community work experience and sought his opinion on projects that many groups presented to her, aspiring for her support. She never claimed to know it all, and was humble enough to learn new things even from a "younger, less experienced guy like [Rapa]."

Because Cory could not accept all the invitations she continued to get, she assigned Rapa to represent her in meetings with high-level officials. His reports and feedback from those meetings became the basis for her decision on which programs and advocacies she would be involved in. He grew into the job and found himself entrusted with more and bigger responsibilities as she chose to be more involved in the formation of coalitions to protect the country's young and newly regained democracy from various threats. He was drawn to sensitive backroom negotiations and meetings to pave the way for a peaceful transition of leadership during both the Estrada and the Arroyo administrations.

Such was the context of the working environment that allowed Rapa to get to know his Auntie Cory better and in a new light. Rapa had grown to be her most trusted assistant. She was no longer just the former president and icon of democracy that he was in awe of. She was now his mentor, confidante, a second mother, and companion in what he describes as "a journey of responding to God's call." He saw at close range, in ways tangible and intangible, her "fidelity to the Lord's calling." He continues to describe what is akin to a spiritual experience for him: that she loved unconditionally and that she was "truly a modern-day imitation of Christ."

For Rapa, this was his own awakening. He saw in the lives of Ninoy and Cory how difficult it was to embrace God's will. He saw what it meant to leave their comfortable worlds and to respond for what the common good calls for. "In Uncle Ninoy's case, it meant seven years and seven months of unjust incarceration" and falling victim to an assassin's bullet.

Drawing from lessons learned in proximity to Ninoy and Cory, Rapa addresses the millennials, for them to appreciate what recent Philippine history, only a generation ago, had yielded. He reminds them that the wonders and the phenomenon of social media may have misled them to be narcissistic, to focus only on themselves. He narrates that his Uncle Ninoy, the charmer, was ambitious and driven, a popular young man in a hurry. He must have drawn much admiration. "But what made him the man that he became were those long days in solitary confinement, where he discovered his God and the mission he was called to do." How appropriate a symbol was his final image on the tarmac, his body and arms forming a cross, just as he embraced life's cross given him.

His Auntie Cory, the grieving widow, became the reluctant president, transforming from the quiet and nurturing spouse and solo parent to their five children. Even during the last years of her life, she was still considered the guardian and protector of the democracy she helped restore, a woman of influence in Philippine politics. She often received harsh criticism from even former allies that the "Cory magic" was long gone. She chose to ignore all these, following only what she believed was right and good.

"It was in death that both of them showed that it is how much we love that matters. It is not about what people say about us and the rewards that the world will give us in our lifetime. In the end, it is how many lives we will touch and how they, in turn, will touch others. It is about how we can journey together and help each find God in our lives," Rapa shares.

What perhaps concretizes what Cory was to Rapa, is the incident regarding her seventy-fifth birthday in 2008. To surprise her, he solicited letters from her friends to form part of a tribute on the foundation's website. He thought nothing unusual nor unbecoming about this, for as he explained in his profusely apologetic letter to her, "The tribute was intended to be a compilation of what many of your friends have always wanted to say about you but may have not had the chance or opportunity to do so."

Instead of feeling complimented, his Auntie Cory was very upset and took offense, despite his reassurance that he received enthused and positive responses. Rapa further explained that he did not tell her about it as it was meant to be a surprise for her milestone birthday. He apologized, "After all these years, I really should have known better, that you really do not wish to bother other people anymore about requests or favors of this sort."

The next day, he received a text message from her, "Okay, Rapa. Let's just get back to our work."

Today, Rapa Lopa continues his leadership role as executive director of the now-renamed Ninoy and Cory Foundation, Inc. and also of the Philippine Business for Social Progress, the country's largest corporate-led foundation for social development. With regard the position he currently holds, he says in a November 2014 interview with the Business Call to Action of the United Nations Development Programme (UNDP): "My current job is really just a scaling up of what I have been doing all my life, which is to engage change agents that will empower those who are less fortunate."

Just as in the Cory Aquino administration, he holds no government position in the present administration. He says he only talks to his cousin PNoy whenever he is called, which is seldom. He was involved in several aspects of managing the campaign and enjoyed most working with Mon and Abby Jimenez in the communication strategy and execution.

One of his former colleagues in the Ninoy and Cory Foundation, Inc. only has generous words about Rapa: "A really good and generous person, with no airs. I never saw him angry or push his weight around. Always accessible no matter how busy he is, he finds time to listen."

He unwinds by watching movies with his family, visiting the family farm, and reading spiritual books especially by his favorite author, Dutch Catholic priest Henri Nouwen who writes about pastoral ministry, spirituality, social justice, and community. His friends rightly label him as "restless." He admits that, owing to his impatience for change, he gets involved in so many things all at the same time. Things must get much better than they are today, and the number of poor people must dramatically be lessened. To him, "The status quo is not good enough."

Appendix

Maria Corazon Cojuangco Aquino

Born on January 25, 1933, Maria Corazon "Cory" Aquino was the sixth of eight children of Jose Cojuangco and Demetria Sumulong, both from politically prominent and wealthy clans. She attended grade school at St. Scholastica's College, and then went to the U.S. for her high-school education. She then moved to the U.S. where she continued her studies at Ravenhill Academy in Philadelphia and Notre Dame Convent School in New York City. At the College of Mount Saint Vincent in New York, Cory graduated with a bachelor's degree in French and minor in Math. While in the U.S., she also volunteered during the 1948 presidential campaign of Republican Thomas Dewey. Returning to the Philippines, she took up law classes at the Far Eastern University, but discontinued this when she married Ninoy.

Known for her deep faith and simple lifestyle, Cory preferred to be on the backstage during her husband's political career, supporting him during his campaigns and his incarceration, even as she endeavored to give their children as normal a family life as was possible.

Cory was eventually put on the spotlight after her husband was assassinated in 1983, as she was seen by many as the force that can unify the opposition. She was eventually prevailed upon to be the united opposition's presidential candidate, and run against Ferdinand Marcos during the 1986 snap election, thereby challenging his two-decade rule.

After numerous protests and rallies against the violence and alleged fraud in the elections, the defection of military officers from Marcos, and mobilization of religious, political, and civic groups who went to EDSA, and the success of the nonviolent People Power Revolution in February 1986, Cory was sworn in as the 11th president and the first woman president of the Philippines.

While her term inherited a country beset by economic and political difficulties, including significant external debts, high inflation, and several coup d'état attempts, several reforms took place under her leadership. The 1986 Freedom Constitution was put in place, until the 1987 Constitution was ratified. The president's powers were limited, and the Congress was restored. Numerous legislations were crafted, including the Local Government Code, Comprehensive Agrarian Reform Law, Build-Operate-Transfer Law, and Foreign Investments Act. The government worked to achieve higher economic growth while minimizing fiscal deficit, debt-to-GDP ratio, and inflation rates.

Although qualified to run again for the presidency as she was not inaugurated under the current Constitution, she opted not to do so. After her term ended in 1992, Cory remained an active voice during consequent attempts at reforming the Constitution to extend the term of the president, as well as allegations of politicians' abuse of power. She continued to give speeches on democracy and various issues, and was also involved in initiatives for low-income population, and served as chair of the Benigno S. Aquino, Jr. Foundation. Cory has also been a recipient of various awards and honorary degrees from institutions locally and abroad.

After battling cancer for over a year, Cory passed on last August 1, 2009 at the age of 76. In honor of the "woman in yellow," thousands of Filipinos lined the routes during her funeral procession, which lasted more than eight hours. From the time she was ill until the day she was laid to rest, yellow ribbons, banners, and confetti could be seen in the streets—the same color that had come to symbolize Filipinos' fight for democracy—as an expression of solidarity in her struggle, and love and respect for the woman who served as the country's icon and champion of democracy.

Ninoy and Cory are survived by their children Maria Elena Aquino-Cruz (Ballsy), Aurora Corazon Aquino-Abellada (Pinky), Victoria Elisa Aquino-Dee (Viel), Kristina Bernadette Aquino (Kris), and Benigno Simeon Aquino III (Noynoy), who is also the 15th president of the Philippines.

The State of the Nation Message of Her Excellency Corazon C. Aquino, President of the Philippines, to the Congress

Delivered at the Batasang Pambansa, Quezon City, on July 27, 1987

M r. President of the Senate; Mr. Speaker of the House of Representatives; members of both Houses of Congress; the Vice President and members of the Cabinet; the Chief Justice and the associate justices of the Supreme Court; Your Excellencies of the Diplomatic Corps; distinguished guests; ladies and gentlemen:

Fifteen years ago, in this season of the year, my husband stood in the Senate and delivered what turned out to be the valedictory of Philippine democracy. He exposed the conspiracy to place the country under martial law, dissolve the Congress, and set the stage for the unremitting plunder of our patrimony and the degradation of our great name and honor.

The dictatorship's last mockery of democracy was committed in this hall, where the loser was proclaimed winner of the snap election. Today, I join you in rededicating this hall to true democracy. [*Applause*]

The route to these chambers was long and difficult, fraught with danger and paved with sacrifice. The electoral contest just completed has been exacting for all and bitter for some. But the nation has spoken. The complete leadership of this country has been chosen; the configuration of their powers and duties permanently set by the new Constitution.

An election is as much an expression as it is an exercise of the national will. We have been made instruments of this will. Our performance will bear witness to its wisdom.

It is my duty under the Constitution to apprise you now of the state of the nation—but henceforth its continuing progress shall be our common accountability.

THE ECONOMIC PROGRAM

When I took power in this country 17 months ago, I was immediately called upon to deal with the dangerous combination of a severely distressed economy and a growing insurgency; threats which fed on each other and on the hopelessness and confusion which prevailed. Production had contracted by 11% for two consecutive years, bringing unemployment rates to double-digit levels. Twelve percent of the labor force, nearly 2.6 million workers, were unemployed. (And up to now, 750,000 join the labor force every year.) Real per capita income had been set back 10 years. New investments had dried up and business confidence was at an all-time low. Interest payments on a $26.3 billion external debt took almost half our export earnings. And as I must stress yet again, no part of this debt benefited, or perhaps was even seriously expected to benefit the Filipino people. Yet their posterity to the third generation and farther are expected to pay it.

Poverty blighted the land. Five million families (or 59% of the total) lived below the poverty line, as compared to 45% in 1971. Dictatorship had done nothing but make more of our people poorer.

It also made us sicker. The prevalence of malnutrition among our young and the incidence of birth fatalities had risen at alarming rates.

In short, I inherited an economy in shambles and a polity with no institutions save my presidency to serve as the cornerstone of the new democracy that we set out to build.

I had taken the oath to be president of a country that had lost everything, everything but honor. With that honor came a renewed faith in national leadership and in the ability of our race to change things for the better given the will and the courage to do it. [*Applause*]

I responded with an economic reform program aimed at recovery in the short, and sustainable growth in the long run. More concretely, it addressed itself to the basic problems of unemployment and underemployment, and the consequent mass poverty.

The program calls for comprehensive structural reforms of the internal economy, complemented by no less important external economic cooperation.

There are two basic features of this program:

The first is its comprehensiveness with respect to structural reforms. We have come to regard the scope of reform not as a problem, but as a challenge, as necessary as it is ambitious; and as realizable as the strength of our commitment allows.

The second basic feature is its reliance on the private sector to carry the main burden of growth. We have reaffirmed our faith in private initiative to propel and sustain our economy. Our premise is that, for as long as free market forces dictate the dynamics of the business environment, the private sector will respond aggressively. As a corollary, the program defines and limits government's participation in the economy.

INTERNAL STRUCTURAL REFORMS

The dictatorship gave special privileges to government corporations and select individuals. In their various forms, these enterprises had several things in common: They enriched the few at the cost of impoverishing the many. They distorted markets and factors of production. And they bore the aspect of legitimacy that made challenge and change impossible.

We abolished these monopolies and special privileges and the effect was felt almost immediately. Fertilizer prices dropped 33% and farmgate prices of copra nearly doubled in 1986. We trace in part the renewed vigor in agriculture and the general economy to these and similar measures.

We committed ourselves to a fair and transparent trade liberalization program that is consistent with our country's continuing weaknesses. Some 1,000 items were released, from a complex bureaucracy of licensing requirements, into a regime of rational tariff protection.

We removed price controls which had been an almost permanent fixture of the past regime. And yet inflation was less than 1% for the whole of 1986 and our estimates place it at an average of 1% for the first half of this year.

We instituted tax reforms to shelter the poor from onerous taxes and equitably redistribute the tax burden. We created an Asset Privatization Trust and a Committee on Privatization to start the divestiture of government control or participation in private business and, with the Sequestered Assets Disposition Authority, the SADA, to help fund the Comprehensive Agrarian Reform Program that I enacted last week.

EXTERNAL COOPERATION

Recession hit the international economy in the early eighties. Every economy suffered, but the heaviest toll was taken on the fragile economies of the developing nations. One of the worst hit was our own. The dictatorship had already borrowed heavily, exceeding the debt ceiling mandated by law, when interest rates shot up. Meanwhile, a material portion of the debt had gone to projects that offered virtually no hope of payback. Conceived to either line pockets or inflate egos, these projects would never contribute to the repayment of the debt.

The domestic structural reform program we have initiated cannot be pursued in earnest unless the necessary financing is made available. Fresh funding is needed to effect adjustments in the industrial structure, to assist new ventures, and to support our social programs. This funding cannot come from the domestic economy. Low domestic incomes cannot generate the required savings. Meanwhile, debt service was taking half our export earnings. Rescue could only come from foreign sources, both official and private.

Our appeal for external economic cooperation was aimed at gaining increased flexibility in our domestic resource management. The program required a reduction in our debt burden and increased support from bilateral and multilateral institutions. Simply put, we needed to buy time for our structural reforms to start paying dividends. And time is money. While a fool and his money are easily parted, we have discovered that our foreign creditors are not such great fools as the past leadership of our country.

It is my sad duty to report to you that the results of the recently concluded debt renegotiations are far short of our expectations and, more importantly, of our urgent needs. Let me put it bluntly. Our extraordinary achievement in fulfilling the first requirement of renegotiation, the establishment of free and responsible government, gained us applause but no substantial accommodation from our foreign creditors. The saga of democracy had made great television, but no appreciable change on their business priorities. We were treated not much better than other debtors, even those who had rejected the austere discipline mandated by restructuring. A discipline we had readily accepted. Incredibly, despite the significant reduction in country risk effected by the democratic restoration, we were not accorded the terms given other countries, which got longer periods, better rates, and greater latitude for growth.

We cannot help but feel that our foreign creditors took undue and unfair advantage of the internal difficulties we have with factions intent on subverting this government and destroying our democracy. Under the continuing threat of a cutoff in trade credits, which would have given new vigor and a signal to seize the moment to the enemies of democracy, we had to relent and sign the accord.

Nothing is more revealing of the tenor of the negotiations than the insistence that our government assume the liability of planters products to a consortium of banks. Their private risk would have to become our public liability. Nonetheless, the demand stood and provided the none too subtle coercion—sign or face the prospect of a protracted delay in the finalization of the debt restructuring program agreed to in March 1987.

We do not bow our heads in shame, for the shame is not ours. Yet even as necessity has forced our hand to agreement, we vow never again to let the patrimony of this nation lie at the feet of these noble houses that have finally shown the true face of foreign finance. [*Applause*]

For the record, our foreign debt stands today in excess of $28 billion. The increase from $26.3 billion when we took power is largely accounted for by the weakening of the dollar against major currencies. In the next six years, we shall have to pay $20.4 billion to our official and private creditors. Net payments could average 5% of our total output. Close to 40% of government expenditures and over 45% of our projected merchandise export earnings, or 27% of all foreign earnings, will go towards servicing this debt. The bottomline, honorable members of Congress, is that we have been left little room for domestic error. It is for this reason that I have yielded more to prudence than desire in the reform measures I have enacted. I have aimed for modest successes to avoid a comprehensive failure.

Still, despite our disappointments in this sector, I am pleased to report certain healthy signs in the economy. Recession bottomed out in late 1986. GNP posted a modest growth at 1.5%; significant nonetheless because of the previous two years' negative performance. Exports posted a volume growth of 21.7% and provided the much needed boost. To be candid, as we must always be, fortuity can account for these improvements as much as the reform measures we had taken. For the low 0.7% inflation rate in 1986 was largely a reflection of the drop in oil prices and the prevailing weak demand and purchasing power.

Our reform measures, however, started to pay dividends in the first half of this year. Our estimate of first quarter GNP is 5.5%. Unemployment declined from 12% last year to 11.2%. The exchange rate remained relatively stable. And gross international reserves at the Central Bank stood at about $2.4 billion as of the end of June 1987, or the equivalent of five months' merchandise imports.

What is important is that this time it is not the world market but a reinvigorated domestic economy that is paving the way to recovery. Investments reversed their contractionary trend of the past three years. The 23% growth rate in investments promise a respectable real GNP growth for the rest of the year.

The current budget has a definite bias for health care, education and social services expenditures. Some 6.9 million people received food assistance from the Food and Nutrition Program in 1986. We began to expand the coverage of Medicare. Teachers' salaries were increased, and a leaner and more relevant curriculum was adopted. Some 5.2 million poor availed of vital services such as self-employment assistance, job placement, and family planning. For 1987, we have made P4.2 billion available for long-term mortgages in support of the national shelter program.

NATIONAL DEFENSE AND SECURITY

The price of security and national honor, no less than liberty, is eternal vigilance. And that too has a price. Our country is threatened by totalitarian slavery on the Left and reversion to fascist terror and corruption on the Right. Meanwhile, the bottom is threatened by secession. On the bomb-shattered reviewing stand of our military academy, I vowed to end all threats to our democracy by the end of my term. We shall make good on that pledge. Meanwhile, it should be clear by now that no one in these struggles has had a monopoly of anguish and no one in these debates has had a monopoly of moral insight. It is in that light that we ventured to settle these issues outside the battlefield. For, surely, in the words of an architect of conflict and peace, "a society becomes great not by the victories of its factions over each other but by its reconciliations." To this end, we shall continue to exhaust measures and avenues that will involve all our people in the task of moral and material reconstruction and national unity.

Still our march towards nationhood must be undeterred and any threat to its progress will be countered with all the resources available to us, wielded with as much passion as self-preservation can muster.

The application of force will be as effective as it is judicious. The operational thrust of our Armed Forces is predicated on deterrence, preemption, and destruction. But the question is: Can we execute? If we have come to ask our soldiers to do battle to secure our way of life, then we have an obligation to equip them sufficiently for the fight.

Having exhausted the avenues of negotiation, we have armed them with the right. Now we must complete the complement with the material, organizational, and physical wherewithal to accomplish the task.

We have directed our immediate attention towards strengthening the chain of command, reinstilling discipline within the rank and file, and upgrading morale in the Armed Forces. We have placed renewed emphasis on training—on the physical and mental readiness of the troops. Area Unified Commands have been established to facilitate force augmentation and complementation within and across the major services, particularly in areas where military operations are either imminent or ongoing.

We do, however, have a dire need to improve our intelligence, logistics, and communication services. Given our limited resources, we must improve our ratio of patrols to contacts, and our capability to maximize such combat opportunities as present themselves. We therefore need ordinance platforms and air transports for ground support, troop mobility, and medevac. We need a truly effective navy to secure our coastlines against fresh infusions of arms to rebel or fascist forces, and to punish any further attacks on our territorial honor and integrity, especially in the south.

Our Armed Forces are asked to do more for less. Defense appropriations are down 1-and-1/4% of GNP from an average of 2% prior to 1986. We have been able to afford this reduction because of the moral victory we gained in the February revolution. Still, our defense expenditures are the lowest in ASEAN, and yet no country's security is so seriously threatened as ours.

Given the realities of our finances and our priorities, we will continue to press for efficiency in the Armed Forces. But we will need a sober assessment of adequacy.

Some will say that force does not address the roots of insurgency. I will answer: Indeed, for such roots are addressed by measures of economic improvement and equitable distribution. But such measures also need time to bear fruit; time that only feats of arms and negotiating from strength can buy us.

We have chosen to improve upon our capability to effectively manage force not so that we who desire peace could wage war, but rather so that those who would war upon us will realize, by the deadliness of our riposte, the virtues of peace.

Thus: "we shall bear arms when the intent of bearing them is just," and, if necessary, we shall mourn our dead by celebrating the birth of generations whose legacy shall be one nation, free, upright, and prosperous. [*Applause*]

I have spoken of our problems and I have sketched our programs, some of which have already borne appreciable results. A more detailed report will be submitted to this Congress. Succeeding messages to Congress will convey the legislative agenda of my administration, particularly the Comprehensive Agrarian Reform Program, whose Congressional complement is eagerly awaited. We have prepared the ground for Congressional action on autonomy in the Cordillera, and we are determined to achieve genuine autonomy, and thus eliminate completely the issues that divide us from our Muslim brothers in a manner consistent with the honor and integrity of the Republic. [*Applause*]

In deference to the Congress, executive orders issued last week have 1-year, 90-day, and 60-day effectivity dates. While we believe these measures merit immediate implementation, Congress may want a second look.

I would also hope that our proposed revisions of the Tariff Code and the rationalization of the government corporate sector shall be among the Congress' first concerns, these being two areas that I find require the common counsel of executive and legislature.

I have also spoken of our continuing vulnerabilities.

Now let me speak of our strength.

The source of the new vigor and energy in the land is the sense of pride and renewed self-confidence of our people; pride in their unmatched political achievements. And flowing from that pride, the renewed confidence that we can improve things given the will and the courage to do what is right.

That pride and that confidence rest, however, on their continuing faith in the one solid and undeniable achievement of the great moral exertion of our people: the establishment of a democratic government under an honest and dedicated leadership. In short, it rests on their continuing faith in a government that will lead them to permanent peace, freedom, and progress.

All the assaults on our government have fallen flat and harmless because the people believe in our government, in its honesty and sincere desire to work for the common good.

When this session opened, the great powers of the State that were united in my person divided, and a portion has flowed to you. I have felt no loss but rather a great sense of achievement. The great work we set out to do, for which the nation made me its single leader, is completed. We have this day opened the door of Asian democracy's most famous home: the Congress of the Republic of the Philippines. [*Applause*]

With the portion of power that has gone to you goes the shared responsibility to maintain the people's faith in government.

While I held total power in my hands, and even after I had scattered the enemies of democracy, I kept ever in mind that power and glory are fleeting. That, in times to come, in the words of Gandhi, "the people will not judge us by the creed we profess or the label we wear or the slogans we shout but by our work, industry, sacrifice, honesty and purity of character." [*Applause*]

In the great debates that will ring in this chamber, remember also those words of Gandhi: "Insist upon truth by loving argument, by the testimony of your own life. Once you are assured of the truth, refuse to recant even to death.".

You are blessed beyond all Congresses of the past or of any other nation. For here, ever to guide you, are the somber shades of the eternal Senators of our Republic: Jose W. Diokno and Benigno Aquino, Jr. [*Applause*] Even as their memory continues to freshen our sorrow, may their sacrifices ever nourish our idealism and commitment to our people, and remind us of the painful lesson that "a government that is evil has no room for good men and women except in its prisons."

This day completes the circle of our democratic achievements. Now Philippine democracy rests solidly upon the three pillars of freedom: the President, the Supreme Court, and Congress. Mr. Senate President, Mr. Speaker, members of the Congress, join me now in expressing our congratulations and deepest gratitude to those who have this day by God's grace given to the nation the fully ripened fruit of freedom: *ang ating mga kababayan, ang mamamayang Pilipino.* [*Applause*] [*Standing ovation*]

The State of the Nation Message of Her Excellency Corazon C. Aquino, President of the Philippines, to the Congress

Delivered at the Batasang Pambansa, Quezon City, on July 22, 1991

Senate President Jovito Salonga; Speaker Ramon Mitra; Chief Justice Marcelo Fernan; Honorable Diosdado Macapagal; distinguished members of the Senate and the House of Representatives; Your Excellencies of the Diplomatic Corps; fellow workers in government; honored guests; *minamahal kong mga kababayan*:

In March 1973, six months after the declaration of martial law, Ninoy Aquino was taken blindfolded from Fort Bonifacio and brought to a place he did not know. He was stripped naked and thrown into a cell. His only human contact was a jailer. The immediate prospect, in such a place, was a midnight execution in front of a grave dug by himself.

The purpose was as clear as it was diabolical. It was not to kill him yet, but to break him first and with him break the compelling proof that men can stand up to a dictatorship.

He came close to giving up, he told me; he slipped in and out of despair. But a power that must have been God held him together. He remembered the words of the epistle, God chose the weak to confound the strong.

On the third anniversary of his incarceration in Laur, the recollection of his pain gave birth to a poem of hope. This is the poem he wrote:

> I am burning the candle of my
> life in the dark
> with no one to benefit
> from the light.
> The candle slowly melts away;
> soon its wick will be burned
> out
> and the light is gone.
> If someone will only gather
> the melted wax, re-shape it,
> give it a new wick—
> for another fleeting moment
> my candle can once again
> light the dark,
> be of service
> one more time,
> and then ... goodbye.

This is the anguish of good men: that the good they do will come to nothing. That pains suffered in obscurity or sacrifices made away from the sight of men, amount to the same, and mock the man or woman who bears them.

Mr. Senate President, Mr. Speaker, members of the Congress, distinguished guests, my countrymen:

That is not true. None of the good that we do is ever lost; not even the light in an empty room is wasted.

From Ninoy's burnt-out candle, and thousands like it in cells throughout the garrison state, we gathered the melted wax and made more candles. To burn—not as long in such loneliness—but much more brightly all together, as to banish the darkness, and light us to a new day.

You might ask, "When will the president stop invoking Ninoy's name?" My answer is, "When a president stands here other than by Ninoy's grace. And not while gratitude is nourished by memory. Not while we acknowledge that it was his sacrifice that gave us back our freedom. And restored the freely elected office whose incumbent must stand every year in this place."

Five years have passed. My term is ending. And so is yours. As we came, so should we go. With grateful acknowledgement to the man who made it possible for us to be here. A man who discovered hope in the starkest despair, and has something yet to teach a country facing adversity again.

It would be foolish to ignore what is staring us in the face. Our march of progress brought us far, but such misfortunes have come upon us as to make us feel that we are not much farther from where we started.

The eruption of Mount Pinatubo is the biggest in this century. Abroad, its effect is so far-reaching as to lower the temperature of the Earth. At home, it is so devastating it knocked off 80,000 productive hectares from our agriculture, and destroyed the commerce of at least three provinces. Hundreds of thousands were driven from their homes and livelihoods, and thrown on the kindness of relatives and countrymen, and on the solicitude of the state. It was an event so powerful it wiped out the largest military base in the Pacific, and changed the nature of our relationship with an old ally. In the wake of the volcanic eruption, more has been revealed about that relationship than was covered by its ash.

Before Pinatubo, there was the typhoon that cut a wide swathe of destruction across the southern regions. And before that was the killer quake that cut off the northern parts of the country, destroying billions of pesos in infrastructure, causing the loss of billions more in foregone economic activities. It leveled the City of Pines and buried children in the rubble of yet another city.

But those natural calamities were preceded by another entirely the work of human hands: the massive December 1989 military revolt that cut short a second economic recovery, after the dislocation caused by the earlier August 1987 coup attempt. That one strangled the powerful rebound of the Philippine economy after the EDSA Revolution.

I mention these calamities not to excuse the perceived shortcomings of my administration nor to brag about my indestructibility. I mention them so that we know where we are, and why we are here, and the exact requirements of the task to build up this country yet again.

I mention them because I will compare them with what we had and lost, and then I will ask, "Was it all in vain?" And I will answer, "It was not; no more than a hero's life is wasted."

By 1985, the economy had contracted considerably, its rate of growth has been negative for two consecutive years. The country was at a standstill, as if waiting only for the last rites to be performed. By 1986, we had turned the economy around—in less than a year. We improved on that performance the year after.

The rate of unemployment was reduced, the volume of new investments significantly increased. New industrial projects were introduced, hitherto idle industrial capacity was fully utilized. The foundation of new regional industrial zones was laid. Public infrastructure and services strained under the load of expanding economic activity.

I mention this, not to offset the shortcomings of the present with the achievements of the past. I mention it to show what can be done in such a short time, and how much improvement was made from conditions far worse than what we have today—the dictator's apologists notwithstanding, that the country is worse off now than when he and his wife were stealing the country blind.

This progress was cut off by the August '87 coup attempt. But the economy quickly rallied, and in two years recovered a great deal of the ground we had lost. We were on the verge of a second takeoff when the December 1989 coup broke out. It drained the last drop of confidence in our future from all but the hardiest spirits, and shattered our image abroad.

Still we persevered, achieving gains that, admittedly, continue to fall short of the galloping needs of a fast-growing population, but real gains nonetheless.

Improved health care, increased housing, and—one of the proudest achievements we share with the legislature—free secondary education: 660,000 youth immediately availed themselves of it; another 200,000 private school students received scholarship grants under another recent law; 80,000 new classrooms have been built—the first preparation of the nation for the future of economic competition, which will take place in the highly educated minds of the youth.

We have made the first serious effort to arrest environmental degradation—already so far advanced in the previous regime that it set up an agency that did nothing about it, anyway. We have pushed agrarian reform beyond the point of no return, almost completing its coverage of rice and corn. Its extension to other agricultural activities is proceeding at a pace consistent with our resolve to achieve for the farmer the prosperity promised by agrarian reform, and not just its bare legal implementation.

Indeed, we started to make up our losses, and kept on going through the Gulf crisis which doubled the price of energy and introduced the element of a tremendous uncertainty, not only about our economy, but that of the world as well.

You might ask, "Having lost so much so easily, what was the worth of all that effort?"

With such reversals of fortune, is progress for our country a hope in vain?

Paul says that suffering produces perseverance; perseverance, character; and character, hope. The good we do is never lost. Some of it remains, if not in material goods, then in a deeper experience, a more practiced hand, and a spirit made stronger by that which failed to break it—stronger to meet greater challenges ahead.

But in one thing we grew from strength to strength—in the enlargement of our democratic space and the strengthening of our democracy.

Every calamity tested the capacity of democracy to absorb distress, find relief, and meet the absolute necessities of the people without the least curtailment of freedom or compromise of rights.

Against our economic gains that are ever hostages to fortune, stands one steadfast, unalloyed achievement: our democracy. Destined, I believe, to outlive our problems and deck with the graces of liberty the material progress of our future. That achievement is better seen from the disinterested distance of foreign admirers, than from the myopic view of those at home who wish to destroy it. [*Applause*] It is an achievement entirely in our power to preserve and enhance.

Visitors from the new Germany asked me what things strengthen democracy. Economic progress, naturally, I said. But the attainment of that depends on external factors more than on the will of a developing country. But there is a way to strengthen democracy that is within any country's reach. That is through the empowerment of the people. This is obvious to a government like ours that came to power by its means, as well as to a people like the Germans who attained complete freedom in the same way.

But empowering the people means more than just giving them elections every three years. It means enlarging their contact with government beyond elections to its daily workings—so that the vast resources of one support the initiatives of the other, and the policies of government are refined by the insights of the people. *Ngunit ang pagkaloob ng kapangyarihan sa mamamayan ay nangangahulugan hindi lamang ng pagdaraos ng halalan tuwing ikatlong taon. Kailangan pagyamanin ang kanilang pagkakadiit sa pamahalaan—sa araw-araw na gawain ng pamahalaan—upang ang malawak na kayamanan ng isa ay makatulong sa mga pagkukusa ng kabila at ang mga patakaran ng pamahalaan ay paglinangin ng mga mamamayan.* By this means the lives of the people shall be constantly improved and the people themselves empowered by the habit of directing their own government. The constant revision of flawed policies and the wider application of good ones are possible only by bringing together the people and the government. People empowerment, through people's organizations, NGOs, foundations, and cooperatives, is the surest means we know to make government mirror the aspirations of the people. [*Applause*]

In the past, the idea was to give the people just enough power to elect their mistakes and suffer the consequences until the next elections. Elections were a safety valve. We want elections to be just one of other more effective means to bring the people into government and government to the people, to make it truly a participatory democracy.

This is the only way to end the character of total war that elections have assumed, where the aim is the division of spoils and the victims are not just the losers but those who voted for them too. Such elections are like Russian roulette where your chances are five-to-one your life will not improve, and one-to-five you will blow out your brains.

Participatory democracy will end the practice of punishing provinces and municipalities for the wrong vote in the last poll. It will separate elections, where the people vote for their favorites, from the provision of public service which every Filipino has a right to expect from the government, regardless how he voted.

This administration has made large steps in that direction. To the disappointment of those who marched with me against the Marcos regime, my administration has plowed resources into regions and provinces where I was cheated in the snap elections. The politics of revenge had had its day. [*Applause*]

The organized participation of the people in daily government may provide the stabilizing element that government has always lacked. Policies have radically changed with each administration, yet the basic needs of its unchanging constituencies have not been met: less bureaucracy for business, more public services and infrastructure support for agriculture and industry, and economic safety net for the common man. The active participation of the people in government will lend proper direction and continuity to policy.

This is what I wish for most. That after me, the continuity of our work is not broken. So that things well done shall be completed, and the same mistakes avoided by succeeding administrations. In this way, nothing done shall go to waste, and the light of a misplaced candle shall still be valued for the light it sheds on the things to avoid.

I am not asking that all my programs be blindly followed by my successor. God knows, we have made mistakes. But surely, our objective is right—the improvement of our people's lives. And the new way is much better than those before. To give the people greater power over their lives is the essence of democracy that we must strive to bring out completely.

These ideas, articulated in the Kabisig movement, may not have been well received by this body. It was wrongly projected. I should make it clear that the Kabisig, and the whole movement of people's organizations that I have tried to encourage, will be campaigning hard for one candidate only—the Filipino people and no one else. [*Applause*]

Give the people power movement another chance, for it will go on regardless. I ask you to consider that we have tried the politics of spoils and patronage for half a century, with no better result than the stagnation of the country in a region where everyone else is racing ahead.

The formula for success is said to be dictatorial government.

But we tried that already, with worse results than the most irresponsible democracy can produce. Besides, the spirit of our race will not accept a dictatorship; and memories, fresh as the scars it left, will not let us consider that option again. Democracy is the only way for us. We must therefore find the ways by which the pitfalls that go with its blessings are reduced, while its inherent strengths are brought to the fore. Of those strengths, the most promising is people power, a reserve for nation-building we tapped only once in our history with such marvelous result.

A detailed report of the performance of government is before you; the legislative agenda—principally the Local Government Code, the Civil Service Code, revenue enhancement measures, and electoral reforms—has been communicated to the Senate President and to the Speaker of the House.

This is the last time I shall address you on such an occasion as this. Let us clear the air between us.

I could have made things easier for myself if I had opted for the "popular."

I could have repudiated the foreign debt, won the passing praise of a greatly relieved people, and the lasting contempt of a devastated country.

I could have opted for outright hostility towards the international banking system and invited its retaliation. But the only result would have been to weaken the present democracy against the conspiracies of the former government which contracted the miserable debt in the first place. I would have taken the chance, if I were the only one at risk, but I had a country to take care of. [*Applause*]

I could have called for an elected constitutional convention.

Surveys showed that an elected convention was the popular choice to draft a new constitution. But I believed it was more important to draft a constitution and submit it for ratification in the shortest time possible, and hold elections immediately. The people and the army needed a full elected government and a constitution around which to rally in defense of freedom.

I could not afford the luxury of the popular by waiting out the endless deliberations of an elected convention, like the 1971 Constitutional Convention. And besides, what was so great about that experience? After a year of talk and scandal, the final draft was prepared in Malacañang, approved by the frightened convention, and ratified in a fraudulent plebiscite.

I could have made things easier for myself if I had allowed the executive to influence the decisions of constitutional commissions. I might have spared myself deep embarrassments by interfering with the judgments of the courts. But I uphold the independence of these bodies. I am convinced it is in all our best interest to respect an independence that may thwart the government's will from time to time—but is yet our best assurance of justice when we will need justice most. [*Applause*]

I firmly believe in the freedom of the press. And I accept the criticisms poured on me, painful as they are, as part and parcel of the hazards of public service, and conducive to its honest performance. True, I have sued for libel, but I did not use the power of the presidency to advance my cause. And this is shown by the fact that four years later my case continues to drag on. [*Applause*] I have not forgotten that what my husband wanted most in prison was for the public to hear the side of freedom, and no newspaper would print it.

I submitted myself to the judicial process as an ordinary citizen, and exposed myself to indignities a president should not endure. But I want to encourage people to seek redress in the law, despite the inconvenience, rather than in vindictiveness, which has no end. I want them to make the cause of justice for one, the cause of justice for all. [*Applause*]

I have consoled myself that great men like Gandhi were not spared criticism either, but—regardless of it—he pursued the path he believed was true, mindful only of harmful effects on the people, but not of the consequences to him. He believed that God demands no less of us than that we follow our conscience. God will take care of the rest.

I could have done the popular thing in the last administration, and arranged a nicer retirement for myself. But my instructions to PNB, DBP, GSIS, SSS, and Land Bank were explicit: no behest loans, and no special favors [*applause*] whether to relative, friend, or political supporter. This accounts for their sterling performance, for the unprecedented public faith in their competence and integrity, and for the incalculable contribution, particularly of PNB and the Land Bank, to the development of cooperatives and the financing of small and medium enterprises, wherein lies the strongest hope of progress in these times.

We can roll back prices at the drop of a hat and spare ourselves all the aggravation, but we learned that hasty rollbacks exacted a heavier, long-term cost on the economy, and, ultimately, on the people, than they had saved.

I could have done any of the things calculated to win a passing popularity at home. I could have thrown away by so-called popular solutions the goodwill we have built up in financial circles by the strict performance of our obligations. This is the goodwill that accounts for the continued support extended to the Philippine Assistance Program [PAP]. Anyway, most of the pledges to the PAP are redeemable in the next administration.

I could have said, "Let my successor be presented with the bill for my popularity today." But it is the people who would pay the price, and I am not made that way. [*Applause*]

I did not always adopt the ideal solutions proposed by those who have the luxury of contemplation. Government often had to do what pressing realities compelled it. And if the government sometimes lacked better choices, it never lacked the sincere desire to do good. [*Applause*]

I could have promoted only military officers popular with the press, and ignored the experience of a democratic government that has been the principal military objective of the rebel forces and an insurgency that just doesn't know when to quit. But I chose instead commanders of proven courage, leadership, and fidelity to the Constitution.

I could do the smart thing still, and do the things my opponents unfairly charge me of preparing—rigging the elections in 1992, the way I did not rig the ratification of the Constitution, the national elections, and the local elections. The way they rigged elections from 1969 to 1986. But my instructions to the military and police are explicit. Let them hear it again:

The right of the soldier and the policeman is merely to cast his vote; his greater and solemn obligation is to assure the right of others to cast their votes and get them honestly counted. [*Applause*] No soldier has the right to combine with his comrades to campaign for a person or party and deliver to them a block of the military vote. No member of the military shall lend his name, prestige, and the influence of his position to anyone's campaign. The same holds true for the police. [*Applause*]

The military has earned the people's trust as the spearhead of their liberation and the constant defender of their democracy. To these honors, it is my aim to add the distinction of shepherding our democracy through its first political succession, by clean and peaceful elections. [*Applause*]

I will not preside as Commander in Chief over the kind of military that cheated the opposition in 1978, and me in 1986. [*Applause*] That would insult the memory of the man to whom I dedicate this last address to the joint houses of Congress, and stain the proud achievement of this nation in 1986.

I specifically charge AFP Chief of Staff General Lisandro Abadia and PNP Director General Cesar Nazareno with the responsibility to assure clean and honest elections. [*Applause*] While they may not fear my displeasure because I will not be president then, they will face the judgment of the disappointed country.

Yes, I could have done all those things that win wide acclaim, exiting as grandly as any president could wish. But while my power as president ends in 1992, my responsibility as a Filipino for the well-being of my country goes beyond it to my grave. [*Applause*] A great part of that responsibility is to do the best I can today, according to my best lights, while I have the power to do it.

As President, I have never prayed for anything for myself; only for our people. I have been called an international beggar by the military rebels. Begging does not become me, yet— perhaps it is what I had to do. I could have kept my pride and held aloof, but that would not have helped our people. And it is for them that I was placed in this office. [*Applause*]

Someone who will do better may stand in this place next year, for I believe in the inexhaustible giftedness of the Filipino people. I only hope that he will be someone who will sincerely mean you well. [*Applause*]

I hope that history will judge me as favorably as our people still regard me, because, as God is my witness, I honestly did the best I could. No more can be asked of any man. [*Applause*]

On June 30, 1992, the traditional ceremony of political succession will unfold at the Luneta. The last time it was done that way was in 1965. I shall be there with you to proudly witness the event. This is the glory of democracy, that its most solemn moment should be the peaceful transfer of power. [*Applause*]

Maraming salamat sa inyong lahat at paalam. [*Applause*] [*Standing ovation*]

Benigno Aquino, Jr.

Ninoy was born on November 27, 1932 to Aurora Aquino and Benigno Aquino, Sr., a politican and landowner from Tarlac. His grandfather, Servillano Aquino, was a general during the Philippine Revolution. He studied at Saint Joseph College, San Beda High School, then at the Ateneo de Manila College of Liberal Arts and the University of the Philippines College of Law.

Before entering politics, Ninoy was a journalist and at 17, served as *Manila Times* correspondent during the Korean War and covered other assignments in Southeast Asia. He also worked for Pres. Ramon Magsaysay and, in 1954, negotiated the surrender of Hukbalahap leader Luis Taruc.

Ninoy married Maria Corazon "Cory" Cojuangco in 1954. The following year, at 22, he was elected mayor of Concepcion, Tarlac, and eventually was elected vice governor (1959) and governor (1961) of Tarlac. In 1967, he became the youngest Filipino to be elected as senator.

At his young age, Ninoy had already served as special assistant under three Philippine presidents. He was also awarded the Philippine Legion of Honor for his coverage of the Philippine Expeditionary

 Force to the Korean War and his negotiations for the surrender of Luis Taruc. In 1960, he was also voted as one of the Ten Outstanding Young Men of the Philippines (TOYM) in the field of public service. Ninoy was also voted as outstanding senator by the *Philippine Free Press* and was elected secretary-general of the opposition Liberal Party.

Ninoy was a well-known opposition leader and critic of the Marcos regime. When Marcos declared Martial Law in 1972, Aquino was detained with other political opponents of the regime. For more than seven years, he was imprisoned in Fort Bonifacio as well as in Laur, Nueva Ecija, with much time spent in solitary confinement. In 1977, Ninoy was given a death sentence by a military court. His incarceration, however, did not stop him from challenging the Marcos government from his cell.

In 1980, he was allowed to go to the U.S. for his triple heart bypass surgery. During his three-year stay in the U.S. with his family, Ninoy became a fellow at the Harvard University's Center for International Affairs and Massachusetts Institute of Technology's Center for International Studies.

Despite being warned of the possible consequences, Ninoy decided to go back to the Philippines and continue the struggle for democracy. But on August 21, 1983, he was assassinated after disembarking from the plane at the Manila International Airport. Around two million people attended his funeral march. His death further ignited public sentiment against the Martial Law regime, and eventually put his widow in the political limelight.

With the passage of Republic Act 9256 in 2004, August 21 has been declared a national holiday, to commemorate the death of Ninoy, who once had said: *"I have carefully weighed the virtues and the faults of the Filipino and I have come to the conclusion that he is worth dying for because he is the nation's greatest untapped resource."*

Undelivered speech of Sen. Benigno S. Aquino, Jr.

Intended for his return from the United States of America on August 21, 1983

I have returned on my free will to join the ranks of those struggling to restore our rights and freedoms through nonviolence.

I seek no confrontation. I only pray and will strive for a genuine national reconciliation founded on justice.

I am prepared for the worst, and have decided against the advice of my mother, my spiritual adviser, many of my tested friends, and a few of my most valued political mentors.

A death sentence awaits me. Two more subversion charges, both calling for death penalties, have been filed since I left three years ago and are now pending with the courts.

I could have opted to seek political asylum in America, but I feel it is my duty, as it is the duty of every Filipino, to suffer with his people especially in time of crisis.

I never sought nor have I been given assurances or promise of leniency by the regime. I return voluntarily, armed only with a clear conscience and fortified in the faith that in the end, justice will emerge triumphant.

According to Gandhi, the willing sacrifice of the innocent is the most powerful answer to insolent tyranny that has yet been conceived by God and man.

Three years ago when I left for an emergency heart bypass operation, I hoped and prayed that the rights and freedoms of our people would soon be restored, that living conditions would improve and that blood-letting would stop.

Rather than move forward, we have moved backward. The killings have increased, the economy has taken a turn for the worse, and the human rights situation has deteriorated.

During the martial law period, the Supreme Court heard petitions for Habeas Corpus. It is most ironic, after martial law has allegedly been lifted, that the Supreme Court last April ruled it can no longer entertain petitions for Habeas Corpus for persons detained under a Presidential Commitment Order, which covers all so-called national security cases and which under present circumstances can cover almost anything.

The country is far advanced in her times of trouble. Economic, social, and political problems bedevil the Filipino. These problems may be surmounted if we are united. But we can be united only if all the rights and freedoms enjoyed before September 21, 1972 are fully restored.

The Filipino asks for nothing more, but will surely accept nothing less, than all the rights and freedoms guaranteed by the 1935 Constitution—the most sacred legacies from the Founding Fathers.

Yes, the Filipino is patient, but there is a limit to his patience. Must we wait until that patience snaps?

The nation-wide rebellion is escalating and threatens to explode into a bloody revolution. There is a growing cadre of young Filipinos who have finally come to realize that freedom is never granted, it is taken. Must we relive the agonies and the blood-letting of the past that brought forth our Republic or can we sit down as brothers and sisters and discuss our differences with reason and goodwill?

I have often wondered how many disputes could have been settled easily had the disputants only dared to define their terms.

So as to leave no room for misunderstanding, I shall define my terms:

1. Six years ago, I was sentenced to die before a firing squad by a Military Tribunal whose jurisdiction I steadfastly refused to recognize. It is now time for the regime to decide. Order my IMMEDIATE EXECUTION OR SET ME FREE.

   I was sentenced to die for allegedly being the leading communist leader. I am not a communist, never was and never will be.

2. National reconciliation and unity can be achieved but only with justice, including justice for our Muslim and Ifugao brothers. There can be no deal with a Dictator. No compromise with Dictatorship.

3. In a revolution there can really be no victors, only victims. We do not have to destroy in order to build.

4. Subversion stems from economic, social, and political causes and will not be solved by purely military solutions; it can be curbed not with ever-increasing repression but with a more equitable distribution of wealth, more democracy, and more freedom; and

5. For the economy to get going once again, the workingman must be given his just and rightful share of his labor, and to the owners and managers must be restored the hope where there is so much uncertainty if not despair.

On one of the long corridors of Harvard University are carved in granite the words of Archibald Macleish:

> How shall freedom be defended? By arms when it is attacked by arms; by truth when it is attacked by lies; by democratic faith when it is attacked by authoritarian dogma. Always, and in the final act, by determination and faith.

I return from exile and to an uncertain future with only determination and faith to offer—faith in our people and faith in God.

Selected Books on Ninoy and Cory Aquino

Aquino, Benigno S. *Letters, Prison & Exile*. [Metro Manila: Aquino Family, 1983.]

Aquino, Benigno S. *Ninoy: Mga Tula, Liham at Talumpati*. Manila: Komisyon sa Wikang Filipino, 2011.

Aquino, Benigno S. *Shenanigans, Syndicates, Stinks – in the Sweepstakes*. [Manila]: Public Information Office, 1968.

Aquino, Benigno S. *Testament from a Prison Cell*. USA: Philippine Journal, 1989.

Aquino, Benigno S. and Simeon G. Del Rosario. *Surfacing the Underground, Part II: The Involvements of Benigno S. Aquino, Jr. with 29 Perpetuated Testimonies Appended*. Quezon City: Manlapaz Publishing, 1977.

August 21: This is Ninoy . . . Know Him Well! Quezon City: Katotohanan at Katarungan Foundation, Inc., 1998.

Bernas, Joaquin G. *A Living Constitution: The Cory Aquino Presidency*. Pasig City: Anvil Publishing, Inc., 2000.

Crisostomo, Isabelo T. *Cory: Profile of a President. The Historic Rise to Power of Corazon Cojuangco Aquino*. USA: Branden Books, 1990.

Cruz, Justin Benigno Aquino. *Ninoy: Art and Essays*. [Philippines]: Justin Benigno Aquino Cruz, 2008.

Fernandez, Yvette. *Ninoy, Cory, and Noynoy*. Manila: Dream Big Books, 2012.

Joaquin, Nick. *Ninoy Aquino in the Senate: Final Chapters of The Aquinos of Tarlac: an essay on history as three generations*. Mandaluyong: Solar Publishing Corporation, 1986.

Juico, Margie Penson. *Cory: An Intimate Portrait*. Pasig City: Anvil Publishing, Inc., 2009.

—————. *Cory: An Intimate Portrait, Book 2*. Pasig City: Anvil Publishing, Inc., 2010.

Komisar, Lucy. *Corazon Aquino: The Story of a Revolution*. New York: George Braziller, 1987.

Laurel, Salvador H. *Neither Trumpets Nor Drums: Summing Up the Cory Government*. Quezon City: PDM Press, 1992.

Maramba, Asuncion David. *Seven in the Eye of History*. Pasig City: Anvil Publishing, Inc., 2000.

Mercado, Monina Allarey. *People Power: An Eyewitness History: The Philippine Revolution of 1986*. Manila: James B. Reuter, S.J. Foundation, 1986.

Policarpio, Alfonso P. *Ninoy: The Willing Martyr*. USA: Isaiah Books, 1986.

Saguisag, Lara. *Ninoy Aquino: The Courageous Homecoming*. Makati: The Bookmark, Inc., 2000.

San Diego, E. Salvador. *Lakas ng Sambayanan (People Power): Alay kay Ninoy Aquino at sa Masang Pilipino*. Quezon City: Sandugo Enterprises, 1987.

Simons, Lewis M. *Worth Dying For*. New York: William Morrow & Co., 1987.

Skard, Torild. *Women of Power: Half a Century of Female Presidents and Prime Ministers Worldwide*. Bristol: Policy Press, 2014.

Sta. Romana Cruz, Neni. *Tales from EDSA*. Pasig City: Anvil Publishing, Inc., 2000, 2009.

Ventura, Sylvia Mendez. *Benigno Aquino*. Manila: Dream Big Books, 1995.

Villacorte, Rolando E. *The Real Hero of EDSA*. Quezon City: Rolando E. Villacorte, 1989.

Yap, Miguela G. *The Making of Cory*. Manila: Cellar Book Shop/New Day Publishers, 1989.

About the Authors

ELFREN SICANGCO CRUZ is the op-ed columnist for "Breakthrough" in *Philippine Star*. He wrote a weekly column, "Framework," for *BusinessWorld* from 1999 to 2010, which won the 2006 Catholic Mass Media Award for Best Business Column. His book *Setting Frameworks: Family Business and Strategic Management* won Best Business Book in the 2006 National Book Awards by the Manila Critics Circle. Elfren was the head of the Presidential Management Staff in the Cory Aquino cabinet, and was governor of the Metro Manila Commission from 1988 to 1990. He received two bachelor's degrees and a Doctorate in Business Administration from De La Salle, and holds an MBA from the Asian Institute of Management. Elfren was a professor of strategic management at the De La Salle University Ramon V. del Rosario School of Business from 1992 to 2014. He is currently the chair of Lockton Philippines Insurance and Reinsurance Brokers, Inc. and a consultant on family business and strategic planning.

NENI STA. ROMANA CRUZ is chair of the National Book Development Board. A freelance journalist and a children's book writer, she has several published books, including a pop culture series and has been anthologized in over twenty books. Neni is a former faculty member of the International School Manila where she headed the Children's Media Center and taught writing to gifted and talented elementary school students. She continues to be a literacy advocate promoting the love of reading as a regular contributor to the op-ed section of the *Philippine Daily Inquirer*, a trustee of the Teach for the Philippines, and a member of the Library Hub Technical Working Group of the Department of Education. She is invited to various speaking engagements with schools on author visits and with Filipino-American audiences in the United States. She is the director of Where the Write Things Are, a writing center for writers of all ages.

Also by the Authors

Elfren Sicangco Cruz:

Setting Frameworks: Family Business and Strategic Management

Neni Sta. Romana Cruz

The Boy Who Would Feed the World

Daughters True: 100 Years of Scholastical Education 1906-2006
   (co-edited with Paulynn Paredes Sicam, Karina Africa Bolasco, and Ma. Ceres P. Doyo)

Don't Take a Bath on a Friday: Philippine Superstitions & Folk Beliefs

Great Lives: Gabriela Silang

Ngalang Pinoy: A Primer on Filipino Wordplay

Philippine Proverbs

Sundays of our Lives

Tales from EDSA: Stories of the Revolution

The Teacher

The Warrior Dance and Other Classic Philippine Sky Folktales

Why the Piña Has a Hundred Eyes and Other Classic Philippine Folktales about Fruits

You Know You're Filipino If…